Guns and ballot boxes

Guns and ballot boxes

East Timor's vote for independence

Edited by

Damien Kingsbury

Monash Asia Institute
Clayton

Monash Asia Institute
Monash University
Victoria 3800
Australia

www.monash.edu.au/mai
monash.asia.institute@adm.monash.edu.au

National Library of Australia cataloguing-in-publication data:

Guns and ballot boxes : East Timor's vote for independence.

Bibliography
ISBN 0 7326 1188 1

1. Indonesia. Angkatan Darat - Political activity. 2. United Nations. Mission in East Timor. 3. Referendum - Indonesia - Timor Timur. 4. Self-determination, National - Indonesia - Timor Timur. 5. Atrocities - Indonesia - Timor Timur. 6. Indonesia - Politics and government - 1966–. 7. Indonesia - Militia I. Kingsbury, Damien. II. Monash Asia Institute. (Series : Monash papers on Southeast Asia ; no. 54).

320.9586

Maps © Monash Asia Institute
Cover photograph © Jason South
Designed and edited by Emma Hegarty
Typeset by Emma Barling
Printed by Brown Prior Anderson

Contents

Introduction i
Damien Kingsbury

Maps ix

Reconciliation, unity and national development 1
Xanana Gusmao

Towards reconciliation 11
Bishop Carlos Belo

East Timor to 1999 17
Damien Kingsbury

The Popular Consultation in the Ermera district:
Free, fair and secret? 29
Anthony Smith

Taking the risk, paying the price 43
Helene van Klinken

The TNI and the militias 69
Damien Kingsbury

The militia, the military and the people of Bobonaro district 81
Peter Bartu

A reporter's view 99
Hidayat Djajamihardja

The United Nations in East Timor: Comparisons with Cambodia 117
Sue Downie

Accountability for human rights abuses in East Timor...................... 135
Annemarie Devereaux

Big states and little secessionist movements 157
Gerry van Klinken

East Timor, Australia and Indonesia.. 169
Scott Burchill

Conclusion.. 185
Damien Kingsbury

About the authors.. 188

Bibliography 189

Glossary.. 198

Introduction

There were moments in East Timor during August 1999 when one could not help but be overwhelmed by the atmosphere of joyous celebration, of shared achievement, of a life's goal on the cusp of realisation. Outsiders were openly and warmly welcomed by the vast majority of East Timorese. Here was a place that since 1975 had received so very few visitors, a mere handful either escorted about on officially conducted and carefully orchestrated tours or who had come, clandestinely, to search out information and to let the East Timorese people know that not everyone in the world had forgotten their plight. But from July 1999, East Timor had become a territory dominated by the United Nations and its coterie of hangers-on, including aid workers, journalists, observers and a few activists thinly disguised as interested tourists.

For most East Timorese, especially those in the larger towns, the first impact of this new 'invasion' was the rapidly escalating prices of basic goods. The UN brought its own economy, inflated to above even a usual Western standard and laid over an environment that at best struggled to provide some of the minor luxuries of 'developed' life. In Indonesia generally it was easy to slip beyond the web of Western style hotels, generic fast-food outlets and discotheques. In East Timor, it was difficult to find even a faint resemblance to this Western generica. For most of its 24 years as a captive Indonesian province East Timor was the country's poorest outpost, so there was simply no way to absorb this inflow of cash other than by vastly inflating prices. Some of the UN-generated profit trickled beyond the largely non-East Timorese business owners into the hands of East Timorese themselves; but most did not. For them, UNAMET and its noisy periphery were a spectacle, albeit a spectacle that brought with it the possibility of ending Indonesia's long, repressive and often bloody reign.

In setting itself up in East Timor, UNAMET employed mostly pro-independence local staff. It could not have done otherwise, when there were so very few people in East Timor who were neutral and such an overwhelming majority was in favor of independence. Indeed, those actively opposed to independence refused to co-operate with UNAMET, so there was little likelihood of their being employed in any case. Despite this, the East Timorese UNAMET workers maintained a high level of neutrality. They could afford to do so, as it was obvious that in any even remotely fair ballot the pro-independence cause would win hands down. Conducting a ballot on the issue of independence was the prime goal of the pro-independence movement. Just letting the process go ahead was enough. So too it was enough for UNAMET. Later accusations of UNAMET bias could be said to be accurate if the point on which the debate turned was not the conduct of the ballot process, which from a UNAMET perspective was free and fair,[1] but whether or not the ballot process should go ahead. By this stage, however, it was too late to stop the ballot process going ahead. Indeed, it had been too late from the moment Indonesia's President Habibie announced to the world that the people of East Timor would be allowed to vote in a 'popular consultation' on whether the territory remained part of Indonesia as an 'autonomous' region, which in reality meant no change, or whether it became independent.

Even the activities of Indonesia's military, so clearly designed to thwart the ballot process through a campaign of widespread violence and intimidation, could do little to alter the outcome of the ballot. For a while it was possible that the military believed they could provoke pro-independence guerillas into conflict and hence cancel the ballot, or alter the balance of the vote by enough to call into question the status of a pro-independence majority. The official military view was that 20% of the population supported independence and 20% supported continuing integration. The remaining 60%, they thought, could be swayed. Similar tactics had worked for the arch political manipulators of the military in other parts of Indonesia in the past. Why couldn't they work again? The problem was that this time the election was supervised by an independent body, and that the people of East Timor already knew which way they wished to vote. In most cases, the violence and intimidation only hardened them in their resolve. The pro-independence organisation, the National Council for Timorese Resistance, did not even want to campaign ahead of the ballot. As its organisers said at the time, it had been campaigning for 24 years. An extra few days were not going to instill the message any more clearly. By comparison, the pro-integration groups were angry and violent, displaying no sense of joy at having their views tested via the ballot box. Their rallies were usually small, lacklustre affairs significant only for their open display of weapons and the unsubtle threats used against the pro-independence supporters. And in the background, homes were burned, tens of thousands of people were turned into refugees in their own land and murder became commonplace.

It was an extraordinary roller-coaster of a time for all involved; the prevailing sense of popular euphoria contrasted with dread and terror, and celebrations of the coming ballot were silhouetted against burned homes, ominous disappearances and grisly bodies. For some there was little or no euphoria at all, their lives wrecked, the tragedy too overwhelming. One Australian police officer based in Maliana and serving in one of the worst militia controlled areas asked, just before the ballot day, if there was a sense it

---

[1] Despite some pro-Jakarta claims to the contrary, it was a clean ballot process by any standard, and especially that by which Indonesia had previously operated. The observer group to which I was attached reported a single, minor violation of balloting procedure on the day of the vote.

was all a roller-coaster why did it never go up? There were times when it seemed the darkness would never lift, although the moments of hope seemed even more bright, perhaps because of the contrast.

Most of the contributors to this volume were in East Timor during the ballot, for differing periods and in different places. Each was deeply touched by the situation as it unfolded there, and by the people whom they met and stayed with. To a lesser or greater degree, those personal experiences inform their contributions, some more obvious than others but in all cases with an underlying value. It would be easy to suggest that this value is implicitly moral and defines right and wrong. Certainly on the ground in East Timor this did appear to be a stark choice. But here there is no such overt moralising. Rather, there are stories and analyses that allow the readers to make up their own minds. If there is a broad consistency of perspective it is because the facts of the situation were too clear and unambiguous for there to be any great division on this point.

Each chapter covers a particular field, helping to put together the jigsaw puzzle that was East Timor during the ballot period. If there is an underlying theme to the papers presented here, it is the issue of state-sanctioned political violence, and of betrayal. Although it was common knowledge that the militias, the TNI and the police were working together, with varying degrees of comfort and agreement, what was most disturbing was that the Indonesian government had promised to provide a secure environment for the ballot. It did not so much fail to fulfill this promise as—through the actions of its agents—lie. Everyone knew that official Indonesian security was a lie, but that did little to make it more palatable.

It is conventional wisdom in state theory that the state reserves for itself the right to employ violence, but in an acceptably functioning, non-predatory state, that violence should only be used within the bounds of an agreed legal code. In Indonesia generally this has been problematic since the founding of the state in 1945, and state-sanctioned but uncodified violence was in particular a hallmark of the New Order government of President Suharto. But East Timor occupies a special place even within a violence-based state such as Indonesia.

From Indonesia's invasion on 7 December 1975 until the last TNI troops left the territory in disgrace on 29 October 1999, East Timor was used as a training ground for Indonesia's armed forces, the place where they could hone their anti-insurgency and anti-civilian skills. There were very few of the limited restraints that applied even in other parts of Indonesia and, amongst a people who always so clearly wanted independence, everyone was suspected of being the 'enemy'. A culture of military impunity reigned. It was with such impunity, with the aid of their militia thugs and the police, that the TNI directed their last vicious campaign against this 'enemy', the people of East Timor. This violence is the back-drop to this, as experienced by the authors. The perspectives differ, but each comes back to the central theme of an official promise of allowing people the right of a vote and then, cynically, punishing those people for exercising that right. It is a bleak unifying theme, but it is an accurate one.

Such bleakness would be completely unrelieved if no insight were available, or no lessons learned, from those events. Insight is a rare commodity, but perhaps there are some glimpses of the evil to which such men are capable of stooping, especially in the name of a greater idea. This evil has a long if undistinguished history and has been a leitmotif of the 20th century. It may well continue, although one would like to think that the progress of civilisation, including open and informed discussion of such evil, will limit its continued journey.

Perhaps the most obvious lesson demonstrated by these papers is that, in the final analysis, public violence cannot hide and will, in the end, be accountable. Whether or not war crime trials are held or whether they secure convictions, the TNI will stand accused in the eyes of the world as a reprehensible force comprised of many evil men. This is not enough, but their exposure is important and will continue to inform the way both the international community and many Indonesians view their own armed forces.

The chapters

East Timor can be said to have two main leaders, one pastoral and the other temporal. Longtime guerilla leader, political prisoner and president of the CNRT, Jose Alexandro 'Kay Rala Xanana' Gusmao recorded his thoughts on East Timor's future for the day of the ballot, which are reproduced here. Facing his people are the twin obstacles of rebuilding East Timorese society in both a material and social sense. In this latter sense, Xanana calls for reconciliation, perhaps the hardest of all hurdles to overcome when there has been so much loss, so much bitterness and so much blood and tears. But, like the East Timorese people, he looks forward, perhaps because looking back is at the moment still too painful, and because there is so much to do. Here the theme of violence is couched in terms of healing past wounds and moving forward.

Having grown as the spiritual leader of the East Timorese people, Bishop Carlos Belo is less concerned for the material development of his nation, but also emphasises the need for reconciliation. However, for reconciliation, he says, there must be truth. For a country with East Timor's past, the truth is perhaps the hardest of all its problems to confront, especially for those who will be exposed before its harsh and unrelenting light. It is this exposure of evil—a term, incidentally, Bishop Belo does not use here—that helps ensure it does not happen again.

A thumbnail sketch of East Timor's history helps to locate the contemporary events to which Xanana and Bishop Belo allude. The history of colonialist enterprise is punctuated by violence no matter where it occurred, including Portuguese Timor. The Japanese interlude, nominally sparked by an Australian military presence, provided a foresight of the horrors to come. But by far the greatest, most intense and most sustained violence was that which accompanied and followed Indonesia's invasion in 1975. If one is ever forced to wonder where the horror of 1999 came from, one need only look to the behaviour of Indonesia's armed forces in the territory over the preceding 24 years. It was the role of the Indonesian military, and the sustained struggle for independence, that led directly to the independence ballot.

From this background, Anthony Smith's personal account as an observer located in the old Portuguese hilltop town of Ermera brings the events in East Timor back to the personal, the local and the immediate. Smith's observations were thematically common to others, but his experiences provide an immediacy and concrete reality that is sometimes lost in the bigger world of ideas. Smith's paper complements and briefly intersects with the experiences of Helene van Klinken, who worked as a UNAMET political officer out of the increasingly troubled town of Gleno, the capital of the Ermera district. Van Klinken's experiences and analysis were broadly representative of events in East Timor in the lead-up to the independence ballot. Political tensions ebbed and flowed and there were moments when it seemed that the ballot could be conducted without too much further loss of life. Yet as if pre-planned, which it was later shown to be, the pro-Jakarta groups became more belligerent and, inevitably, violence escalated. Van Klinken's chapter brings together a chronicle of factual developments in that district, analysis of why they took place and, movingly, her personal responses. It was not a place about which one could be dispassionate and still claim to enjoy normal human emotions.

My study of the links between the Indonesian military and the militias is also tinged by personal experiences as far apart as Los Palos in the east and Maliana and Balibo in the west of the territory. This demonstrates, if nothing else, that the escalation of militia/TNI thuggery was common to the whole territory, even if it was notably worse towards the west. In this paper again there are moments of hope and joy, punctuating and otherwise almost unrelieved backdrop of murder, rape, displacement and intimidation. But rather than being purely or even mostly descriptive, this chapter looks at some of the evidence that linked the TNI to the militias, and explains how and why events unfolded as they did.

More firmly rooted in Bobonaro district, which encapsulated the militia strongholds of Maliana, Balibo and Batu Gade, Peter Bartu, a veteran of the UN Transitional Authority in Cambodia, writes of his experiences and insights as the UNAMET political officer in what was widely seen as the most difficult and confronting district in the territory. Bartu's time in Maliana put him at the forefront of the TNI–militia anti-independence campaign and, according to many in East Timor at that time, until his departure he was more intimately acquainted with the detail of the conflict than any other UNAMET official. At a time when killing in Bobonaro was becoming commonplace, Bartu dug into his diplomatic reserves and secured 48 hours of peace ahead of the ballot. As a veteran of Cambodia's bloody transition to elected government, it was telling when he said, one morning on his first day off in eight weeks: 'It's been tough, mate. It's been really tough.'

Contrary to the secrecy and disinformation that characterised what had happened in East Timor in the preceding 24 years, journalists played a critical role in bringing the unfolding events to the world. This exposure ultimately influenced foreign governments to commit themselves to sending a military force under the auspices of the UN to end the uncontrolled violence. Included here is the story not just of a journalist in East Timor, but of an Indonesian journalist who lives and works in Australia, bringing to the subject a unique and perhaps the least subjective of viewpoints. Hidayat Djajamihardja has a souvenir of East Timor, a large but otherwise nondescript rock. On a day of uncontrolled rioting and killing in Dili four days before the ballot, it smashed through the window of his car and hit him in the back, thrown by a militiaman who had wanted to shoot him.

Many observers were struck by the similarities between East Timor and Cambodia, although they are a long way apart in terms of culture and geography. This ranged from the political and later military role of the UN to the remarkably high level of voter registration and, against the odds, an even more amazing turn-out by happy, enthusiastic voters. And then there was the 'Year Zero' scenario, in which an out-of-control political organisation embarked on a campaign of terror and mass murder, effectively kidnapping and transporting a huge proportion of the population and almost totally destroying of the built environment. Sue Downie worked in Cambodia from the late 1980s throughout the UN period there, and was repeatedly struck by the similarities between the two places. Most importantly, perhaps, she also saw the repetition of UN activities that, in Cambodia, eventually led to longer term problems for the society it set out to protect. Her paper here notes those similarities, as well as differences, and points to areas that the UN will have to consider in its longer term role in East Timor.

Another observer in the town of Ermera, Annemarie Devereux, brought to bear her perspective as a human rights lawyer on the activities of the militia and the TNI during and after the ballot period. As Devereux notes, there is in East Timor, under international law, a case to be made for a war crimes tribunal or for charges to be laid for crimes against humanity. At the time of writing, the gathering of evidence was severely hampered by security, administrative and natural impediments, while the Indonesian government and the TNI have always shown themselves unwilling to be judged by procedures over which they ultimately have little or no control. But, as Devereux makes clear, the violence in East Timor was not simply a matter of civil conflict or the maintenance of security—crimes in a conventional legal sense were committed. Regardless of the outcome, the actions of the militias and the TNI will always be understood by the international community in criminal terms.

Gerry van Klinken's assessment of Indonesia's problematic and somewhat arbitrary construction views East Timor as the most obvious site of dissent within a deeply challenged unitary state. In one sense, East Timor was the most troubled and reluctant of Indonesia's territories, but it was only one among many. It has been suggested that if Jakarta's responses to East Timor had been more conciliatory and inclusive the independence movement might have withered. But its responses in East Timor, while undoubtedly the worst, were characteristic of the central government's responses to all its restive outlying provinces.

Longtime critic of Australia's policy of appeasement towards Indonesia over East Timor Scott Burchill dissects how Australia's policy unfolded and where it went so disastrously wrong, including identifying some of the key proponents of that policy. Perhaps Australia's role in influencing Indonesia has been overstated, but clearly Australia's recognition of East Timor as first a *de facto* and then a *de jure* part of Indonesia gave comfort to a government presiding over a brutal military occupation. Australia's policy about-face and the future of relations between Indonesia, Australia and East Timor also come under consideration here. This rounds out a package of thoughtful and at times provocative essays that are valuable for their insights, their analysis and their first hand accounts of what it was like to be in East Timor during the ballot period. This volume is, therefore, largely a primary record of events that led to the bloody birth of a new state, which leads us to consider a confluence of the most demanding of moral issues to confront the international community in the last and perhaps defining moments of the 20th century.

Thanks

The preparation of this volume is in large part due to the support and assistance of the Chairperson of the Publishing Committee of Monash University's Centre for Southeast Asian Studies, Associate Professor Stuart Robson, and the Monash Asia Institute's Publications Officer, Emma Hegarty. Thanks to Jason South for providing the photograph on the front cover, and to Gary Swinton for drawing the maps. I would also like to thank Pat Walsh of the Australian Council for Overseas Aid Human Rights Office, the co-ordinator of the Australia East Timor International Volunteer Project, Stancea Vichie and the AETIVP observers I had the honour of working with in East Timor during the ballot process. This book is dedicated to our East Timorese friends, too many of whom are no longer with us.

Damien Kingsbury
Melbourne, January 2000

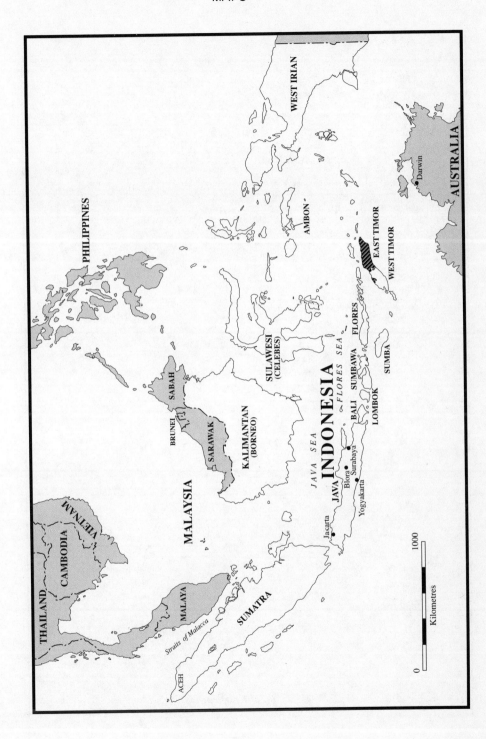

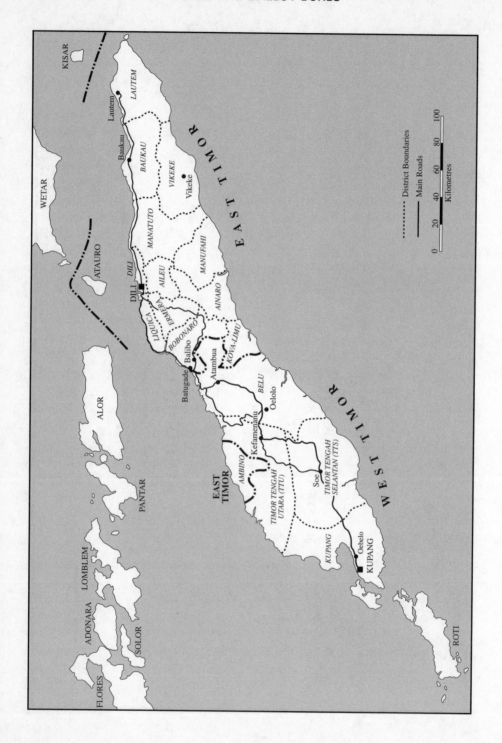

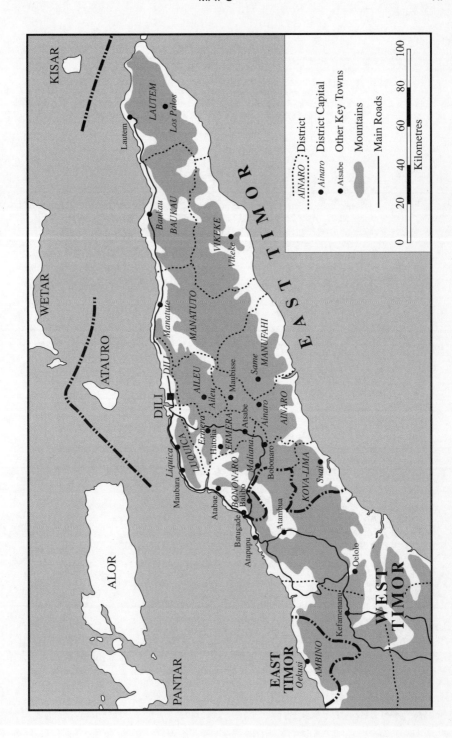

Reconciliation, unity and national development in the framework of the transition towards independence[1]

Jose 'Kay Rala Xanana' Gusmao

A few days from now (30 August 1999), the people of East Timor will cast their vote in the Popular Consultation, organised by the United Nations, to democratically choose their destiny. A long chapter in the history of our people's struggle for the affirmation of its culture and firm determination to choose its own future is reaching its conclusion.

The patriotic engagement of thousands of freedom fighters and anonymous citizens in this glorious struggle for the independence of our country is the expression of our ancestors' fighting spirit over centuries. The blood of the Timorese nation is made of heroic deeds and the abnegation of all those who have given their lives in the name of freedom. It has been a difficult process, a source of mourning, destruction of families, that marked generations.

Reconciliation and national unity

The birth of the Timorese nation cannot take place in the midst of division, discord and rancour. Regardless of past political positions, all citizens are called upon to embrace the need for harmony, and to show forgiveness and tolerance towards their brothers for the sake of our national interests. The difficulties endured to this day cannot remain a permanent shadow obstructing our future.

Our nation will be greater if each and every one of us is able to forgive, including those who have committed the most reprehensible acts. In such an exalting time, each of us is called upon to overcome differences and bury hatred. Let's embrace each other and join hands in an unbreakable chain of brotherhood and love. For Timor's future to be one of joy and prosperity, we must be united around our nation.

Peace, reconciliation, understanding and harmony are fundamental for the political stability, for the social and economic progress of our country. All citizens are thus called upon to demonstrate brotherly understanding and solidarity towards the less fortunate and most needy. In the new era which is

---

[1] This chapter was written by Xanana Gusmao just before the 30 August 1999 ballot. It was a speech to the people of East Timor, recorded and broadcast from prison in Jakarta about ten days before the ballot. It addresses the main issues that continued to focus the attention of the CNRT after Indonesian forces left the territory on 29 October 1999.

before us, all East Timorese are indispensable in eradicating the misery and under-development that characterise a large proportion of our population.

The construction of the East Timorese state

The eradication of illiteracy and the construction of a prosperous society with a modern and self-sufficient economy will be the main foci of our struggle in this new phase. All East Timorese are called upon to dedicate their skills and energy to the strengthening of our country.

The objective of our struggle for independence was to build the state of Timor Lorosae that fights for peace, democracy and prosperity for all, regardless of political or religious convictions, race, colour or social and cultural origins.

The state of Timor Lorosae will respect the universal principles relating to human rights, gender equality, freedom of speech and information and of assembly as they are defined in international conventions and treaties. Independence will be consolidated through the establishment of the rule of law. The state of Timor Lorosae will fight for the separation of powers and defend the independence of its judiciary.

The state of Timor Lorosae will respect and protect the right to ownership of land and goods legally acquired in East Timor by individuals or groups, nationals or foreigners, and will encourage the economic players to consolidate and expand their ongoing economic and social activities. It will promulgate laws that will regulate in a balanced manner public and private interests, social and individual objectives and will guarantee the freedom of movement of people and goods.

Market economy

With the objective of promoting economic growth towards self-sufficiency, the state of Timor Lorosae will advocate the development of a market economy with selective intervention of the state to ensure equity, transparency and efficiency. The state will encourage the building and strengthening of the private sector in all social spheres, with particular emphasis on support for private Timorese entrepreneurs.

To overcome Timor Lorosae's backwardness and underdevelopment is a very difficult task that will require determination, persistence and a strong individual and collective effort. The scarcity of resources and the high level of illiteracy are preoccupying. However, this must not dampen our enthusiasm and will to overcome under-development.

Economic and social development

Politic and economic development will follow an approach promoting higher production, prioritising rural development, which concerns the overwhelming majority of the East Timorese people. Integrated rural development will be based on the reinforcement of the towns and villages, on the improvement of living standards, and on the introduction of techniques and technology that will increase productivity and, consequently, the rise of agricultural production, the exchange of goods, always bearing in mind the equilibrium and preservation of the environment.

The objective of the economic policy of the state of Timor Lorosae will be to transform the East Timorese economy, predominantly an agrarian and subsistence one, into a more diversified and developed economy. For such purpose it will promote a better use of natural resources such as forests, cattle and fisheries, the exploration of mineral resources and development of tourism.

With a view to stimulating job-creation, and generating greater income for the state budget, the Government of Timor Lorosae will draw maximum benefit from the country's geo-political and economic situation, and of the confluence of the commercial route between Asia and Oceania, in the midst of thousands of islands situated between the Indian and Pacific Oceans, taking advantage of the ample market of the Southeast Asian countries, among which are countries that have experienced significant economic growth in the past 30 years.

In this context, the Government will define a policy of fiscal and custom incentives that encourage and stimulate investment in the production sector so as to replace imports, increase exports and stimulate employment. In pursuit of this economic policy, the state of Timor Lorosae will facilitate the creation of some special economic zones in order to stimulate employment for the East Timorese, though the development of an off-shore centre consisting of a modern financial hub.

Attracting foreign investment

The state of Timor Lorosae will encourage the transfer of resources available abroad and their channelling into fruitful investments in the country. To this end, a specific bill protecting national and foreign investments will be enacted. As it is the practice in international banking, the state will protect banking secrecy by law.

With the intention of attracting foreign investment to complement domestic resources and of creating jobs, the Government of Timor Lorosae will develop technical, scientific, economic, social and cultural co-operation, on the bilateral and multilateral level, with different countries and international institutions.

The appearance of Timor Lorosae on the global economic stage will permit access to the experience and knowledge achieved throughout the world and thus reinforce the capacity of the East Timorese people to confront the challenge of globalisation.

The Transitional Government of Timor Lorosae will prepare a plan of national development for the years 2000 to 2005, in the context of a strategic plan over 20 years. The plan will confer priority to the development of national initiatives promoting better exploitation of natural resources, local capacity and initiative, making the most of internal savings as a contribution to the realisation of investments in the country.

Public administration

The public service will be gradually restructured according to the demands of the independent state of Timor Lorosae. Public administration has to be efficient and operational, proportionally in keeping with our objectives and means. Public administration will be managed with transparency, raising the level of professionalism with full and regular accountability.

In this context, the state will modernise all of its services, simplifying the administrative procedures to better serve the national economy. It will encourage the expansion of domestic and international commerce and stimulate the modernisation of the financial and banking sectors as well as other services such as transportation, communications, water and electricity, sanitation and urbanisation, and will build the necessary infrastructure.

Good governance will also aim to reduce bureaucracy and prevent corruption. The government initiative will also aim to encourage projects generating employment and wealth, which will bring about prosperity and well-being.

The state of Timor Lorosae will promote a culture that confers value and dignity on work in all sectors of activity. Recruitment of public servants will be kept strictly within budget limits, for a rational management of human and financial resources. In the context of its economic program, employment will be generated mainly through development of small-scale enterprises in the agricultural and industrial sectors, in commerce and traditional crafts.

Training

With the independence of our country, governance will require scientific and technical know-how to ensure that the economic and social life of the country follows the appropriate course. We are thus calling on all citizens, and in particular on the youth, to resume or pursue their studies at all levels.

Bearing in mind our history, the current, geo-economic and cultural reality to which our country belongs, we must strengthen Tetum, our mother language, disseminate and perfect the command of Portuguese language, as well as maintain the teaching of the Indonesian language. Success in education and training in any socio-professional sector will ensure positive results on the social and economic issues.

With regard to the eradication of illiteracy, the Government of Timor Lorosae will give priority to adult education and the training of East Timorese, focussing on the youth, enabling them to obtain professional, technical and vocational qualifications to enhance their entrepreneurship, be it of their own initiative or in the context of entrepreneurial associations or co-operatives.

Relations with ASEAN and Indonesia

The state of Timor Lorosae will strive to participate in the dynamics of regional co-operation for peace and development in the ASEAN framework, reinforcing political, defence and security alliances, as well as economic, social, scientific and technical relations.

Taking into account its history, as well as the imperatives of peace and multifaceted co-operation, Timor Lorosae will establish privileged co-operative relations in the different economic and financial, social and cultural sectors with a democratic and multiparty Indonesia, formalising bi-lateral agreements in the economic sector (among others), scientific and technical co-operation agreements, an agreement of mutual protection of investments and agreements in the economics and finance areas.

Relations with Portugal and CPLP

The solidarity between the peoples of Portugal and East Timor is unbreakable. Relations with Portugal constitute a wealth of knowledge, historic and cultural inheritance as well as an emotional bond close to our hearts that we have preserved in all circumstances. We wish this relationship to remain strong, through new relations of co-operation, as two peoples, free and equal. We were deeply touched by the declaration of the Portuguese that they will take responsibility to ensure that the existing institutions in East Timor continue to function.

Bearing in mind the profound solidarity forged with the Lusophone countries during the most difficult years, we will join the forum for co-operation linking Southeast Asia, Africa, Europe and the Americas.

International relations

The state of Timor Lorosae will practise a policy of peace, peaceful co-existence, solidarity and mutually beneficial international co-operation with the greatest possible number of countries. Timor Lorosae will formally seek membership of the UN, APEC, the South Pacific Forum as well as ASEAN and the CPLP. The state of Timor Lorosae will ratify the agreements signed by the member states of these organisations safeguarding the country's situation of transition. Within these organisations Timor Lorosae could develop wide ranging regional co-operation, reinforcing political alliances of mutual defence and security, as well as reinforcing economic, social, scientific and technical relations.

The state of Timor Lorosae will establish mutually beneficial relations with all independent countries, and will foster relations at various levels with Australia, the United States, Japan, the European Union, and Portugal in particular, and the member countries of the Community of Lusophone Countries (CPLP).

The state of Timor Lorosae will also establish political and diplomatic relations with all independent nations, based on mutual respect and national sovereignty and equality, entering into mutually beneficial agreements.

The state of Timor Lorosae will seek membership of the International Monetary Fund and the World Bank institutions as well of the financial institutions established in the framework of ASEAN and the countries with which bilateral and regional co-operation have been developed.

The national liberation fighters

The Falintil, the liberation fighters of our nation, will deserve the eternal gratitude of our entire people. Not a single one of us fought expecting rewards of any kind or nominations to top posts in government and public administration. For us the greatest reward will be to attend the ceremony at which the flag of freedom will be raised in our free and independent nation. Our Government, with the support of the international community, will give priority activities aimed at the social and economic integration of the freedom fighters, creating the conditions and opportunities for them to receive professional training, so that they will not depend exclusively on the state budget.

Top priority tasks

General amnesty and tolerance

At this promising and unparallelled moment in the history of our people, as we prepare to face a new future, it is imperative to ensure political and social stability in the country. This requires a peaceful and harmonious transition, as well as the reinforcement of the spirit of equanimity and national reconciliation.

For reconciliation to become effective, we will proclaim general amnesty for all political crimes committed until now. This decision is a mature one taken after careful consideration. This act of generosity transcends our emotions, heals wounds and elevates the soul of our people! I wholeheartedly appeal for an immediate end to violence.

So as to ensure stability during the period following the vote, the Transitional Government will pay particular attention to the integration of East Timorese currently in the TNI and Polri ranks, as well as the paramilitary groups. Training will be available to those who wish to enter, together with other citizens, the Timorese police force for the protection of law and order and the safety of the citizens.

We have fought against an oppressive system that has antagonised us. At no point have we fought against the people of Indonesia. We are on the eve of a new era. All East Timorese citizens will thus be able to consider one another with trust and join hands for the growth of our nation.

Ensure the continuity of operation of the country

In the current phase, it is essential to ensure the normal operation of the institutions, businesses and other services. We call on public servants in particular, on businessmen, all Timorese nationals and foreign residents in Timor Lorosae to:

1. Ensure that the institutions continue to function:

   It is indispensable that all public and private institutions continue to operate in the period immediately following the Popular Consultation to ensure the regular distribution of goods and service provision to the population. There must be no moving backwards. Services must improve particularly in the health and education sectors.

2. Maintain the regularity of supply:

   It is essential to pay particular attention to the uninterrupted supply of goods, including that of imported goods, to the population.

3. Maintain production levels:

    To avoid paralysis of the economy, it is essential to ensure the replenishment of the necessary reserves up to the next harvest and its commercialisation. Maintaining in full operation of industrial plants and services is equally important, particularly water and energy supply, health centres and others catering to the people's basic needs.

Negotiations with Indonesia

The Transitional Government will negotiate with the Indonesian Government to reach an agreement on issues that are essential and of high national interest so as to:

- Maintain the Indonesia rupiah in circulation in the country at least during the transition period;
- Define the status of the East Timorese civil service (including military and police) and the employees of partly state-owned companies in the service of the Indonesian state, so that their rights and obligations are respected;
- Define the rights and obligations of the Indonesian citizens working in state institutions as well as parastatal companies (including banks and state telecommunication, water, electricity and transport companies) who wish to remain in the service of the new state of Timor Lorosae. They are welcome to contribute to the building of the new state;
- Reach an agreement on the public institutions and parastatal companies operating in East Timor.

Dear East Timorese brothers and fellow countrymen,

The independence process demands the participation of all the sons and daughters of Timor Lorosae. We call upon all the political leaders regardless of their differences and to the leaders of all the East Timorese associations to lend their skills, their knowledge and energies to contribute together to the building of the Nation.

We are all indispensable to the construction of our independence. Let's make Timor Lorosae our common banner. We have to face the challenge of the affirmation of our political and cultural identity, which causes us to face complex problems linked to economic and social development. Therefore, we must redouble our efforts to win our fight against poverty and under-development.

The struggle against under-development is a long and complex one. By fighting together we can successfully contribute to the creation of a dignified and prosperous Timor Lorosae. Due to the democratic nature of the popular consultation, the decision to build or not an independent country concerns us all. All citizens, in the interest of the nation, must respect the outcome of the vote and pledge to put their skills and energies at the service of the Timorese nation.

Timor Lorosae will welcome in its bosom all the East Timorese, regardless of the positions they assumed in the past. I particularly refer to those who are part of the pro-integration paramilitary forces (PPI).

I here reiterate my solemn commitment to guarantee the amnesty and reconciliation between the East Timorese for the security and tranquillity of all.

It is time to build the future!

Towards reconciliation

Bishop Carlos Belo

It appears to me that the problems of East Timor are not unique to East Timor. They occur in many countries in these final years of the 20th century. There are special characteristics to the present culture of violence throughout Indonesia and East Timor, as there are to other places in the world where people live in fear. To paraphrase Leo Tolstoy, it seems that each country is unhappy in its own way.

I want to talk to you about reconciliation and the processes involved in reducing conflict, and moving from fear and anger to peace and development. Reconciliation is not simply made of shaking hands and speaking some fine words. It certainly does not involve forgetting the past and marching on regardless. Reconciliation means much more than that. It is not easy. It is hard, strenuous and difficult. It is also necessary. In fact it is crucial if societies that are split apart by politics and terror are to regenerate and become places where human dignity is respected.

I am indebted to the work of American theologian Robert Schreiter for his insights into reconciliation through his work for the Caritas network, the organisation that has brought me to Australia for this occasion.[1]

Other prime sources of insight can be found in the transcripts of the South African Truth and Reconciliation Commission. In that Commission ordinary people have the chance to tell their story. It is an open, public process that relies strongly on a widespread desire to heal wounds, not exact retribution.

I will not talk about the crimes that have been committed in my country, East Timor. Although enough can never be said on that subject to satisfy the many victims, I want to concentrate on the future and perhaps to suggest some ideas about working for a true and just peace through processes of reconciliation.

Reconciliation is a word that is used a great deal in Christian writings, for it comes to us directly from the life and example of Jesus Christ. In the short time that I have been here I have noticed that reconciliation between indigenous and non-indigenous Australians is a subject of considerable importance in Australia. You have a Council for Aboriginal Reconciliation. Other countries too have adopted the words and practices of reconciliation: South Africa, Chile, Rwanda to name only a few. But it is clear that reconciliation in Australia is not straightforward. Setting up a national

---

[1] This talk was given just before the ballot to a gathering of Australian supporters in Sydney.

institution does not necessarily affect the feelings and understandings that lie in the hearts of ordinary men and women.

Sometimes the word reconciliation is linked to the word truth. South Africa has a Truth and Reconciliation Commission. That is an extremely important conjunction of meanings, truth and reconciliation. For it is only through establishing and agreeing on the truth that we can achieve reconciliation.

Take the story told by Reverend Mpambami to that Commission:

Peter and John are friends. It happened that Peter stole a bicycle from John, and then after three weeks Peter came to John saying, "John let's talk about reconciliation."

And then John said, "I don't think we need talk about reconciliation at the present moment until you bring back my bicycle. Where is my bicycle?"

And Peter said, "No, let us forget about the bicycle, let us talk about reconciliation"

And then John said, "We cannot talk about reconciliation until my bicycle is back."

We cannot deal with reconciliation until the people who are victimised sit down around the table and talk about what happened first. The bicycle may be replaceable but the dead are not. We cannot go to a shop and buy back those people who are dead. Nelson Mandela has said: 'To make peace with your enemy, one must work with that enemy, and that enemy becomes your partner.'

What does he mean by that? Simply that in order to make a new start to lives fractured by violence and fear, we must talk with our persecutor. Recognition must be made by the perpetrators of crimes of the facts of what happened, and victims need to be prepared for the recognition that crimes in which they suffered need to be put to rest and the burden of shame, fear and anger can be relieved. This needs to happen in a mutual process based on equality and dignity for all concerned.

Living in fear, faced every day with violence, creates victims paralysed and captive to the past. Our concern must be to break the cycle of violence. There are many parts of the world where the violence continues for many years after the initial events, think of the Middle East or of Northern Ireland. Our concern must be to create new living conditions where the victims can become survivors. To do that requires true reconciliation, both individual reconciliation and social reconciliation.

The last 20 years have seen numerous attempts by governments to establish truth and reconciliation commissions. In many of these the Church has played a leading role, particularly in South America. Some 25 official commissions have been established, relying mainly on public hearings where victims can present their cases. These have been situations where there was an urgent need to establish clearly the truth of what happened because many governments refuse to recognise the truth. They develop the capacity to lie on a grand scale, to distort facts, to divide people. When that occurs we need a process of restoring a moral order to society. A moral order grounds civil society and it uses the law to institutionalise its morality.

It is amazing how powerful a weapon the truth is in the fight against dictatorship. Take the example of Argentina, where a military dictatorship ruled throughout the 1970s and into the 1980s, conducting a war against its own people, who merely wanted an open, democratic country. The crucial event that more than anything else brought about the downfall of that dictatorship is found in the actions of the grandmothers and mothers who started to meet outside the Presidential Palace in the capital, Buenos Aires. They were the grandmothers and mothers of children who had disappeared, and they carried photographs of their loved ones. They were asking for information as to their whereabouts, and they continued to meet for many months in that very public place. The authorities did not dare oppose them through confrontation, and their continued presence, with the photographs of their children, brought home the truth of that regime to many millions of people.

Telling the truth through a public process is the first element of reconciliation. In many countries, not just Indonesia, or Australia, the factual truth of what happened, perhaps hundreds of years ago, lives with us now. If that truth is not recognised, or it has been distorted by the political process, it becomes very difficult to agree on the facts of what happened. When governments state that certain events have not happened, and yet we have the victims before us to testify that they did, government loses its credibility, and it loses its authority. We see before us today governments that lack natural authority and have to make up for that by the use of force. They do not have the support of the people because they are not trusted by the people. We hear many fine words seeking national unity, co-operation and harmony, yet, almost in the same breath orders are given to military units to shoot civilians, protesters are rounded up, many disappear, many are tortured. No government which governs by the use of force can survive except by force. There is no going back, because force begets force, and the perpetrators of crimes live in fear that they might become victims in their turn.

People torn apart from each other by violence and discrimination can only resume peaceful humane relationships if they recognise the events that have caused so much harm. There is a need to recognise the truth of what happened and then come to an agreement about how future relations are going to be handled. But if the truth remains unrecognised, those relations will be constrained for as long as memories survive. It is clear that such memories survive a very long time. Even today, victims of the Holocaust in Europe retain the memory of what happened to them 50 years ago.

The life and example of Jesus Christ teaches us that the victims should be our first concern. Victims of violence bear more than physical scars. The psychological burden can remain for the rest of their lives, and sometimes it is so overwhelming that it results in suicide. Such cases are well documented. I understand that Australia has become home to many thousands of people from war-torn countries bearing these burdens. I thank God that a refuge is available and that its people will welcome the survivors.

But the life and example of Jesus Christ teaches us more than to take care of the victims. It teaches us that the victims themselves bear more than simply the burden of their mistreatment. We learn that it is the victims themselves who must start the process of reconciliation. Jesus Christ was Himself a victim of violence. He was crucified by the Roman state, experiencing a horrible painful death. In His resurrection we see the victim overcoming his pain. His friends and disciples, in great fear themselves, abandoned Him in the hour of His greatest need. In His return to life He approached the disciples and brought them to the understanding that they must spend the rest of their lives spreading the word of His teachings. They overcame their fear. They recognised their own abandonment of Jesus and they built new lives. We read in the Gospels of the transformation that Jesus underwent through His death. Victims need to transform themselves into survivors, and ultimately some are able to approach their tormentors without hatred.

I have heard that many stories of transformation of victims have been recounted during the South African Truth and Reconciliation Commission hearings. One story is that of a man who accidentally met his former torturer in a car sales room. He was initially tempted with the idea of killing him with a knife, but his anger was dissipated when he talked to the man and found him to be poor, sick and friendless. He arranged for him to get to hospital, but the former torturer died soon afterwards. The survivor now felt able to shake off the burden of bitterness and hatred and was able to move forward with his life. The former torturer felt relieved of the burden of shame that his work had placed on him.

That is an example of reconciliation between two former enemies. It is based on recognition of the facts of what happened and then the mutual need to move on to a new life unburdened by the past. The past is never forgotten; but its burden is lessened.

When we have whole societies needing to reconcile the difficulties become even greater. The effort being made in South Africa to create a public debate on reconciliation is a great step forward. Their Truth and Reconciliation Commission has a very open process. It is not bound by legalities such as courts of law impose, but is closer to the oral traditions of Africa, allowing ordinary South Africans to recount their stories in a public way, first of all to establish the truth of what happened. There has been discussion about reparations, of vengeance and of justice. Observers have sometimes been overwhelmed by the expressions of magnanimity and generosity shown by those who have suffered. I think we in this part of the world have a lot to learn from this new experience. For what is required of us is that we come to some sort of public judgement about the past and start the process of building on that judgement so that we can start new lives in the new millennium.

I have read too about your Human Rights and Equal Opportunity Commission and its report on the Stolen Children. This report recounts many stories of suffering, perhaps not so much of physical violence, but of psychological violence. It seems to me that the capacity to tell these stories, in a public way, shows great courage. Undoubtedly the survivors gain by relieving the burden of secret memory and bringing it into the open for all to see. Their private knowledge has now become public knowledge. This new public knowledge acknowledges a truth that had not been widely known before. It seems to me that there is no going back to a time when those stories were not public. Those truths are now part of the public discourse of your society. No-one can pretend that these events did not happen. The effects of government policy are now clear.

In Indonesia we have lived for so long under a regime that distorted facts and language every day that we will need many such reports to be able to establish that sort of clarity. To tell the truth in a public process will require peace and the abandonment of the use of force by government before people will be willing to co-operate. The political process needs to establish a new governmental mechanism in East Timor. Our greatest fears are that this is not yet underway and that in fact we have more violence to meet before that can even start.

I have not spoken about justice. I think we need to think carefully about different types of justice. A process of reconciliation presents to us the idea of a restorative justice, not a justice of retribution. Let us compare the two and seek the best way forward. I do not offer any particular solution. We should observe carefully what happens in other parts of the world where the fighting may have ended but the conflict continues.

Neither have I spoken today of forgiveness. It would be quite wrong of us to demand forgiveness from those who have been hurt so deeply. That is not something that is within our power. Individual acts of forgiveness are proof of the grace of God.

Pope John Paul II captured the relationship of truth to justice, especially as it relates to forgiveness, in his message for the 1997 Day of World Peace. He says that there are two things required to bring about forgiveness and reconciliation: respect for the truth and a justice 'that is not limited to that which is right among the parties to the conflict, but looks above all to re-establish authentic relations with God, with the self, with others'. Truth prepares the ground for justice.

East Timor to 1999

Damien Kingsbury

East Timor's history is more complicated than many, at least for such a small (19,000 square kilometres) and relatively obscure place. Prior to the Portuguese establishment of a Dominican religious order and trading ports in the mid-16th century,[1] Timor (*Timor Loroe Sa'e*—Land of the Rising Sun) was a collection of small and competing kingdoms. Even until the middle of the 19th century, petty kingdoms not only continued to exist but frequently acted against each other and the Portuguese. The southern part of Timor was predominantly Polynesian in ethnic make-up, the north mostly Melanesian and the central regions largely aboriginal. Added to this ethnic mix, Chinese traders seeking sandalwood had been visiting the island for centuries before the Portuguese arrived, while traders from other nearby islands were regular visitors. As a result of the ethnic variety and the rugged, difficult terrain, some 16 separate linguistic groups, along with around 35 further dialects, developed in that last area controlled by the Portuguese, corresponding to contemporary East Timor (see De Matos 1974; Leitao 1952).

During the 16th and 17th centuries, the small kingdoms of Timor were frequently at war with each other, primarily in bids to control the island's lucrative sandalwood trade. Their reception of the Portuguese was little different. Portugal only gradually extended its control over the island, facing several rebellions. By the time it had managed to subjugate most of the *liuri* (local kings), the Dutch had begun to expand their regional interests into this Portuguese territory. In two agreements following conflict, in 1859 and in 1913, Timor was partitioned along its present lines, leaving the enclave of Oecusse within the Dutch territory (Hiorth 1985:6–7). This was the state of the island when Japanese forces occupied Dutch Timor in February 1942. The Japanese had left Portuguese Timor alone, as it was a colony of the sympathetic but otherwise neutral fascist Portuguese government. However, Australia, concerned about the potential for Timor to be used as a base for the launch of an invasion, violated Portugal's neutrality by sending 400 commandos to operate in the territory on 17 December 1941. In the ensuing conflict, many local people supported Australian commandos in their work against the Japanese. The price for these people was that some 40,000 of them were killed by the Japanese in retribution, with many more dying in later Allied bombing (Jardine 1995:21–22; see also Hastings 1999). It was from

---

[1] Portuguese explorer Duarte Barbosa was one of the first Europeans to visit the territory, arriving in 1518.

this time that many Australians began to identify a special relationship with the people of East Timor, which both assisted and complicated East Timor's bid for independence in the last quarter of the 20th century.

Portuguese Timor's post-war period was quiet, with the colony being the least developed of Portugal's overseas possessions. However, the cost of retaining its colonies burdened Portugal and, with the winds of change sweeping the Iberian Peninsula, on 24 April 1974 the fascist Salazarist dictatorship of Marcello Caetano was overthrown in a military coup that quickly took on a leftist character. The intention of the Revolutionary Council was for Portugal to cast off its colonial dependencies and, as a consequence, political parties began forming in the colony. Founded on 20 May 1974, the Timorese Social Democrats, soon renamed the Frente Revolucionaria de Timor L'Este Independente (Revolutionary Front for an Independent East Timor), better known as Fretilin, was the biggest and most popular party. It was trailed by the Uniao Democratica de Timor (Timorese Democratic Union—UDT), founded 11 May 1974, comprising small businesspeople, property owners and officials, which initially supported continued integration with Portugal but soon opted for independence, and later for integration. The Associacao Popular Democratica de Timor (Apodeti—Timorese Popular Democratic Association) was founded soon afterwards on 27 May 1974. Other minor parties also came into existence, including the Partido Trabalhista (Workers Party), Associacao Popular Monarquia de Timor (APMT—Popular Association of Timorese Monarchists) and the Associacao Democratica Intergracao Timor-Leste Australia (Aditla—Democratic Association for the Integration of East Timor into Australia) and Klibur Oan Timur Aswain (KOTA—Sons of the Mountain Warriors). Of these, Partido Trabalhista had perhaps a dozen members, APMT was unpopular and quickly became the party known as KOTA, while the Aditla received a negative response from Australia and, subsequently, folded. Kota and Apodeti supported integration with Indonesia and were essentially a product of Indonesia's military intelligence (Dunn 1996:65–6; Hiorth 1985:21–23; see also Nicol 1978:35–147; Joliffe 1978:chs2–5). Between them, these smaller parties accounted for less than 10% of popular support.

Fretilin and UDT were initially not radically different in their aims, and managed to come together in an alliance in January 1975, seeking independence. An election for a popular assembly to oversee decolonisation was planned for October 1976. But with Indonesian intelligence conspiring against the more left-wing Fretilin, the UDT was led to believe Fretilin would soon launch a coup. To forestall this possibility, on 11 August 1975, UDT, supported by local police, made a pre-emptive strike against Fretilin in what was called the 'Revolutionary Anti-Communist Movement of 11 August'.

However, Fretilin enjoyed the support of around 3,000 Timorese (Portuguese army) soldiers and some 7,000 local militia (Dunn 1996:38). Fighting was fierce but it was over within days, costing some 2,000–3,000 lives. The Portuguese administration fled to the nearby island of Atauro and then to Portugal. Never great colonial masters, the Portuguese left the colony in abject retreat. Portugal, however, continued its claim to East Timorese sovereignty (which it finally relinquished to the UN at the time of Indonesia's formalisation of separation in late 1999). In late August and early September 1975, UDT–Apodeti–Kota–Trabalhista (pro-integration) remnants fled to West Timor from where, with the fulsome assistance of the Indonesian military, they began cross-border raids the following month. In this post-'civil war' period, Fretilin put back together the machinery of government and, apart from the security problem in the west, life resumed close to usual under an interim administration (see Dunn 1996:chs 8, 9).

The first Indonesian–pro-integration raids in early October 1975 were on the northern coastal border town of Batu Gade, which was abandoned by Falintil[2] troops in the face of superior numbers and tanks. This then provided the base for a more sustained attack in mid-October, when Indonesian troops and anti-Fretilin irregulars attacked the town of Balibo, about 20 kilometres southeast of Batu Gade. It was in this attack that five Australian journalists were killed by the invading force, which increased Australian interest in the territory (and would continue to have implications almost a quarter of a century later). Despite these forays by Indonesian-backed forces across the border, Falintil put up an unexpectedly stiff resistance, prompting Indonesian military planners to reconsider their approach to what was by now an obvious desire to occupy the territory of Portuguese Timor. On 24 November 1975, Fretlin asked the UN to push for the withdrawal of Indonesian forces from its territory, and four days later declared East Timor an independent republic.

On 30 November UDT and Apodeti announced their support for integration into Indonesia. On 7 December 1975, Indonesia launched its formal invasion of East Timor, starting with a parachute landing on Dili ahead of more than 40,000 troops invading the territory. The wholesale slaughter of East Timorese people by Indonesian troops that immediately followed presaged a major campaign of violence and dislocation. It has been variously estimated that 60,000 people were killed in the first two months immediately following the invasion. On 22 April 1976, the UN voted for Indonesia to withdraw from East Timor. In May 1976, selected East Timorese village chiefs and others who supported integration, including representatives of

---

[2] Falintil—Forcas Armada de Liberacao Nacional de Timor L'Este (Armed Forces for the National Liberation of East Timor)—was the armed wing of Fretilin, and now of the Council of National Timorese Resistance.

UDT, Apodeti, Kota and Trabhalista, were chosen by the occupying Indonesian force to vote for East Timor's incorporation into Indonesia. These delegates were claimed by Indonesia to represent the wider East Timorese community. Their decision was formally endorsed by Indonesia's President Suharto on 17 July. This decision was never accepted by the UN, which voted on 28 November 1976 and again on 17 July 1977 and 20 November 1978 for East Timor to be allowed an act of self-determination. In an act that led to deep divisions within Australian society, on 20 January 1978, Australia gave *de facto* recognition of East Timor's incorporation into Indonesia. This move was significant as Australia had initially led criticism of the invasion and incorporation, and as the closest neighbour was seen to have a moral responsibility in the issue. This recognition was later confirmed, in 1985, when the Australian government shifted this *de facto* recognition to *de jure* recognition of the legitimacy of incorporation. This recognition paved the way for Australia and Indonesia to reach agreement on the Timor Gap Treaty for the exploration of oil and natural gas in the region between Timor and Australia.

Despite the overwhelming presence of Indonesian armed forces in East Timor, Falintil kept up an active military campaign throughout the later 1970s. Quickly abandoning conventional warfare, Falintil opted for guerilla tactics, which were relatively successful in holding back more than 20,000 Indonesian troops. On 31 December 1978, however, Falintil's leader, Nicolao Lobato, was killed after a six hour gun battle on Moutn Maubisse. Lobato's death was thought by Indonesian forces to herald the end of Falintil. However, in the face of continuing resistance, in the late 1970s and early 1980s, the Indonesian forces instituted a policy of relocating villagers believed to be supporting Falintil to 'secured' sites. Without adequate food, water or sanitation, by the early 1980s the International Committee of the Red Cross estimated that tens of thousands of people were on the edge of starvation. By late 1981, these sites were later estimated to have contributed to around half of the deaths of more than 200,000 people, around a third of East Timor's population[3] (ACFOA 1991:3).

Development?

Under Indonesia, East Timor, or Timor Timur as it was known in Indonesian, underwent a number of profound changes. Apart from the massive violence and social dislocation, that on a per capita basis exceeded even the atrocities of the Khmer Rouge in Cambodia, Indonesia moved to put its stamp on the territory. The first step was for senior military figures to take

---

[3] Indonesia's own official assessment estimated a drop in population from 626,546 in 1973 to 555,350 in 1980, a decline of 15%, not including expected population growth (DPR1987:17).

over or set up businesses that traded directly with Singapore, by-passing Jakarta and hence the need for taxation or other forms of accountability. For example, the military held a monopoly on East Timor's export of coffee, until the development of gas and oil took over as by far its most profitable trade. This military-dominated economy proved to be a lucrative source of income for many officers, although it had the effect of further impoverishing the already poor territory. Businesses and property once owned by Portuguese citizens were taken over by Indonesians. The military made considerable profits by selling established businesses to new Indonesian owners, even though the new owners never legally held title.

Under Indonesia, education was expanded and the number of secondary schools increased rapidly. In part, this policy of educational development was intended to inculcate in the East Timorese a sense of their belonging to the greater Indonesian 'nation'. The medium of education was Indonesian, which did have the effect of introducing as a common language Indonesian amongst virtually all East Timorese who went to school during Indonesia's occupation.

Indonesia also built a number of health clinics, although ordinary East Timorese felt little benefit from them, especially in the earlier years of occupation. What the clinics and, increasingly, the schools did serve was the influx of 'transmigrants'—those officially encouraged to relocate from more crowded islands—and economic migrants from around Indonesia. By 1998, it was widely estimated that more than 150,000 non-East Timorese lived in East Timor, with up to two-thirds of them centred on the capital of Dili. Administrative jobs were created to run the territory, but these were often given to non-East Timorese. Those who were brought to East Timor on government business received a 'hardship' allowance of 99% of their salary, which boosted local inflation and artificially inflated the average income of people in the territory. The standard of living for some East Timorese did rise under Indonesia, but for many it did not. Even the roads that Indonesia built in East Timor, for which it was unduly proud, according to resistance members served in large part to transport troops and equipment from district to district. According to aid workers in East Timor in 1994,[4] many of the major bridges and water supply projects were built with foreign aid.

Throughout all of this, East Timorese people were often regarded as less than human by their new Indonesian masters. Women were raped almost as a matter of course, opponents to Indonesian rule murdered and people continued to disappear, presumably killed, with a monotonous regularity. At no stage did the vast majority of the East Timorese people ever feel that they lived in other than an invaded territory, while the Indonesian armed forces

---

[4] When the author first visited the territory.

continued to act like an insensitive occupying force rather than as the guardians of the state and protectors of the peace (see AETA 1983:10–17). Meanwhile, Falintil continued its guerilla campaign from the mountains, reduced in the 1980s to a small and desperate force of a few hundred. It was rebuilt from the late 1980s as a small but tough and highly-disciplined military group consisting of four semi-independent units totaling perhaps 2,000.

Political changes

In 1981, after the Indonesian army's notorious 'fence of legs' campaign in which East Timorese civilians were pushed in front of Indonesian troops advancing on Falintil positions, the political parties were more closely co-ordinated under the overall banner of national liberation. This policy rejuvenated the independence movement and, briefly in 1983, the Indonesian government agreed to enter into peace talks. However, General Benny Murdani, who became commander-in-chief of the Indonesian armed forces in that year, cancelled the peace talks and stepped up the military campaign against the resistance movement. As head of military intelligence, Murdani had been one of the two key proponents and architects of Indonesia's invasion of East Timor[5] and was regarded in Indonesian military circles as militarily aggressive. He was not the sort of military leader who opted for discussion. The East Timorese resistance had little choice but to unite if it was not to disappear entirely (Jardine 1995:54–57; Singh 1995:145–6).

As the senior ranks of Falintil thinned out as a consequence of Indonesia's continued attacks. In 1981, leadership was formally handed to regional guerilla leader Jose Alexandre Gusmao, known by his *nom de guerre* Kay Rala Xanana. Gusmao was born on 20 June 1946 in Manatuto. As a young man he trained at the Jesuit seminary near Dare, just south of Dili. As one of the territory's few well-educated young men, he quickly joined the then newly-established political party the ASDT, later Fretilin. By August 1975 Gusmao was working for Fretilin's Department of Information and was elected to the party's central committee. However, following the Indonesian invasion in December, Gusmao fled to the east of the island, to a stronghold behind Mount Matebean, from where he led the armed resistance movement in that area.

Gusmao's first major initiative as leader was, on 26 April 1986, to establish the Council of National Maubere Resistance (CNRM) as a clandestine coalition of all East Timorese groups, including Fretilin, UDT and

---

[5] The other had been Murdani's mentor, General Ali Murtopo, who was head of Opsus (Special Operations), a secretive quasi-military organisation.

the student group Restencia National dos Estudantes de Timor L'Este (Renetil). Maubere, which means 'older brother' in Tetun, was used to describe the relationship between the active pro-independence fighters and ordinary East Timorese. In theory, Falintil was to look after the interests of ordinary East Timorese under this arrangement. In practice, what it meant was that Falintil worked more openly with East Timorese people, especially in terms of political education, and relied on them more closely to provide a support base for their activities. This paved the way for the independence movement's next step.

The next major move in the political delineation within East Timorese politics was the formal separation of Falintil from Fretilin in 1987. This division did not reflect any ideological division between the political and armed groups, but rather a recognition of the need for the armed resistance movement to represent all anti-Indonesian political groupings. Despite being Falintil's commander, it was also from this time that Xanana Gusmao led the independence movement to reorient itself away from open armed conflict, towards a policy of civil disobedience. The cost of the armed conflict, in terms of lives, and the slim chance that Falintil would ever be able to defeat Indonesia's military in the field, pushed Gusmao to look at attracting international attention to their cause, while still keeping up pressure on the Indonesian authorities within East Timor. The recruitment of young, urban East Timorese—in most cases those born in the years since Indonesia's invasion—into the pro-independence ranks breathed new life into the independence campaign. It was from this time that independence started to look like a faint possibility. The adoption of this policy also stamped Gusmao's personal authority on the pro-independence movement, elevating him from the status of guerilla leader to cult figure within the pro-independence community.

The Santa Cruz massacre

Despite the already long and bloody history of Indonesian atrocities in East Timor, perhaps the issue that most galvanised world opinion on East Timor was the killing of protestors at the Santa Cruz Cemetery in Dili on 12 November 1991. The protesters were, in theory, attending the burial of a student who had been killed two days previously. However, the event was also clearly an opportunity to protest against Indonesia's continued occupation of East Timor and active repression of its people. The attack against the protesters also corresponded to a planned (but abandoned) visit to Dili by a Portuguese delegation. One version of events had it that the massacre was prompted by the former commander-in-chief of Indonesia's armed forces, Benny Murdani, as a means of embarrassing his son-in-law, (then) Lieutenant Colonel Prabowo Subianto, who was at that time stationed in Dili. It was also a sign that the army would continue to take a tough line against protesters in East Timor. The incident backfired against this suggested plan, arousing even greater antipathy towards Indonesia amongst the people of East Timor, while Prabowo was not held accountable for the incident and two key Murdani supporters lost their jobs. A more conventional interpretation of events was that the army was solely trying to reassert its authority over dissident East Timorese, although this seems unlikely given the public nature of the attack (see Kingsbury 1998:119–20).

The outcome was that, regardless of the motives behind it, almost without warning, soldiers opened fire on the protesters at close range. They later bayoneted wounded protesters and were alleged to have gone to a nearby hospital where they killed the wounded who had been taken there. Parts of the massacre were recorded on videotape and broadcast throughout the world. It was a public relations disaster for Indonesia, and aroused considerable international sympathy for the East Timorese cause. The Indonesian government exacerbated the situation by initially claiming that only 19 had been killed with 91 wounded, later raising that number to 50 dead after a formal inquiry. However, other accounts put the final death toll from this encounter at 273 (Grant 1996:40).

It was far from the most bloody of Indonesia's massacres of East Timorese, but it did come at a time when the issue of East Timor was widely thought to have been resolved. In fact, what it showed the international community was two things. The first was that Indonesia's army would not hesitate in using brutal force against unarmed civilians. The second was that popular opposition to Indonesian rule in East Timor continued to be widespread. This in turn reflected the new policy on the part of Falintil to shift the focus of its campaign against Indonesia from direct armed conflict back to the towns of East Timor, through civil disobedience campaigns. It was a high price to pay, but the Santa Cruz Massacre refocussed world attention on East Timor in a way it had not been focussed since, or perhaps even including, 1975.

It was also from around the time of the Santa Cruz Massacre that the Catholic Church, already converting East Timorese at a quick rate, began to take on some of the traits of the radical version in Latin America, liberation theology. Most ordinary East Timor claim the Church was slow to accept the independence struggle, but as the ranks of its congregations swelled with pro-independence activists it was transformed from the bottom up. Although he had already begun speaking cautiously about the possibility of a referendum on East Timor's future, by 1992 Bishop Carlos Belo was still very cautious about his role and the role of the Church in pressing for independence.

However, within three years he had become an outspoken advocate of the human rights of East Timorese people and, by extension, an opponent of continued Indonesian occupation. In 1996 he and Fretilin's international spokesman, Jose Ramos Horta, were awarded the Nobel Peace Prize.

The capture of Xanana Gusmao

As a part of the independence movement's policy to bring the struggle from the countryside to the towns, Gusmao moved to Dili in 1991. It was from there that he personally directed the civil disobedience campaign. However, living in Dili was a high risk strategy, which came undone on 20 November 1992. Betrayed by an informer, Xanana was arrested. It was initially thought he would be charged with subversion, which carried up to the death penalty in Indonesia, but the charges were later modified to those of rebellion, illegal possession of weapons and separatism. He was initially sentenced to life imprisonment but, following international pressure, in 1993 his sentence was commuted to 20 years in prison.

While Fretilin and UDT had worked closely together since the mid-1980s, there had been some reluctance on the parts of their members to form a full coalition. This was based on the ideological differences of the two organisations, lingering animosities flowing from the August 1975 'civil war' and UDT's association, however forced, with the Indonesian army for some years thereafter. However, with UDT increasingly firmly in the pro-independence camp, it became clear to both UDT and to Fretilin that, in order to secure international support, they needed to present a cohesive front. This was done through the establishment in 1997 of the Conselho Nacional de Resistencia Timorense (Council for Timorese National Resistance—CNRT). CNRT became the primary vehicle through which aspirations for independence could be channelled. Leaders from both parties joined the CNRT, which became, in effect, a peak body. Both Fretilin and UDT continued to exist as separate political parties. Falintil shifted its political association to the CNRT, bringing some UDT members into its ranks in the process. The make-up of the CNRT included both Fretilin and UDT members at its top level, but Jose 'Xanana' Gusmao, the leader of both Falintil and Fretilin while still in jail, was elected to the position of President of the CNRT, while retaining his title of 'Supreme Commander' of Falintil.

The 'Popular Consultation'

Following the resignation of Suharto as Indonesia's President in May 1998, his successor, Habibie, moved to assuage concerns of the international community over a range of issues, while also instituting some liberalising procedures. Apart from releasing some political prisoners, lifting many media restrictions and making fitful moves towards cleaning up the most obvious cases of corruption and nepotism, Habibie began to look for something to further placate a restive international community. The cost of maintaining East Timor, in terms of the military presence, the infrastructure required to support both the military and the Indonesian bureaucracy and what the Indonesian government claimed was its investment in human infrastructure, through education and health, was higher, at US$50 million a year, per head of population than for any other province. However, 'a lot poured out of it, into the pockets of corrupt military and civilian officials' (McBeth 1999c). Some estimates suggest as much as 30% of spending was lost on corruption. In terms of revenues locally raised and expenditures, 7.6% of local government expenditure was raised within East Timor, with 92.4% coming from Jakarta (Tesoro 1999). But this did not account for the redirection of a massive proportion of East Timor's economy, nor for the disparities in income distribution that were clearly defined along ethnic lines.

As a consequence, and because of the international concern expressed over Indonesia's continued involvement in East Timor, on 20 June 1998, President Habibie offered to free Xanana Gusmao, withdraw troops and create a state of special autonomy for East Timor if the world recognised it as a part of Indonesia. It was only the first step in a protracted negotiation, and one that was quickly rejected by Gusmao as 'diplomatic blackmail'. Portugal, however, quickly jumped at the opportunity to re-open dialogue on East Timor, saying 'If Indonesia is aiming for democracy, it is their duty to guarantee the East Timorese people the right to choose how they want to live' (Spencer 1998). Discussion continued and by November it was becoming clear that Habibie was looking for a genuine resolution to the issue. On 27 January 1999, Habibie announced that the people of East Timor could decide their future. They would be given the chance to vote on whether they wished to remain as a part of Indonesia, with what was claimed would be a wide-ranging autonomy, or to opt for independence.

However, while this offer was at one level widely appreciated, most commentators, including the jailed leader of the CNRT, Gusmao, asked for a longer time-frame in which the process could be undertaken. The UN, which was to supervise the ballot, also asked for a longer time-frame. However, Habibie refused, locking the UN into conducting the ballot within seven months. In part, Habibie's refusal to allow a longer time-frame acknowledged that at a later time he would probably no longer be President and that his successor might have a very different policy on the status of East Timor. At that time, Habibie's most likely successor was Megawati Sukarnoputri. Megawati had already made clear her opposition to East Timor's becoming independent, a position she reiterated in East Timor just days before the ballot took place.

Further, the agreement that formalised the arrangement, signed on 5 May 1999, precluded the UN from having an armed presence in East Timor. (UN 1999a: pt 4). The Indonesian police would, the Indonesian government claimed, guarantee security. Yet before the 5 May agreement had even been signed, the security situation in East Timor had begun to deteriorate seriously. This reflected a deep reluctance on the part of many senior TNI figures, including the commander-in-chief of the TNI, General Wiranto, to accept Habibie's decision on East Timor. It also reflected a deteriorating relationship between Wiranto and Habibie and what amounted to competing visions for Indonesia's future. Thus the stage was set for the establishment of the TNI-backed militias in East Timor, the violence of the pre-ballot period and the arrival of the United Nations Assistance Mission to East Timor (UNAMET). The last bloody phase of East Timor's bid for self-determination was about to unfold.

The Popular Consultation in the Ermera district: Free, fair and secret?

Anthony Smith[1]

Between 17 and 31 August 1999 I was based in, or around, the township of Ermera to participate in the Popular Consultation as an Observer with the Australia East Timor International Volunteers Project (AETIVP). For the first half of the trip I was with Annemarie Devereux, a law lecturer from the Australian National University. For the second half I was paired with David Glasgow, a retired teacher from Darwin. While in the Ermera district we functioned as witnesses to events that occurred in the run-up to the Popular Consultation. This chapter concerns the conduct of the United NationsAssistance Mission to East Timor (UNAMET), as well as the pro-autonomy and pro-independence campaigns. Some mention will also be made of events on 30 August, the date of the referendum, and the immediate aftermath in the area.

It is the judgement of this observer that UNAMET did its best to remain neutral, despite charges to the contrary, and that the ballot stands as a free and fair result and accurately reflects the will of the people of the area that I observed. Major breaches of the voting rules did occur in the run-up to the ballot; however, this primarily came from the pro-autonomy campaigners. Therefore, the final result to reject autonomy would appear, given what occurred in the townships of Ermera, Gleno, Poetete, Fatu Bolo, Fatu Bessi and the immediate environs, to stand despite violations of the rules intended to swing the vote in the other direction.

The conduct of the UNAMET staff

Upon arriving in the area, Annemarie Devereux and I observed the voter education program that was conducted by the UNAMET staff. This generally consisted of UN volunteers presenting voter education through the use of local interpreters. The education programs generally included the following elements:

- stressing the importance of the vote to East Timor's future;
- emphasising that there would only be one vote per person;

---

[1] This report has been written after consultation with Annemarie Devereux. The author wishes to express his thanks for her assistance.

- explaining which identification documents needed to be brought to the polls (including the procedure for dealing with lost or stolen registration cards);
- stressing the complete secrecy of the vote, including guarantees that there would be one result for the whole of East Timor and no regional or village level break down of results;
- demonstrating how to mark or punch the ballot paper and place it in the ballot box correctly;
- reminding the people that they must vote on 30 August between 6am and 3.30pm (the time was later extended to 4pm);
- tellinging the people about successful United Nations missions around the world to overcome the fact that to many local people the UN was an unknown quantity;
- attempting to counter the effects of psychological coercion: audiences were reminded of Bishop Belo's statement in the Ermera church that the people were free from any 'blood oaths', to vote a certain way, that may have been signed under duress;
- informing the participants that there would be a period before the election where they could check the registration lists for their own names, and make objections to others if they did not believe they met the criteria to be on the list.

Great emphasis was placed on persuading the local people of their unique chance to decide on their future in an election that was freer and fairer than any they had experienced in the past.[2] Overall there was never even a hint that the UNAMET were instructing people who to vote for; instead, the emphasis was on voting as one's conscience dictated in an impartial election. In some villages the people clearly indicated their voting preferences by a clap of hands or comments, and in other cases they were more circumspect.

In my discussions with UNAMET DEOs it was apparent that DEOs had not been provided with a script for the civics education, only the general topics to be covered. It is thus possible that regional variations occurred. However, Annemarie Devereux and I witnessed two different teams of DEOs provide this education and it was of a consistently high standard. I witnessed further programs at a later date by other teams, and while the content remained largely the same, the presentation of the material differed. The education was simple, made good use of symbols and handouts, and was

---

[2] As an aside, this observer saw the voting figures for the Indonesian election for the town of Fatu Bessi that were still on the wall of the village administration centre. Of more than 3,000 votes cast in this town, all but six went to the Golkar Party.

undertaken with sufficient support in terms of translation. There was adequate time at the end of the sessions for questions and answers. For most civics education, there was adequate notice to the *kepala desa* (village head) and the residents to permit large attendances, though *ad hoc* education sessions were carried out in smaller villages. UNAMET staff were also able to monitor the way in which their literature was passed from village to village to ascertain whether the education was being transmitted to villages not directly targeted for education.

Another message stressed by the UN staff was that UNAMET would not leave East Timor after the Popular Consultation, regardless of the result—contrary to rumours that were in circulation around the Ermera district. This undertaking was based on the assumption that the Indonesian security forces, principally the Republic of Indonesia Police (Polri), would provide ongoing security for the UNAMET operation. In every case the local people seemed happy that UNAMET made this undertaking. There were, however, concerns expressed at UNAMET's inability to provide security for those wishing to travel on the polling day. People expressed concerns over road-blocks and the threat of having their homes burned. It was explained that UNAMET's over-riding priority would have to be to protect the ballot boxes, for without them, the whole process would be for nothing. I am satisfied that the voter education was done in an impartial manner.

One aspect of the education was to distribute radios where possible. These radios, donated by the Japanese government, were usually left with the kepala desa with a sheet listing the transmission frequencies and times of daily UNAMET broadcasts. Sometimes this meant one radio per village or hamlet, but due to shortages the giving of radios had to be targeted to where the greatest need was expected. A greater number of radios and education teams would have enabled more adequate coverage of the area. Use was also made of audio aids—including UNAMET educational tapes that could be broadcast through the sound systems of UN vehicles.

In the week prior to the poll itself, those registered to vote could check the lists to ensure that their name was present and correct. They could also object to those that they believed should not be on the registration list. During my observation of lists at Fatu Bolo, Poetete and Ermera, an overwhelming majority of people came to the polling centres to see that their name was there. This process was extremely successful. There was not a single objection to the lists in the whole of the Ermera district, but many people found that their names were spelled incorrectly.

In the area around Gleno the Civilian Police (CivPol) did a lot of follow up work on incidents. This was clearly a difficult job given that many witnesses were reluctant, there seemed to be little Polri support to follow up on incidents involving militia, and many incidents turned out to be little more than rumour. On one occasion I travelled with the New Zealand CivPol of the district into the Railaco area as a translator to investigate reports of intimidation in the area. The CivPol sent a clear message to the local Indonesian military (TNI) commander that they would regularly patrol the area and maintain a presence there through to voting day.

UNAMET staff in the district capital, Gleno, played a major role in negotiation with TNI, Polri, the militia, the pro-autonomy campaign leaders and the National Council for East Timorese Resistance (CNRT). In the run up to the referendum, for the most part, these negotiations played a crucial role in ensuring that relative peace was kept throughout the Ermera district. This 'understanding' suffered a serious breakdown, but those links forged ultimately ensured the safety of international and local UNAMET staff and observers. The charge arose just a few days prior to the vote that UNAMET and CNRT were in collaboration to ensure that the election result was in favour of rejecting autonomy, leading to separation from Indonesia.[3] This serious allegation was followed up in subsequent days with threats to UNAMET staff, principally the local workers. It also accounts for the siege that occurred in Gleno the day after the vote was taken (see below). Allegations of 'collusion' (to borrow one official Indonesian observer's pun on the reformasi movement's criticism of Suharto) between UNAMET and CNRT led to clear resentment from UNAMET staff. Ironically, the charges, and most of all the intimidation, led to a complete lack of respect for the local militia and some involved with the pro-autonomy campaign. It remains the opinion of this observer that while many UNAMET officials, from a vast array of countries, drew their own private conclusions about the different sides in this referendum process, there was no question of this spilling over into their roles as impartial UN staff.

The campaigns

Observing the political campaigns was an important part of observing the referendum process. In Ermera, Gleno and the immediate surrounds, it was very clear the vast amount of campaigning was undertaken by the pro-autonomy supporters. On almost a daily basis, autonomy supporters would leave the town bound for one of the campaigns in the district, and on one occasion, a large campaign in Dili. By contrast the CNRT supporters cancelled all but one of their rallies (which was held in Gleno), although a 'birthday celebration' for Falintil in the hills behind Fatu Bolo on 20 August functioned, for all intents and purposes, as a second.

---

[3] This included the district-wide distribution of written materials repeating the allegation.

From 17 August, Indonesia's independence day, the red and white Indonesian flags proliferated around the district and they remained standing through the election period. These flags were found in every village and hamlet, even in very remote spots. There was also a very wide dissemination of red and white tee-shirts and caps with the word *autonomi* written on them, which large numbers of people wore (this was even spotted in the Falintil camp near Fatu Bolo). The CNRT presence was less visible in this sense, with a small number of posters—usually featuring Xanana Gusmao. In Ermera town these posters were confined to one corner of the village. The CNRT supporters did conduct a systematic door to door political campaign in the area in order to combat the limitations on other types of campaigning. Students, on leave from studies elsewhere in Indonesia, were often involved in this type of work.

The actual campaign rallies also differed considerably in their nature. The pro-autonomy organisers would usually use transport (local trucks for coffee workers or minibuses) to move their people around to the appropriate meeting point. Between two and four pro-autonomy rallies were held each day within the Ermera district. These rallies would typically open with a good deal of traditional East Timorese dancing. The people either dressed in traditional clothing or in the red and white of the Indonesian flag. Tee-shirts and caps would be distributed, and at one rally I witnessed, at Poetete on 18 August, rice was brought in to give to the supporters that had gathered. One organiser openly admitted that the rice that was being trucked in was to be a gift for the pro-autonomy supporters. These rallies consisted of no more than 200–300 people, and often less.

There were a number of illegal rallies held by the pro-autonomy campaigners. Illustratively at Fatu Bessi and Fatu Quero (19 August), Eraulo, Gouldo, Mau Ubu, Urahow and Lisabat (20 August), and Railako (21 August). Annemarie Devereux and I personally witnessed the illegal rally at Fatu Bessi, where the pro-autonomy supporters arrived earlier than the planned UNAMET civic education program to take advantage of the assembled crowd. This delayed the start of voter education in Fatu Bessi and constituted a serious breach of the referendum rules.

The CNRT rally and the Falintil birthday celebrations were far different. The one rally in the district, which occurred in an established settlement area, in the weeks running up to the referendum, was in Gleno on 27 August. Most supporters walked or caught public transport and the rally attracted about 2,000 people. After speeches they marched past the central police station and the *Bupati*'s office. This march took place under duress, with supporters having to delay their march while a large number of pro-autonomy vehicles circled around in the near vicinity, probably on their way to Dili. Another threat had been delivered via the Gleno police chief, Lieutenant Colonel Gultom, who had stated to a senior CNRT member that Polri might not be able to guarantee the safety of pro-independence marchers who were civil servants. By implication Polri would not be able to protect them from the TNI. This sparked alarm among the UNAMET staff, prompting a CivPol presence to ensure safety. This, and the presence of other UNAMET staff, may have fuelled further speculation that there was collusion between the CNRT and UNAMET; however, those in attendance felt that their presence was of some necessity given the fresh threats to pro-independence supporters on that day.

The earlier birthday party for the Falintil on 20 August 1999 marked a real turning point in the district, because it is from this date that the troubles began to arise. On this date the Falintil held a celebration of their struggle against Indonesian armed forces since the invasion/integration of 1975. This occurred in the hills behind Fatu Bolo, about one hour's walk from Ermera. Annemarie Devereux and I decided that it was important to witness this event in the lead-up to the Popular Consultation, having attended the local pro-autonomy rally in Poetete several days earlier. Between 15,000 and 20,000 people were in attendance in the day-long celebrations. I also visited the Falintil camp on a subsequent visit. In my discussions with Falintil commanders and CNRT officials, the following things were clear. There was the need for reconciliation after the vote and that probably only some of Jakarta's leading generals and Suharto himself should face war crimes charges. There was favouritism shown to the establishment of full democratic governance in an independent East Timor. There was also the prevailing opinion that Falintil could meet the militia groups on their own terms, but not the Indonesian military, which remained the most significant problem. It was indicated that Xanana Gusmao had called a halt to all violence, including retaliation against the militia. There were two reasons for this: (1) the general commitment to not escalating violence and ensuring a free and fair vote on 30 August and hope for future reconciliation; and (2) the fear that retaliation for any Falintil action would be directed at the surrounding villages rather than at the guerrillas themselves. This course of non-violence by the pro-independence supporters was followed completely in the area around Ermera town and Gleno. Not a single recorded incident of violence, provoked or unprovoked, occurred from the pro-independence side in Ermera in the immediate run up to the referendum.

The Falintil celebrations contained one other notable feature—the presence of Indonesian officials as invited guests. In attendance were three members of Indonesia's Taskforce, seconded from the Ministry of Foreign Affairs, one senior member of Polri and one senior officer from TNI intelligence. All five were there in civilian clothing with observer status—which is to say they were not there in their official capacities. They were, however, adorned with 'uniform' Indonesian observer caps and vests, which clearly marked them as official Indonesian observers. At the end of the day the Falintil military commander, Ular,[4] actually embraced the senior TNI officer. Inviting Indonesian officials to such a gathering was an act of reconciliation that was not observed among the various pro-autonomy campaigns. The over-riding message was that violence should be renounced—obvious displays of past military glories within the camp notwithstanding. This was in direct contrast to violence and intimidation that occurred subsequent to this event, which was clearly initiated by the various militia groups.

Parliamentary visits

While I was in the Ermera district, three parliamentary visits were made to the area to observe the ballot process. They were: the New Zealand parliamentary delegation on 24 August; the Australian parliamentary delegation on 27 August; and a combined European Union parliamentary delegation on 30 August.

My primary contact was with the New Zealand parliamentary delegation, which was in the middle of a ten day tour of East Timor. The five members of parliament were Roger Maxwell (National, delegation leader), Phil Goff (Labour), Matt Robson (Alliance), Ken Shirley (ACT) and Rana Waitai (Independent). Also present were members of the New Zealand Ministry of Foreign Affairs and Trade, including the Ambassador to Jakarta, Mike Green. While in Gleno the delegation made calls on the *Bupati* and the police commander, Lieutenant Colonel Gultom. With a couple of exceptions, the questioning was generally diplomatic and some of the comments were complimentary on the way in which a lot of violence had been avoided in the Ermera district (this line was taken in accordance with advice from CivPol). The delegation also witnessed a civic education program near Gleno, arriving unannounced, much to the surprise of the local people. At the end of the address, Rana Waitai, a Maori member of parliament, led the delegation in singing the traditional Maori farewell song 'Po Kare Kare Ana'. Given the cultural and linguistic similarities between the Maori and the East Timorese, this had a great impact. Many locals were moved to tears, as there is a very similar song in Tetun. Later, at the airport on 2 September, the delegation made a brief report on some of the incidents that I had observed.

The Australian delegation visited on 27 August, and the delegation included Tim Fischer (former Deputy Prime Minister and former leader of the

---

[4] A *nom de guerre* meaning 'snake' in Indonesian.

National Party), Laurie Brereton (Labour, Shadow Spokesperson on Foreign Affairs), Australian Ambassador to Jakarta, John McCarthy, and other members of parliament and government officials. The European Union delegation was led by Dr Kimmo Kiljunen, member of parliament for Finland, and arrived at the Fatu Bolo polling centre to observe the voting process.

Incidents

While I was stationed in Ermera and Gleno, there were a number of incidents that can only be described as a breach of the voting process, if not a breach of the law:

1. At 4pm on 21 August 1999, I returned to Old Ermera to discover that a pro-autonomy militia group had attacked both the UNAMET outpost there and the church property in which I was staying. At around 10am, according to eye witnesses, members of the local militia surrounded the UNAMET office and threatened the local staff. A militiaman with a large knife chased one interpreter, who only avoided harm by outrunning his attacker. The militia also went around the corner to the aforementioned church building. They attacked this building to harass some students staying in another wing. They smashed one window and one door, and took some of the students' campaign materials. The rooms of international visitors were untouched. During the whole incident, which included a warning shot from a home-made gun to a UNAMET worker with a video camera, the 'internationals' were essentially left alone. UNAMET vacated the town for one night (much to the disappointment of the local people). This event was in clear response to the massive turn-out to the Falintil party the day before. The police, some 200 metres away, failed to act during this event in what became a familiar pattern. The church house was revisited by the militia on several other occasions over the next week.

2. The TNI and militia established a road-block near Ermera on 21 August. A Portuguese observer was threatened when a TNI regular soldier pointed a gun directly at him.

3. From 21 August, gun shots were fired in the main street every day, usually one around mid-morning and one at night.

4. Local militia and militia groups from out of town would ride into town in the afternoon, usually waving guns in a thinly veiled threat to the local population. On one occasion a militiaman also waved a gun in the air within about five metres of my position, chanting in Indonesian that 'UNAMET is useless'.

5. Immediately prior to voting day the militia rode into town chanting that 'UNAMET is stupid and UNAMET will die as a result of its stupidity'.

6. Through the UNAMET communications system, I observed many similar situations in the other villages in Ermera, often being reported as they happened. One particularly serious incident I heard reported live was at Letefoho, where the militia fired sustained bursts of automatic weapons fire and then torched a church building. The response time of the police, two minutes walk away, was 30 minutes.

7. A couple of days prior to the vote, a drunken policeman walked into the polling centre at Ermera town and threatened the staff there. He was made to apologise later in one of the few incidents actually followed up by police (the difference in this case perhaps being that it was one of their own).

8. During a number of serious incidents in the Ermera district on polling day, usually involving the militia, the police failed to take significant action. This included an incident witnessed by me where shots were fired by the militia near the polling centre at Fatu Bolo and the police escort advised UNAMET to leave, despite the fact that the police heavily outmanned and outgunned the militia (see below).

9. The pro-autonomy supporters would hold illegal campaigns (as notification and approval had to come from UNAMET and Polri), often taking advantage of assembled crowds waiting for UNAMET DEOs to arrive for voter education. They would take the opportunity to instruct the people how to vote.

What is significant about all of these breaches of the peace is that the police failed to act in the majority of cases. The total lawlessness of the situation was astounding. If one pulled a gun in Jakarta, or any other place in Indonesia, and fired a shot into the air, one would feel the full force of the law. In Ermera, this became a part of everyday life.

Preparations for 30 August

In the three days prior to the vote it was important for UNAMET to undertake two objectives: (1) educate local staff, specially employed for the vote and therefore not UNAMET employees, on voting procedures and (2) co-ordinate the observers to cover as much of the district as possible. The role of the Catholic Church in urging for a successful vote was also an important facet of the led-up to the Popular Consultation.

Dave Glasgow and I observed the education of polling staff at three polling centres: Fatu Bolo, Ermera, and Poetete. In each case the locals were instructed that they were to be impartial to the entire process. There were clear restrictions laid down on their actions, including a wholesale ban on informing others how to vote, and instructions not to watch how others voted, and not to wear any clothing that expressed support for either side. At Fatu Bolo several staff had to be told they would have to remove items of clothing (baseball caps) that expressed their preference for autonomy. While the local staff obviously all had views on the issue at hand, they were under strict instructions not to portray this as an official position, given the history of 'guided democracy' in Indonesia.

Co-ordinating the observers was another important job. Around the Gleno area the observers were generally viewed as falling into three distinct categories: the internationals; the official Indonesian observers (who were clearly pro-autonomy, although some expressed concern over the violence and lawlessness); and the 'local' observers (who were judged by Indonesian officials as completely biased towards independence—a view not totally without grounds). The political section of UNAMET's *Markus Besar* headquarters facilitated the co-ordination of the international observers, although the groups themselves determined the actual details. Given that the international observers could not cover the entire territory, it was decided informally that two principles should govern the placement of observers—that an observer team of two should go to each large polling centre, and that those observer groups that were mobile should make fleeting visits to the smaller centres whilst checking the roads for militia road blocks. The principal groups involved in this division of labour were the Australia–East Timor International Volunteers Project (AETIVP), the International Federation for East Timor (IFET) and the Portuguese official observer mission. The latter two groups were mobile. This co-ordination worked out rather well, but was complicated by the fact that a number of observer groups kept arriving unannounced a day or two prior to the poll. Given that there was no central co-ordination at UNAMET's headquarters in Dili of arrivals in the field, this complicated things considerably and made plans extremely fluid. As there was no problems at all with co-operation in the field, all groups were able to work together successfully in the end.

The role of the church is ensuring a free and fair election was crucial in Ermera and the surrounding areas. In July, Bishop Belo had informed the people that they had no moral obligation to follow through with 'blood oaths' that were taken under duress. A forced promise, the Bishop declared, was not binding in the sight of God and that people should vote as their conscience led them. The people of the area surrounding Ermera town had had difficulty getting to church in the weeks prior to the referendum due to the disruption to local transport. However, on the Sunday prior to the poll, 29 August, thousands of people came to Ermera to celebrate mass. The crowd was so large that mass had to be held outside the church. Some AETIVP and ANFREL (Asian Nations for Free Elections) observers were present at the service and invited to sit in the front row as honoured guests of the occasion. The church service involved the reading of a nationwide message in Tetun, Portuguese and Indonesian. The message was an appeal to vote with one's conscience and to respect the individual consciences of others. There was also a message of reconciliation between the two sides and the desire for peace.

Polling day

Starting in the early hours of the morning of 30 August, large numbers of people were moving to the appropriate polling centre. Upon arrival at polling centres in Ermera between 5.00 and 5.30am, UNAMET staff and observers encountered hundreds of people already 'queuing' (to use the word loosely)—although in Fatu Bolo, the largest centre, at least half of the 6,000 had already assembled. People were extremely anxious to vote, often surging and pushing, but almost everyone went through by the early afternoon. Voting levels were in the high ninety percentiles in just about every case.

The great festival of democracy was marred by a series of ugly incidents, perpetrated by the militia, in just about every polling centre in the immediate surrounds of Ermera town and Gleno. At Fatu Bolo a nearby village was set on fire and the militia started firing rifles 1.5 kilometres from our position at 3pm. Fortunately the voting had finished by this time, and the 40 heavily armed police advised staff simply to pack up and leave. At Ermera, plain clothes servicemen attempted to mingle with the crowd. At Poetete the militia set up a road block for much of the day and threatened the life of a CivPol officer who had attempted to disarm them close to the polling centre. In Gleno a number of threats were made and a local militiaman fired into the centre with a homemade rifle, slightly wounding the deputy political officer for UNAMET. Sustained automatic weapons fire was also heard throughout the night in Gleno. All of this constitute a serious and concerted attempt to intimidate voters by the militia in the general area. In my opinion it all added up to an effort to undermine the notion that the people's will is sovereign in this instance. It also amounted to cheating.

The official Indonesian observers told me that they had witnessed local staff instructing registered voters how to vote by escorting them to the actual polling booths, and they believed that instructions given were to vote for independence. I was later to discover that this accusation was levelled at UNAMET across the whole of East Timor and constituted a serious formal challenge to the impartiality of the process. One polling centre cited was Fatu Bolo. I was stationed at Fatu Bolo all day on 30 August and never saw this particular breach occur. Given the presence of pro-autonomy items of clothing on some of the local staff a few days earlier, it is somewhat presumptuous to assume that if they did speak with votes at all it was therefore necessarily to promote independence. If this particular breach did in fact occur, it was not observed by this witness and therefore, it is reasonable to conclude, cannot have been widespread at Fatu Bolo to say the very least. What is of greater import, however, is the attempted disruption by the pro-autonomy militia groups, who largely issued either direct threats or indirect threats via the discharging of weapons at the polling centre of Ermera district. Therefore, the final result stands in spite of the intimidation to vote in a direct way—at least as far as Ermera is concerned.

The aftermath of polling day

The day after polling day, the Ermera district became something of a flash point area. The town of Ermera was quite deserted and it was obvious that road blocks were preventing any traffic from coming through. The night before, the Gleno militia had attempted to actually seize the ballot boxes as they were being loaded onto one of the UNAMET helicopters.

Dave Glasgow and I were escorted by the Ermera town police chief, Danny Koan, down to Gleno to make our way back to Dili. On the way down there were torched homes and a road-block on the outskirts of Gleno—which we only passed due to our armed police guard. We arrived at the Gleno *Markus Besar* at 9.30am to discover everyone in a tense and emotional state, many still lying on the floor, after some threats from the militia (this particular group coming in from Dili). Staff anticipated getting into a convoy and leaving Gleno, but the convoy was unable to leave because the militia were 'unable to guarantee UNAMET safety'. This was the beginning of an 8–9 hour hold up of a convoy of about 21 vehicles and more than 120 UNAMET staff and observers. CivPol tried negotiating with Polri to get road-blocks cleared and assurances that we could pass through unharmed, but without success. Polri failed to take any action to clear the road, despite the presence of at least 30 heavily armed police beside the *Markus Besar* and 100–200 in the town itself. The main issue seemed to be that the militia wished to prevent the departure of local East Timorese UNAMET staff. There also seemed to be a suggestion that the militia groups were punishing UNAMET for its supposed collusion with CNRT. As we waited we saw militia burning at least two houses in Gleno (in addition to several homes of known CNRT supporters torched in Gleno the night before), and once again Polri took no action. It was reported that some of the militia were from Dili and that it was difficult to negotiate with different militia leaders, who seemed to ignore police requests. At around 2pm a group of 25 militia marched up the road towards our position, forcing all occupants into the UN building, although we saw no weapons with this group. Again Polri failed to act to turn them away. This created a tense situation in the UNAMET headquarters, with people told to take shelter by sitting on the floor. After negotiation between CivPol, Polri and the militia, staff were allowed to return to the vehicles, but the convoy was not allowed to leave. After UNAMET alerted the international media, and with the continuing failure to deal with the militia, the military commander of East Timor, Major General Kiki Syahnakri, arrived via helicopter to try to break the deadlock. The crisis was only settled when the militia chief was allowed to inspect the line-up of vehicles, insisting that one minibus with local registration stay behind with the remaining UN vehicles. This clearly angered many of the UN personnel, who expressed their disgust that such a demand by the militia was agreed to. We were finally 'allowed' to leave at 5.42pm and arrived at the UN headquarters in Dili at 7.30pm.

Conclusion

In conclusion, from my perspective, the Popular Consultation to determine the future status of East Timor, was, despite the violence and intimidation, a largely free and fair process. It does not defy the impartiality of this observer to suggest that every single breach of the election rules observed in Ermera town and its surrounding area came from militia groups presuming to represent the pro-autonomy side of the debate. As time drew closer to the polling day, the abuses of law grew worse, which may have been a sign of desperation that people were defying the threats and intimidations—the numbers at the respective rallies clearly bears this out. As the level of support for independence became more and more apparent, so did the angst of the militia groups. Polri did little, or nothing, to prevent this attempted intimidation, in events that, in a microcosm, tragically mirrored the wholesale destruction and murder that occurred after the announcement of the result. Some credit should go to Polri for ensuring the personal safety of internationals involved in the process—but little more. As the events described in this chapter demonstrate, the militia were given a free reign over the villages and hamlets in the Ermera district. Polri failed to stop this general lawlessness from pro-Jakarta militia groups, which culminated in the serious detention incident at Gleno on 31 August in which 120 UNAMET staff and observers had to stay holed up at the UNAMET headquarters to ensure their personal safety. In the final analysis, the result of the Popular Consultation was a success for a free and fair election, in spite of militia attempts to threaten, bribe or cajole the people in another direction—or at least as free and fair as it could be under the circumstances.

Taking the risk, paying the price:
East Timorese vote in Ermera district

Helene van Klinken[1]

In mid-June 1999, I arrived in East Timor, to work as a political affairs officer with the newly established United Nations Assistance Mission in East Timor (UNAMET). Political officers were stationed in eight regions where UNAMET had headquarters. I was delighted to be sent to the beautiful district[2] of Ermera, situated in the hills one hour's drive south of Dili. As you approach the district centre, Gleno, Mt Ramelau, the highest mountain in East Timor, dominates the skyline. It is a picturesque, fertile, coffee-growing area. Farmers spread their coffee on the road for passing vehicles to drive over and hasten the removal of the outer husks. People are friendly and open, and the welcome to UNAMET was unbelievable. Children would pop out of fragrant coffee gardens as we drove past, waving and calling in chorus, 'UNAMET, UNAMET!'

My job as a political affairs officer was to meet everyone: villagers, Indonesian government, police and military officials, church leaders, pro-autonomy and pro-independence supporters, students, militia and Falintil, and report to the Dili headquarters what they were saying, and whether or not it was possible for the popular consultation to proceed.

UNAMET was given the task to conduct a popular consultation to ascertain if the people of East Timor wished to accept or reject the autonomy proposal offered by Indonesia. The term referendum was deliberately avoided,

---

[1] This essay is dedicated to Ana, a wonderful East Timorese friend. The views in this article represent the author's own and are not necessarily the official UNAMET position.

[2] East Timor is divided into 13 districts (kabupaten). Ermera is a district. Each district consists of several sub-districts (kecamatan). Each sub-district is made up of several villages (desa), which in turn consists of several hamlets (kampung or RK). In Ermera there are five sub-districts, with about 50 villages.

Each level of organisation has its own administrator. District head (bupati), in Ermera Constantino Soares, sub-district head (camat), village head (kepala desa).

At district level there is a district police headquarters (polres), and district military headquarters (kodim).

The heads of these are respectively: the district police commander (kapolres), in Ermera, Lieutenant Colonel of Police Erry TB Gultom and district military commander (dandim) in Ermera Colonel Muhammad Nur

There are military and police equivalents at sub-district level. In each village there is also a military official, a non-commissioned officer (babinsa). There is no police presence at village level.

The district council (muspida) consists of representatives from civilian government including judiciary, police and military.

as Indonesians had long refused to permit a referendum on independence.[3] More than 500 United Nations volunteers from many nations formed the electoral staff who registered the 450,000 eligible voters over a period of 22 days from 16 July to 6 August 1999. After that they conducted voter education, informing people of the voting process, especially that it was secret and votes would not be counted in villages or districts. Finally, they organised the vote on 30 August 1999. Prior to the vote the two sides, those who accepted autonomy, and those who rejected autonomy, could campaign for approximately ten days, up to 28 August. The United Nations volunteers were assisted by local Timorese staff as drivers and interpreters, as well as many others who helped with registration and especially on voting day.

I will never be able to fully put into words my experience in Ermera. It is without doubt the most challenging and amazing job I have ever done. To be forced to suddenly leave, without even saying good-bye, filled me with dismay and disbelief. Not to know the fate of those wonderful people I knew so well continues to distress me.

The two sides

Indonesian authorities presented the problem in East Timor as two sides opposed to each other. There are many divisions in Timorese society, including rivalry between families and village groups, and this has always been exploited by Indonesia. In 1975 the Indonesians encouraged the brief civil war. In the lead-up to the vote they again fanned these rivalries.

Pro-independence resistance groups in East Timor joined together in the late 1980s under the umbrella group the National Council for Timorese Resistance, CNRT,[4] to which most well-regarded East Timorese leaders gave their allegiance. The armed wing, Falintil, commanded the respect of most of the population.

The opposing side, according to Indonesian authorities, should consist of all public servants, who were supposed to be loyal to the government that gave them jobs. In reality many public servants were 'disloyal', so Indoinesia created supporters in the form of militia.

Who were the militia?

Militia have long been part of policing and defence in Indonesia. In Indonesian law they are referred to as 'trained civilians'. The term 'militia' became popular with the foreign press as East Timor came to international attention, but they have been part of the military strategy in East Timor since

---

[3] Sometimes the term ballot will also be used to refer to the Popular Consultation.
[4] The name was CNRM until they became the CNRT in 1998.

1975. However, beginning in late 1998 many more were conscripted, bribed and forced to join their ranks, and each district had its own militia.

There were groups already operating in Ermera, but in early April 1999 they joined together and expanded their ranks to become the Ermera based Darah Integrasi, (Blood of Integration). Militia from other districts helped in its establishment and the CNRT supplied UNAMET with the names of the main military organisers. The CNRT also claimed they heard that Darah Integrasi was often considered a rather ineffective militia. Other militia, such as Besi Merah Putih, BMP (Read and White Iron) and Mahidi (Dead or Alive with Indonesia) were considered more successful in getting results from their intimidation.

Darah Integrasi called itself a battalion. In each sub-district there was a company of the Darah Integrasi. In Ermera, Darah Merah (Red Blood), in Atsabe, Tim Pancasila (Pancasila Team), in Hatolia, Naga Merah (Red Dragon) or Kompi C (Company C), in Railaku, Kompi E, in Letefoho, Darah Integrasi. On the walls of their headquarters in Gleno was a diagram showing the command structure and membership. They claimed there were 1,500 members, but according to informants the number of committed members was in the low hundreds. Whenever UNAMET witnessed militia gatherings, the numbers were much smaller than those claimed. They were supposed to be paid Rp100.000 per month as well as receive ten kilograms of rice. When they did receive rice, according to reliable sources, it was the rice that Indonesia received cheaply for humanitarian aid to the many displaced people already in East Timor.

Miguel Soares Babo was the commander of Darah Integrasi, and his brother, Antonio dos Santos, was second-in-command. Antonio was a low ranking TNI officer who said he was on 'civilian duties'. He was the real force and spokesperson. Miguel was often drunk and prone to use abusive language. He would give instructions to his followers at public rallies, such as, 'if you see a student shoot them, the CNRT are communists, if the CNRT open an office burn it down'. He always carried a weapon and regularly discharged it into the air.[5]

Militia did not always keep to their designated districts and there was even competition between them. In northern Ermera a group of Aitarak (Thorn) operated, though their base was in Dili. Many were local youth, coerced into joining, yet wanting to live in Ermera rather than Dili. They also claimed they

---

[5] The police were unhappy with this, but nevertheless indulgent of Miguel's behaviour. They viewed him as a drunken eccentric, but because he was commander of Darah Integrasi they felt they could not arrest him, as it would have led his followers to revolt. According to them, this was also why they let certain CNRT and Falintil members escape the law.

were protecting the local people from the unpredictable and vicious BMP thugs operating just over the border in Liquica, as well as preventing BMP from establishing a base there.

The difficulty for UNAMET was to understand the exact nature of these militia. In early June 1999, when UNAMET asked, they were at first compared to PAM Swakarsa.[6] Then they became the People's Resistance—Wanra.[7] These were attempts to describe the militia in terms of existing categories in the Defence Act.[8] In Ermera in about August we were told we now had to refer to the militia as Forces Struggling for Integration—PPI. AT this time they mysteriously evolved into a guerilla army, which, we were led to understand, had formed spontaneously to fight for integration with Indonesia. Interestingly they organised themselves copying the Falinitl command structure, in four regions. The 'supreme command' was in Balibo.[9] The difference was, as many in UNAMET noted, Falintil was outlawed, whereas this 'similarly lawless' group was accepted and encouraged by Indonesian authorities.

While the rationale may have changed over time, the militia were the same militia—trained, armed, paid and directed by the Indonesian National Armed Forces—TNI,[10] and the elite commando unit, Kopassus. The militia themselves said their task was to protect people from Falintil. In reality they were free to intimidate and kill without reference to the law, anyone who was suspected of engaging in any pro-independence activity.

One of the security conditions that UNAMET believed needed to exist for a free and fair ballot was that the TNI would stop their support of the militia. Therefore the TNI's relationship with the militia was a dilemma for the Indonesians attempting to explain them; the links needed to constantly be adjusted, concealed and denied.

---

[6] PAM Swakarsa were formed in January 1998 from Islamic groups to defend the Super Parliament for the election of Suharto for his seventh term in March of that year. They later were held responsible for burning and looting in Jakarta in May. Such groups have long been in use in East Timor. This was the first time they were employed elsewhere.

[7] Perlawanan Rakyat or Wanra for short

[8] The 1982 Defence Act sets out the role of trained civilians (rakyat terlatih or ratih). The total population has the responsibility to enforce the law. People receive rudimentary military training and can be called on to assist government, military or police for particular tasks.

[9] The commander was Joao Travares. Balibo is his home district.

[10] TNI, Tentara Nasional Indonesia, were previously called ABRI. I will use the term TNI throughout.

Ermera prior to April 1999

In June 1998, President Habibie first mentioned offering wide-ranging autonomy to East Timor. The people of Ermera district, and elsewhere in East Timor, came out instead in support of independence, and a referendum. Falintil were able to take advantage of the confusion in Jakarta by, for the first time, openly patrolling the roads leading in and out of Ermera. Also for the first time, the CNRT opened an office, with a fully functional organisational structure at district level, as well as sub-district and village. They even talked about having established a 'parallel government'.[11] University students who came from Ermera travelled round the district holding demonstrations and calling for a referendum on independence. A foreign visitor described the atmosphere to me as a 'Prague Spring'.

On the other hand, many Indonesians living in Ermera felt frightened. Some local youths caused distress by calling openly for them to return home. The wife of one high government official told me that youths came into the yard of the local primary school and used a megaphone to tell Indonesians to leave. After February, her young school-aged children refused to attend school in Gleno. Other Indonesians said that while people were worried, nothing really happened. In other places, especially Dili, pro-independence supporters did burn shops, businesses and sometimes the homes of collaborators and non-Timorese. Also some lawlessness prevailed, with motorcyclists refusing to wear helmets, and youths sometimes not paying for taxi rides and blatantly stealing from shops. Ermera was relatively free of such behaviour.

In Ermera, long-standing East Timorese supporters of Indonesia made peace with their Timorese bothers and sisters, joining the pro-independence side. Even Timorese soldiers who had fought for Indonesia sought reconciliation with Falintil. I was told that Timorese in Ermera were united. Some even told me they used to say they did not need a referendum as they already had independence. This unity amongst East Timorese represented a dilemma for Indonesians, and fear of Falintil and pro-independence actors was well established in their minds. The district police commander, an Indonesian, without any guile, told UNAMET that Ermera in August 1999 was a much safer place than in August 1998, when the independence side had the upper hand.

It is difficult to say for what reason the military allowed this space for independence supporters to flourish. Were they pre-occupied with events in

---

[11] Indonesian police claimed that the problem was that the CNRT extorted money. I know little about the CNRT's tax collecting ability at that time.

Jakarta and still recovering from Suharto's downfall, or wondering how to deal with the criticisms levelled at them, or even suffering from loss of confidence? It certainly allowed them to see the strength of support for independence in East Timor, and identify the main players.

In an attempt to help resolve the tensions between East Timorese and the district council, the ex-district head of Ermera, Thomas Goncalves, sponsored reconciliation meetings between the various parties.[12] The CNRT's documentation of the agreement to respect each other and work together, signed on 24 March 1999, was later burnt when their office was destroyed.

Towards the end of February 1999, 11 people were killed in Ermera. The true story of the deaths of these people was not known, although several suspects were arrested by the police. It was reported that the victims were militia.[13] The police commander said he suspected pro-independence Ermera youth. In all of our conversations with Indonesians about atrocities perpetrated by militia, these killings were always mentioned to remind us that both sides were involved. The bodies were not found or not disclosed for some time. At the end of April, the decaying corpses were placed in the local health clinic in Gleno, where flies blackened the windows, to the horror of the whole town. The Indonesian authorities used these deaths to portray the CNRT as a dangerous, vicious movement that could not be trusted.[14]

April–May 1999

Attacks on CNRT

With the likelihood of a popular consultation, a savage crackdown began in Ermera on 10 April, when a CNRT youth, Antonio Lima, was killed and the CNRT office burnt down. People said that the killings were by Indonesian police and military in uniform, who patrolled the streets shooting and

---

[12] Thomas Goncalves was a long-standing supporter of Indonesia, also involved in establishing militia. However, eventually he could no longer support the cruel tactics being employed to ensure an Indonesian victory. After the attacks in April he fled Ermera and is now in hiding in Macau, where he has confessed to his involvement in forming militia.

[13] Kompas (1999) suggest they may have been Aitarak members.

[14] It was difficult to get information about these 11 murdered. I concluded that those murdered were militia, and that Falintil, CNRT or their followers were somehow involved in the murder, but whether it was ordered by the leadership, of course I do not know. The CNRT protested that the police insisted on investigating these murders but refused to even hear the evidence of the many pro-independence people killed by militia, police and military. The CNRT said that, if the reason for not investigating the latter was that it was a state of war, then the former also should be considered in that light. They disputed the fact that the Indonesian police investigated the murders as a criminal matter, but then used them as a political tool. The Indonesian police claimed that perpetrators of the murder were hiding in the forest pretending to be political refugees.

searching for CNRT leaders and well-known pro-independence supporters, to kill them. These killings began five days after the widely reported massacre of CNRT supporters in a church in nearby Liquica. The Ermera district CNRT leader, Eduardo Barrito, was arrested. He was later jailed for 'extorting money and coercing people to join the CNRT'. All remaining CNRT leaders fled to the hills around Ermera. CNRT members told me they were disappointed by the Indonesians' betrayal of the 24 March reconciliation agreement. The Indonesians responded that the death of the 11 justified their actions, as according to them, the situation was getting out of control.

During the days that followed many more pro-independence people were killed. The CNRT estimate 39 but they can't be sure of numbers because until the ballot about 2,500 people were still hiding in the hills, and it was difficult to know who might still be alive. Killing continued in different sub-districts of Ermera throughout April and May. The CNRT gave UNAMET detailed lists of confirmed deaths and the names of perpetrators; many were military personnel, and the CNRT asked us to look at gravesites.[15]

In some areas of East Timor, Falintil had managed to maintain long-term control of a few villages. Military posts stationed in these areas reached some sort of modus vivendi with Falintil, and they did not 'disturb' each other. One such 'liberated area' was Fatubolo village, close to Gleno. On 10 April all senior Ermera CNRT office-holders fled into this Falintil controlled territory, though some went to Dili, which was also considered safe. In the Falintil base I met a sub-district head, many village heads, successful business people, and other important people in their communities. One office bearer of the CNRT, Germenino Amaral dos Reis, who had some protection as he was a member of the local parliament, was asked by the organisation to return to Gleno to be the spokesperson for the CNRT in Ermera district.[16]

Civil servants who were prepared to sign statements promising to support autonomy could come out of hiding on 24 April 1999. Those who refused were threatened that they would loose their jobs or even be killed. Hence many stayed hiding in the hills. The CNRT itself was forced to disband on 26 April. They had to engage in a (chicken) blood-drinking, oath-taking ceremony declaring that they disbanded and did so voluntarily. Later they told me that they had no choice but to do this—killing of their members would continue as long as they refused to capitulate.

---

[15] UNAMET had no mandate or resources to investigate these crimes. Unfortunately many of these documents were lost when the Dili headquarters were evacuated in September 1999.

[16] In 1997 he was elected as a member of Suhartos's Golkar party in the local assembly (DPRD II). After April he was excluded from the assembly.

Militia and TNI posts

While there have always been military outposts in remote areas of East Timor, the numbers of these posts in Ermera was now greatly increased, many of them established after the crackdown in April and May. A military post was usually a simple structure of bamboo and local materials, with the tell-tale tall communications antenna. At a post there were often stationed four Indonesian officers and about ten East Timorese TNI members.

A group of about 20 militia, mostly locally recruited, was also stationed at the post, thus demonstrating once more the close link between militia and military. When UNAMET visited villages, the militia would often hide in the coffee gardens or in a house, and refuse to come and talk to us. The local people would always secretly indicate their presence.

The arrival of UNAMET

The political office had to assess whether the situation was secure enough to proceed with registration. As the time for registration approached it was clear this was not the case, and registration was delayed for several days. However, nothing significant changed in the proceeding days. In New York the United Nations decided to proceed but reassess half-way through registration, after ten days. In Dili the political office drew up a list of eight security conditions, all of which needed to be addressed for the vote to be fair. One of those was that TNI would move out of village posts and back to their barracks.

Military back to barracks?

The new military posts established in April and May were in villages where support for Falintil had been strongest. In these villages the people were the most aggressively pro-independence, and on the arrival of UNAMET they were often the ones who complained most. The following stories of contact with several villages best paint a picture of the relationship between UNAMET and the military in the period mid-June to mid-July.

Talimoro village

On my first day in Ermera, a group of people from Talimoro village, situated on the mountain slopes directly behind our district UNAMET headquarters, came with a complaint. Their location made it somewhat easy for them to sneak into our headquarters, out of sight of the police mobile brigade who were guarding us, stationed directly across the road.[17] They

---

[17] Members of the Police Mobile Brigade (Brimob) are something like riot police. Indonesia was responsible for security and a large force, called Kontingen Lorosae, was sent to East

complained about a meeting in their village organised by the village military official, and the village head, and guarded by soldiers from the military post in their village.

The village head told the meeting that UNAMET would be present for only two months so wouldn't be able to protect them, and if they didn't choose autonomy they would all be killed, including women and children. They were worried because they were told they had to attend another such meeting in a few days, when the names of those who supported the position of the village head would be collected.

UNAMET police contacted the Indonesian police complaining that such a meeting broke the tripartite agreement in that there were threats and compulsion to attend a meeting in relation to the ballot and 'campaigning' was taking place prior to the allocated time.[18] On the day appointed for the follow-up meeting I accompanied the UNAMET police to this village. We discovered the meeting had been cancelled and the military post vacated. We all were very pleased, and we naïvely thought that this would be the pattern as we fanned out into more remote villages—TNI would move out of villages back to barracks, at least at sub-district level.

Ten days later, the villagers from Talimoro returned in alarm to tell us that the soldiers were back at their post. When the UNAMET military liaison officer asked the sub-district military commander about this, he was told that the military official from Talimoro had requested the return of the soldiers to help guard the village against Falintil.[19] From that day on, we received numerous complaints from the Talimoro villagers of the activities of soldiers. In the middle of the night they would throw stones on the roofs of houses of people known to have housed Falintil soldiers in the past. They would shoot randomly into the air to intimidate people. They would break into houses, saying they had received information that Falintil soldiers were attacking the occupants. Most often they were drunk, and frequently terrorised female members of the household, sometimes spending all day lying round drunk in a house, making it impossible for the owners to care for their children or cook.

Timor for this purpose. Every registration centre, UNAMET headquarters and UNAMET staff accommodation were guarded by a police from this mobile brigade.

[18] The tripartite agreement was signed in New York between Indonesia, Portugal and the United Nations on 5 May, laying the conditions for a vote on the autonomy proposed by Indonesia for East Timor.

[19] In Ermera there were three UNAMET military liaison officers who were the contacts with the Indonesian military. Everywhere they went they were supposed to be accompanied by TNI liaison officers.

Urahau and Mau Ubu villages

A few days after registration began we became aware that no-one had registered from Urahau village. We were told by the district head that the reason they did not register was that they were too afraid of the Falintil guerillas to travel to the registration centre. The people we came to in the first hamlet of this village were more terrified than any villagers we had ever met. No one dared speak to us. However, with some urgency they encouraged us to go to the hamlet situated further down the mountain. As we approached this hamlet, one of the people with whom we had previously spoken—he must have scaled down the mountain at a tremendous rate—suddenly appeared and jumped into our car. He told us that of course they weren't afraid of Falintil, but TNI. They had been told to accept autonomy in August or they would all be killed, including children. He told us the village head organised the militia and had been given weapons by TNI.

When we arrived at the hamlet we had been directed to, we came across more than 200 people lining the street, obviously waiting for us—men on one side, women on the other, who clapped as we approached. It was a very moving experience to be the first UNAMET presence there. The people were in poor health and hungry, and the children malnourished. They told us that 150 homes had been burnt in April on the lower slopes, and those villagers had moved to this higher hamlet and were sharing the homes of families and neighbours. They were unable to return to pick their coffee or work their gardens. They could travel to the market along the main road that led out of the village, but without their coffee crops and gardens they were short of money to buy food and medicines. Their condition was miserable.

One brave leader, W, acted as spokesperson, and complained that they were afraid of the soldiers at the military post. The TNI Liaison Officer who accompanied us asked W if the soldiers had actually done anything to the people in the past two months. When W replied negatively, he was asked why then was everyone afraid. W replied that they were still waiting for instructions from above (the military post was located higher up the mountain) before they dared to move. I thought of what one priest had recently told me, 'soldiers with guns represent intimidation to the people—they don't need to do anything'. The TNI Liaison Officer told them they should put the fears associated with the past behind them, look to the future and return to their gardens and also register. He said he would visit the soldiers at the TNI post and instruct them not to threaten people. But he warned the villages that the post would only be withdrawn if Falintil laid down their arms. This Liaison Officer later became very upset with the enthusiasm with which the people registered, but he stuck to his word. The people were left undisturbed until the day of the vote.

We proceeded to Mau Ubu, the adjacent village, where the people were not quite as severely traumatised and afraid to travel to the registration centre. While the UNAMET military liaison officers talked with the soldiers at this military post, I was free to stroll along the length of the village chatting with some women, who readily complained about their treatment at the hands of the soldiers. Suddenly, I was shocked to meet two Falintil guerillas. Behind a wall we talked with them, barely 100 metres from the TNI post, until the scouts keeping guard must have thought there was danger, and like mountain goats, they disappeared from sight.

I believe that the people in these two villages were no less than prisoners, gathered together so their contact with Falintil could be minimised.

Contact with government officials

The many government officials, sub-district and village heads and village secretaries who remained in hiding and refused to sign statements supporting autonomy were replaced by the Indonesian authorities with people who were persuaded and bribed to support integration with Indonesia. As village heads are supposed to be elected, these officials were all unofficial. I met one local sub-district head about whom I had heard from UNAMET electoral staff that he was totally uncooperative in helping them find suitable centres. Indonesian authorities agreed they would cooperate with UNAMET to provide office headquarters, accommodation for staff and centres for registration and polling. This same official, whom I met in the home of friends and family, was a totally different man and he impressed on me how I had to keep his secret. He could see no hope in the current process, nothing would work, and the vote would be a disaster. TNI was in control, they would never change. I felt very sad for him. Amazingly, he assured me that most of the other 'pro-autonomy' officials in the district, right to the highest level, were just like him.

By contrast, Amaral and other CNRT leaders were inspiring people who did not sell their souls, even though they lived with constant threats and in fear. They would express their disappointment about their fellow countrymen who had capitulated to the pressures. They believed leaders had a responsibility to stand up for and protect the little people, who were the ones who always suffered. Amaral would always say that Timorese have to be honest but tell a few lies; while they are afraid they must also be brave. When facing a tiger, you have to be careful or you'll get caught by one of his teeth.

Some village heads had the presence of mind to take with them the stamp of the village office when they fled, so their substitutes were unable to perform their official duties. One particular village head spent his days carrying out his official duties, operating from his motorcycle, skirting round police and military, his stamp firmly secured on his person. He had a very high profile during the registration period, when many people needed that official stamp to register. However, each evening he returned to Dili, too afraid to sleep in his village.

Some village heads managed to maintain their positions yet were very good. Some told us how they accepted the large sums of money they were given by the district head to use to persuade the people in their village to vote for autonomy, but then told their people they had to support independence. They said they accepted the money as it was needed to develop their village.

Contact with ordinary people

The general population was traumatised and fearful when UNAMET arrived. Streets were deserted, the market was scarcely operational, very few people ventured out at night. The UNAMET local staff told of the overwhelming welcome they received in mid-June when they first ate at a stall. They were given money and a free meal. People told them how glad they were that the United Nations had finally come. Soon after the market became once more the busy hub of town, and people were seen out along the roads, doing more than just the essential.

Indonesians seemed to have no idea of the breadth of support enjoyed by the CNRT. One Balinese government official honestly told me that he believed that 70% of people in Ermera supported autonomy.

Contact with militia

By contrast with pro-independence supporters, militia in Ermera made no attempt to contact UNAMET on our arrival in June. Mostly because we were overrun with information and complaints from the pro-independence side, it was some time before we were able to initiate contact. They weren't hard to contact as they hung around town as grass cutters, or just loitered around their headquarters.

Over a period of time, we were able to develop personal relationships with the militia. I often visited their headquarters and had cordial conversations with their members. The commander hooted with delight on one occasion when I turned up in a red T-shirt and white jeans, and suggested he would not mind if I wore red and white, the Indonesian colours, rather than United Nations blue. Some militia members told me they believed that Timorese could be united because they were all brothers, which is not exactly inaccurate. Give any Timorese a few minutes and they will find a family relationship, even if remote—grandmothers are second cousins.[20] The commanders especially wanted to be involved in the reconciliation process that UNAMET was encouraging, and they requested UNAMET presence in a meeting with Falintil.

CNRT's efforts to find a place in the sun

On the first day of registration people turned out in their hundreds, queuing like sardines in a tin. It was as if they were finally doing something they really wanted to do. Parties were held at registration centres. They were joyful places. In one sense registration was too successful. After the ten days it was as if the Timorese people had taken the decision into their own hands. No matter what the security situation was like they were going to vote in what they believed was the only chance they had.

We also had to make a judgement as to whether there were equal opportunities for both sides. For the CNRT in Ermera it was a constant struggle, though they philosophically said, 'we've been campaigning for 24 years. Our people know what they want'. Nevertheless they were not passive, and engaged in strategies to raise their profile. Compared with other districts, they were given little space. In most districts, by the time of the vote the CNRT had opened an office in town, but in Ermera they were too afraid to do so.[21] There were never any Xanana or CNRT posters displayed in town as there were in some other districts, and they did not dare to openly distribute their election material.

Return to town

The CNRT in Ermera decided in July, in the middle of the registration period, that the leadership and members who had been displaced since 10 April 1999 would return to their homes to participate in the popular consultation, and to open their offices. They sought the support of the Ermera district council in doing this, citing the 5 May agreement between Indonesia, Portugal and the United Nations that as the representatives of the pro-independence side they should have equal rights with the pro-autonomy side and be able to operate openly. They invited the police commander to attend a ceremony to be conducted in the hills above Ermera. The Falintil commander, who intended to wear his full Portuguese general uniform, would 'hand over' the CNRT members to the district police commander in a ceremony

---

[20] Finding, sometimes by stretching possible links, distant relations is a common custom amongst strangers in Timorese society. (Ed)

[21] Many of the offices operated for only a short time before they were attacked or burnt.

signifying that, while they had been protected by Falintil since April, now their safe-keeping would be in the hands of the Indonesian police.

They were very excited about this event, hoping to encourage the many other displaced people in East Timor to follow their example. They were adamant that they would not leave the hills only to live in a compound, with police protection, as was the case for the internally displaced people who had undertaken a similar 'reconciliation' in Suai. They talked of returning triumphantly in a convoy of 600–800 people, before the international media, thereby putting Ermera on the map. They wanted to meet with the district council in the town hall, then return to live at home with their families. Senior UNAMET officials from Dili agreed to attend as observers, and a date was set. At the very last minute the plan had to be cancelled, as the district military commander said he could not guarantee their security, and possibly he did not want attention to focus on the numbers of displaced persons in Ermera district. The CNRT was very disappointed, but they also now had to face the reality that the Indonesians, because of the military hard-line position, would fail to fulfill their obligations to create a safe security situation for them to operate freely.

Registration and campaigning

As the CNRT had no office and their leadership was in hiding, the pro-autonomy actors felt they had the upper hand. During the registration period the CNRT put all their effort into registering the people. CNRT members who had to stay in hiding took the opportunity to register wherever they could, mostly in areas where Falintil held control. The CNRT hired trucks to transport hundreds of the old, infirm, pregnant and nursing mothers to registration centres. Young men in hiding to evade being drafted into militia were also helped to register. These latter often requested the protection of UNAMET, but we were unable to offer them even this basic security. Falintil members also wanted protection to register, but again UNAMET could not give them any special considerations.

If Falintil wanted to register, UNAMET told them, they had to take risks like the rest of the population. On a pre-arranged day, the registration centre at Fatubolo, in Falintil territory, opened early. Over 150 active Falintil members crowded into the building, their weapons stored in a nearby house. They were very nervous, afraid of a possible TNI attack. As most had been fighting in the forest for many years they had no documentation. For several hours the centre turned into an 'affidavit factory',[22] every available writing utensil put to work.

---

[22] To register voters were required to produce a birth or baptismal certificate to show they were born in East Timor, and some form of identification, usually an Indonesian ID. As many

By 9am, most of the guerillas had melted away into the forest. The police mobile brigade who always guarded the centre had kept their distance. It felt like a small victory that at least these Falintil members had been able to register.

Registration was a resounding success, numbers far exceeding estimates. I did not meet any Timorese in Ermera who had wanted to but been unable to register. As a result of this success, in some ways UNAMET slipped into a false sense of what we could achieve. We would tell people, 'you were intimidated during registration yet that was successful. Let's just face the next step'.

That next step was the campaign, a period of about ten days prior to voting day. Each district had a campaign committee that set the timetable for local campaigns and handled complaints.[23] In Ermera the autonomy group, as they were called, suggested a timetable where the two groups could campaign on alternate days in sub-districts, and this was agreed on. They presented a program that covered all the villages, with many meetings. The CNRT decided to hold only six rallies. However, two of the CNRT rallies did not fit into the timetable previously agreed on, and they refused to change their plans. The autonomy side insisted that the CNRT follow the agreed arrangement. It was unclear to UNAMET members of the campaign committee why the CNRT refused to reorganise their schedule, or whether indeed they actually felt they had agreed to the timetable. Many frustrating hours were spent discussing the timetable. In the end the CNRT had to cancel those two meetings and, as it turned out, the autonomy side never followed their own timetable.

Militia provided the 'crowds' at the autonomy campaigns, and public servants, who were obliged to support autonomy, led the rallies. The militia travelled round all day in several trucks, conducting random campaigns whenever and wherever they could find a crowd. They frustrated the UNAMET electoral officers by 'stealing' the crowds who had gathered for UNAMET voting information meetings, which were always arranged to avoid clashes with campaign rallies. The autonomy representatives on the campaign committee were embarrassed by the behaviour of their supporters, but they were unable or unwilling to challenge them.

---

internally displaced people had lost their documents when their houses were burnt, and others could not return home to collect theirs, they were permitted to obtain an affidavit. This required only the signature of an official, such as village head, and another of a previously registered voter, acquainted with the person involved.

[23] The Regional Campaign Committees consisted of observers, representatives from the two sides, Indonesian and UNAMET police, and was chaired by UNAMET.

Militia numbers were in the low hundreds on these occasions, nothing like the numbers alleged. The militia complained to some UNAMET local staff about having to 'yell party slogans all day', without even being given food. The militia also told staff they were too afraid not to take part, but assured them that 'what we say with our mouths is not necessarily what we believe in our hearts'.

In the end the CNRT cancelled two other planned meetings, because the leaders were worried about threats to ordinary people who attended rallies, especially when they were held far from the main UNAMET headquarters. One rally was held in Railaku in the north on 18 August. The participants, mostly students from Gleno, were escorted the half-hour drive there by UNAMET and Indonesian police after their convoy was threatened by militia. No locals dared attend. People felt somewhat safer attending a second rally in Gleno, and on 26 August approximately 2,000 local people gathered.

As it happened, on that particular day all public servants from Ermera were told they had to attend an autonomy rally in Dili. The previous day a well-attended CNRT rally was held in Dili. It seemed that the autonomy side wanted to match them. The militia compelled all drivers of local transport in Ermera to take their vehicles to Dili in convoy even if they were not full of people. Some drivers refused and fled to outlying areas. Others had their licences confiscated, to be returned only if they joined the rally to Dili.

As the CNRT were about to begin their rally, one of their leaders was called by the district police commander, who told him that he could not guarantee the security of public servants who took part in the rally, and he suggested they withdraw. (This was a problem as all the speakers at the rally were public servants.) The CNRT confronted him, arguing that pro-autonomy public servants were participating in the autonomy rally, and CNRT public servants should have equal rights. The problem was that these public servants had signed up to support autonomy on 24 April. Government officials could not complain to UNAMET about this.

The district police commander told UNAMET that he was worried about 'inflammatory' speeches by CNRT leaders. The CNRT continued to demand a police guarantee of security. All sides were aware the threat came from TNI, so both the police commander and the CNRT, through colleagues in the Peace and Stability Commission,[24] contacted TNI members and militia, and in the end the rally went ahead without incident.

---

[24] The Peace and Stability Commission was established as part of the 5 May tripartite agreement. It had membership from both sides as well as Indonesian police and military. It was to be a forum for both sides to present their problems, and to try to bring about reconciliation.

In spite of the threats, the speakers were very strident, demanding an end to colonialism, corruption, collusion and nepotism in East Timor. As people paraded they chanted: 'Dead or alive we demand independence'. Police mobile brigade members (most having been in East Timor for a short while only) remarked to local UNAMET staff: 'The autonomy side have already lost—they don't have any people who support them. On their side it is only the militia who run around shouting. The CNRT have no weapons and don't use force, yet mobilise all these people in a disciplined rally. When the autonomy side have a rally, they threaten the people and cause trouble.'

Reconciliation

Timorese traditionally often solve disputes through reconciliation involving the mediation of a third party, and there were strong indications that Timorese from both sides wanted to resolve their differences peacefully. In this they requested the mediation of UNAMET. The militia commanders were particularly keen to meet with Falintil. The district police commander was supportive of such a meeting. In mid-June he visited Falintil in the area controlled by them, and saluted Ular,[25] the commander of Region II, before shaking hands. The Timorese were jubilant about this meeting, claiming it was the first time in 24 years an Indonesian official had openly recognised Falintil. Several times meetings were arranged between Falintil and Darah Integrasi, but each time postponed. Each side was suspicious and anxious about the intentions of the other. However, after some time it became clear that the district military commander was against any such rapprochement. He would always say he could not guarantee security.

After Falintil moved into cantonment, the militia talked of doing so but did not.[26] However, they claimed they had gone further than Falintil by surrendering weapons.[27] Civilian leaders of the pro-autonomy parties with whom I spoke about surrender of weapons appeared distinctly uncomfortable, knowing the exact opposite was the case. They defended the obvious continued use of a weapon by the Darah Integrasi commander, Miguel Babo, by saying that he was entitled to keep his weapon as long as Falintil kept theirs, as he was a fighter from 1975. Miguel and his brother, the deputy commander, would show weapons at campaign rallies to remind voters that this is what they faced if they rejected autonomy.

---

[25] Ular (Snake) is the code name of the commander.

[26] Cantonment is an area where military agree to confine themselves, along with their weapons.

[27] BRTT (East Timor People's Front) and FPDK (Front for Peace, Democracy and Justice). They were formed to take part in the Popular Consultation.

UNAMET sponsored several reconciliation meetings. At the first of these the militia leaders expressed their surprise that the CNRT attended. They said the CNRT had declared to the people that they no longer existed, on 26 April 1999, and as religious people, their thought oaths declared before God should be respected. They said that the autonomy group could not accept the CNRT's opening their office again and continuing their activities, because the CNRT had used killing and intimidation in the past.[28] The CNRT spokesperson responded by saying that crimes by both sides had to be put aside otherwise there would be no end to the problem. The two groups needed to solve the problem together, and that's why the CNRT needed to operate.

At first the Ermera militia refused to recognise the CNRT had any rights, until it was pointed out to them that autonomy leaders in Dili were making concessions to the CNRT under a code of conduct for the campaign signed by both sides on 9 August 1999. At last they agreed on a statement they could all sign a few days later, on 12 August 1999. They agreed to stop threats, not carry weapons, respect legal authority and not take action themselves if they had grievances.

Leaders of the autonomy political parties claimed they could not control 'their people'. Discussions on these matters were a finely tuned performance. The militia had no popular following, but this could not be mentioned. The other truth carefully skirted round in this performance was that the autonomy leaders and even the police had no control over the militia, who received orders from the military. The military weren't present, but their hand as the master puppeteer subtly directed the action.

Cantonment, celebration and flag raising

So how did the CNRT convey their message to the people, given that the rights to campaign and open an office were basically denied them? At every sub-district and village level were CNRT secretaries, who carried the message, albeit clandestinely. Priests and nuns also gave moral courage and leadership, many at great personal risk. The local priests sent letters and met us in person, presenting the complaints of the people. One of the most moving experiences I had in East Timor, and there were many evocative moments, was during and after attending mass where over 1,000 people gathered and knelt on the rocky ground in Letefoho town. Immediately after mass the priest invited me to his house. He told me about threats by partisans against

---

[28] This was a reference to the killing of the 11 and also a trumped up 'hostage taking' incident for which the CNRT leader in Ermera received a second jail sentence. In his defence in court, the CNRT leader said he held the six militia members for their protection (not as hostages) because he was afraid they could be killed, as the 11 had been, and then it would cause more trouble for the CNRT.

villagers, young men being forced to join militia, threats against him and his colleague. In the middle of this conversation two Indonesian policemen burst into the room, and sat down without being invited, telling me to please continue. The Timorese said it was outrageous, that even soldiers didn't just burst into people's houses, let alone a priest's. Eventually I was able to sort out with this policeman the issue of UNAMET staff reporting to sub-district police, and the rights of local people to talk freely with UNAMET. It was very difficult for the Indonesian security to come to terms with such intrusion by UNAMET, threatening their unchallenged authority of 24 years.

The priests and bishops also used Sunday mass to convey their message.[29] On the occasion that Bishop Belo came to Ermera he told the people that this vote was a once-only opportunity given to them by the international community. They should not be afraid of people with guns, it was a secret ballot. They could not be intimidated or forced to vote for a particular position (referring to forced oath-taking ceremonies). They should vote according to their conscience, not just thinking of their own safety but remembering they were choosing the future for their children and grandchildren.

Also a group of university students was instrumental in spreading the message. Some 200 of them from Ermera returned to their homes and villages at the commencement of registration to explain to people the registration and voting process, and gather information about human rights abuses. They were in constant conflict with the authorities, who claimed they 'angered' the 'people'. What they meant was that their effectiveness angered the Indonesian government and military and their militia agents. They were subject to threats, bashing, arbitrary arrest and in some cases were chased out of town.

After an agreement between Falintil commanders and senior Dili UNAMET officials, Falintil guerillas moved into cantonment. One of these areas was located in Ermera, in Poetete village.[30] On 10 August, this movement was celebrated in style with a large party to which UNAMET officials were invited from Dili and Ermera. A short time later, on 20 August, they were again partying. It was Falintil's 20th anniversary, and the first time ever they had been able to celebrate it. Unfortunately UNAMET had to forego attendance. We did not attend the 17 July Integration Day activities, marking

---

[29] The university students mostly belonged to Dewan Solidaritas Mahasiswa Timur Timor (East Timorese Students' Solidarity Council). The Ermera branch was called Dewan Mini Mahasiswa Ermera (Ermera Students' Mini Council). Some belonged to East Timorese organisations from outside East Timor, mostly Java, Bali and Sulawesi. In Ermera they were very well organised.

[30] Ermera is in Region II of the Falintil command structure. Region II is the largest region, located in the west. There were north and south cantonments, the northern one being close to Gleno town.

the official integration of East Timor into Indonesia, in the name of neutrality. This disappointed and angered some Indonesian officials, and for several weeks after that relations were tense. For that reason we decided we should not attend this anniversary. In other regions UNAMET was criticised for attending CNRT flag raisings, after declining to attend Integration Day ceremonies.

For many East Timorese this was the first time they had been able to meet with the guerillas. This party coincided with the campaign period, and I know the CNRT did not just eat, dance and play games on the sports fields constructed by the many able-bodied young men no longer going on patrols. It was the pinnacle of the CNRT's confidence, and from one perspective it was no less than a campaign rally of 18,000 people. For a brief time they put aside their fears of what lay ahead. Victory was in view. They had registered and survived the campaign. There were no serious shootings or grenade attacks at rallies, as they had feared. They were all alive to vote.

On Falintil Day the shops and streets of the hill-top town of Ermera were deserted. The militia, the police and TNI escorts campaigning for autonomy were angry to find no-one at the village where they had planned a rally. On their way home the next day, they vented their anger by attacking villagers and destroying homes of people who had just returned from attending the Falintil anniversary celebration.

On the last day of the campaign and two days before the vote, the CNRT held a flag raising in the cantonment. Falintil soldiers in the cantonment and many supporters attended. A Portuguese-speaking Italian priest, who lived in Japan and was in East Timor as an observer, said mass. It was a very solemn event. As the flag slowly rose under the intense tropical glare, Men hugged each other, their tears flowing unashamedly.

Again because of tense relations with Indonesian security forces, UNAMET staff had to be careful about how often we visited the cantonment. We could be accused of bias and giving overt support to the pro-independence side. The cantonment was by far the most interesting place in Ermera, alive with hope and indeed forgiveness. There was fear of the future, but there was also great hope. I felt the people were serene and genuine, and there was no need of pretence.

Police action against crimes committed by militia and TNI

Incidents reported to UNAMET involving militia were passed to the Indonesian police, as they were responsible for investigation. There was little action taken, despite the promises, and never an arrest of a militia member. After the vote, the police commander told the UNAMET police commander that he had been ordered 'from above' not to interfere with the actions of the militia. This led to a ludicrous situation on the day of voting, after the centre in Gleno was attacked by militia. The district police chief secretly confided that he could solve the militia situation in 24 hours if given a free hand. Instead of being able to do this, it seemed the only thing he could do was take personal responsibility. He sat in the sun for hours in the Gleno polling station grounds ensuring the militia allowed voting to continue. I observed militia standing nearby.[31]

Many Timorese reported to UNAMET, incidents of TNI acting together with militia in threatening and bashing, as well as crimes of April and May by TNI. After some time the UNAMET police were told by the Indonesian police that any incidents involving TNI needed to be passed to the military. Indonesian law stipulates that crimes by military must be handled in a military court.[32] Indonesian police also said that policing did not apply prior to 5 May as a state of war existed in East Timor. According to them, Xanana Gusmao, the Falintil commander, ordered his troops to take up arms after the killings in Liquica on 5 April, therefore until 5 May, when the tripartite agreement was signed, the two sides were at war. UNAMET military liaison officers duly reported complaints about TNI members and incidents involving them to the Indonesian military commander, but there was never any feedback or notification of action.

Polling day and its aftermath

Voting day, Monday 30 August, unlike registration, was not a jubilant occasion in Ermera. Bishop Belo, in a pastoral letter read in all churches the previous day, exhorted people to go home and pray, and keep on praying. Don't do anything to provoke, he told them. By 7.30 we heard on our UNAMET radios that most people were already waiting in line to vote, and this was the case everywhere in East Timor. Many people had travelled the previous evening to their polling centres as people had to vote at the place they registered. A small percentage of people were intimidated after registration and left the areas where they had registered, so were unable to vote. Despite all the fears that voting might be disrupted, 98.5% of registered voters were successful in casting their votes. This was a tremendous result.

---

[31] Also standing by were the leading pro-autonomy supporters. Some were present when the polling station was attacked, and they assured me that had they not been there the situation would have been a lot worse. They claimed they encouraged the militia to stay calm.

[32] UNAMET police and complainants had to report to the Indonesian police. Many Timorese were not prepared to do so, in fact they were often astonished by this procedure. One deposed village head was prepared to report three murders of people in his village by TNI; however, the police refused to accept it. The district police chief told me that there were complications in this village because three TNI members had been killed, but I had no information about this.

The militia attack on our Gleno polling station at midday that day came as a surprise, as Ermera was by this time considered safe, although it was always a knife-edge situation. The US ambassador, Roy Stapleton, had come to view voting there, and was in the yard when shooting broke out and rocks were thrown at the walls of a polling station. The Timorese could hardly believe their luck, to have the ambassador of the superpower actually witness this attack. After several hours and an attempt to address the militia's complaints, the polling station was reopened.[33] Just before closing time, a phone call was received from the district military headquarters. Several soldiers had been busy all day and needed time to change out of their uniforms. East Timorese TNI members were entitled to vote as long as they didn't show up in uniform. Contrary to regulation, one polling box was kept open for them beyond closing time. It turned out that two were registered elsewhere. It was an absolutely immutable rule that people could only vote at their registration centre, but these two also demanded to vote. UNAMET staff observed them becoming agitated, and speaking on their mobile phones. There appeared to be some movement again by the militia, so UNAMET decided to allow them to vote, rather than risk a second attack when the polling boxes could have become targets.

Meanwhile in a distant sub-district of Ermera, Atsabe, over three hours drive away, a very disturbing attack was taking place. At the close of the Baboi Leten polling station, a TNI officer and militia all armed with automatic weapons began to close in on the polling station. They demanded the local Timorese staff be handed over to them, accusing them of forcing the people to vote to reject autonomy. The lone UNAMET police officer was unable to defend the local staff, and witnessed two being bashed with poles and kicked. Two police mobile brigade members stood by doing nothing, but the UNAMET police officer was quite convinced that if they had interfered they would also have been attacked by the militia. One of the victims was taken with UNAMET staff when the police escort arrived to take them back to Atsabe town, but he died later. The UNAMET police officer believes that the other was killed and almost certainly also a third who was taken off in the car of the TNI member. The next day it took many hours of negotiation for the local Timorese staff with the ballot boxes to be evacuated by helicopter from Atsabe to Dili.

Even the boxes in Gleno were not removed without incident. New militia[34] arrived in town the day after polling. The rumour was that Darah Integrasi

---

[33] About 300 of the registered voters at this polling station were too frightened to return after the attack.

[34] We were never able to talk to these militia and find out their identity. We asked the district military commander if they were Aitarak, and he seemed to agree.

was never an 'effective militia'. They surrounded the helipad, where the boxes were to be collected. UNAMET staff tried to foil them by landing the helicopter in the dry riverbed behind the compound. Unfortunately timing went wrong, and before the boxes were loaded the militia arrived and the attempt had to be aborted. As the helicopter lifted off to avoid rocks thrown by the militia, some ballot papers fluttered down like confetti. Fortunately all except two were successfully collected. During this attack, UNAMET staff saw police mobile brigade members handing traditional weapons to the militia.[35]

A landing at the original helipad was negotiated, but before the helicopter could take off, UNAMET had to agree to a militia search to see if Amaral, the CNRT leader, was on board. The landing site in the riverbed was directly behind his burnt-out house. Perhaps the militia thought we had been attempting to collect him. Amaral was by this time safely in the cantonment. Later the district military commander explained that the militia did not want the CNRT leaders to leave as they had done in 1975. He mentioned Jose Ramos Horta as an example. They should stay with their people, he thought. The plan in fact later became clear, that CNRT leaders were to be captured and killed.

The evening after the vote, the burning of houses of CNRT leaders began. A 12-year-old girl came to the UNAMET headquarters to tell us about her house that was burnt, together with their store of rice and corn. She described the grenade planted by a militia member in her mother's flower plot, which was supposed to prove her father was a Falintil member. This provided the pretext for burning her parents' house.

UNAMET staff were never able to visit the families whose homes were destroyed. During the day we were basically prisoners in our compound. All staff had to move together into one of two areas well-guarded by the police mobile brigade. We could only travel between our houses and the headquarters, along one main route. Militia roamed round Gleno with jerry cans of petrol looking for the next house to target. A UNAMET police patrol was threatened by machete-wielding militia, so that was the end of patrols.

Somewhat to my surprise, we were able to make one last visit to the cantonment, on Thursday 2 September, after the vote but before the announcement of the result. While there were militia road-blocks north to Dili, and we needed police escorts to travel to Dili, there were none to the south. The only people we saw on our trip were militia. The markets were closed in the towns through which we passed. All houses had their shutters

---

[35] Many CNRT members said they suspected that some members of the Kontigen Lorosae police mobile brigade were militia.

locked and were deserted, many already burnt. No one was going about their work, and no children greeted us from the coffee gardens. It was as if winter had come to Ermera.

It was comforting to see so many people were safe in the cantonment, but they feared for their friends. There were many requests to check the whereabouts of family members. We were asked what was happening about security. They implored us to tell UNAMET that peace-keepers were needed before the announcement of the result. Could UNAMET help with food and medicines, as people were already flocking there? It was difficult walking away knowing there was nothing we could do to help.

On 3 September I went to Dili never imagining our headquarters would be burnt in just over a week and that I would not be able to return. As the situation deteriorated, the counting of votes was accelerated and the announcement of the result brought forward to Saturday 4 September, in the hope that a clear result might help stabalise the situation.

On the day of the announcement, an uneasy calm had settled over Dili, like the calm before a storm. No one went into the streets to celebrate the clear 78.6% victory for the pro-independence side, an astounding victory against all the odds. Even as the announcement was being made, a group of angry militia from Atsabe, where the three Timorese UNAMET staff had been killed on polling day, arrived in Dili demanding their complaints about the vote be heard and considered in the final count. They left in a rage and razed Atsabe. In Dili that day I answered the phone in the political office. One caller, monitoring military radio, reported he'd heard that attacks on the CNRT and independence supporters would begin at 1pm. Several people phoned saying they had been told they had to get ready to leave immediately for West Timor, and asked what UNAMET advised them to do. Tragically, we could do nothing.

In Ermera the district police commander finally told the remaining UNAMET staff he could not guarantee UNAMET security, and the office was evacuated on 9 September. UNAMET military liaison officers returned to Ermera district weeks later. Most of Gleno and Atsabe were burnt. All the relatively new and valuable government, military and police offices and essential facilities in Gleno were destroyed. Other towns still had some buildings standing.

People in the cantonment survived, eating cassava and sweet potato. Their greatest fears were for up to 30,000 people who were transported out of Ermera district to West Timor. Reports of killings, including that of a prominent female CNRT leader, filtered in but were difficult to confirm. There was a report that some refugees from Ermera were being held in West

Timor at a border town by the militia from Ermera. People drifted back to their villages. The military liaison officer met the first secretary of the CNRT wandering the streets of Gleno, surveying his burnt-out coffee store. This was his first visit home since he fled to the hills on 10 April.

One can only be filled with respect and admiration for those who struggled for independence for East Timor. They abided by the agreements. They offered a reconciliatory hand to all Timorese, even extending it to Indonesians. They remained patient and brave in the face of military belligerence. They took this incredible risk, yet when they won they still had to stand silently by and watch their families removed, their homes destroyed. Only by this did East Timor not dissolve into civil war as the Indonesian military planned. Only after it was over did the international community act. Such was the price of victory in East Timor.

The TNI and the militias

Damien Kingsbury

The United Nations Assistance Mission to East Timor (UNAMET) went into the troubled territory as a neutral body to conduct a ballot on whether or not East Timor would remain a part of Indonesia. Neutral, too, were the independent observers who went to act as witnesses to the ballot process. Neutrality was the key idea in the conduct of the ballot. Yet heaped onto this were the violent activities of the pro-integration militias, who worked closely with the Indonesian armed forces, Tentara Nasional Indonesia (TNI) and the Indonesian police, who were supposedly there to maintain security. At every turn the anti-independence groups acted to thwart the ballot process, attacking and intimidating innocent civilians, burning homes, setting up road-blocks and abrogating just-signed agreements. East Timor turned out to be a difficult place in which to be neutral, not least because the simple act of allowing a people to vote was itself seen as partisan.

Throughout East Timor, in the weeks leading up to the ballot there had been an atmosphere of celebration, despite the violence. Simple birthdays were turned into feasts, parties were held to celebrate parties of the day before, and even the usually cautious Falintil invited thousands of people to its camps to mark its 24th anniversary. One aid worker who attended the Falintil Zone One party described it as a 'Falintil Woodstock', being three days of peace and music, and it did seem like that. The murder continued, the house burnings and the rape proceeded apace. But for a people who had lived with such hardship for a quarter of a century, there was no way to disguise their joy.

Behind the scenes, however, moves were afoot to try to derail the ballot process. President Habibie's move to offer the people of East Timor a vote was not widely appreciated in Indonesia, least of all by the powerful armed forces and in particular its Commander in Chief, General Wiranto.

Wiranto, Habibie and East Timor

The public falling out between Wiranto and Habibie in early 1999 occurred over Habibie's announcement of the vote. The idea for the East Timor ballot had been developed between Habibie and his advisor, Dewi Fortuna Anwar, and then presented to Habibie's cabinet. Yet the fall-out between Wiranto and Habibie had already become well established and, in many respects, Habibie's announcement on East Timor only cemented their poor relations. Wiranto had supported Habibie's becoming President following the resignation of Suharto because this offered a constitutionally acceptable formula for moving on from Suharto through a transitional period. However, Wiranto at no stage ever regarded Habibie's presidency as anything other than transitional.

Not unusually for a politician, although Habibie initially recognised his transitional status, he began to have thoughts of himself as being a longer term President. To strengthen this position he needed to remove Wiranto. His opportunity, or so he thought, came in November 1998, when protesting students occupied the MPR (People's Consultative Assembly) building in Jakarta. Wiranto refused to use force against the students, and their continued opposition to Habibie caused the latter great embarrassment. Habibie offered the position of commander of Indonesia's armed forces to Wiranto's close associate, Major General Susilo Bambang Yudhoyono if he would act to remove the students. However, as Wiranto's then protégé, Yudhoyono refused and the student protest was later peacefully settled. The battle lines between Wiranto and Habibie were drawn.

The next major incident between Wiranto and Habibie occurred at around the time of Habibie's initiative on East Timor. Either just prior to or just following the announcement, Habibie asked Wiranto to resign as head of the armed forces, to be replaced by Wiranto's former close associate Major General Hendropriyono. In this case, Hendropriyono was enthusiastic about the appointment, but Wiranto simply refused to budge. Then there was the actual announcement of the East Timor ballot, which gave material substance to the rift between Habibie and Wiranto.

As TNI commander, Wiranto was not advised of the proposal prior to its being presented to the cabinet before being publicly announced, which he regarded as not being consulted at all. It is believed that Wiranto said nothing during the cabinet meeting, reflecting his anger at the decision. It was from the time of Habibie's announcement that East Timor's 13 TNI-backed pro-integration militia groups became active. Wiranto was later criticised for having failed to contain the activities of pro-integration militias in East Timor. The general belief was that Wiranto was both well aware of what was happening in East Timor as the situation started to deteriorate there and that, by failing to act against it, despite the explicit wishes of Habibie, he endorsed or even ordered the activities. It became increasingly clear that not only was Wiranto aware of events in East Timor, but that he had an active role in them.

Two days after Habibie's announcement on East Timor, a 'Crisis Team on East Timor' was established to wage a 'dirty war' against pro-independence groups. This team was headed by Major-General Zacky Anwar Makarim. Zacky had stepped down as head of military intelligence (BIA—*Badan Intelijen ABRI*) to take up the new position. Zacky was head of intelligence in East Timor at the time of the Dili Massacre in 1991 and had widespread experience there. With Zacky in charge, the 'Crisis Team' set up a series of 'militias', comprising around 6,000 paid and press-ganged East and West Timorse in 13 organisations. The militias included the better known Aitarak, Besi Merah Butih and Lahorus Merah Putih/Halilintar respectively in the districts of Dili, Liquisa and Bobonaro. Naga Merah dan Darah Merah was set up in Ermera, Laksau Merah Putih was established in Kova Lima, Mahidin was based in Ainaro, Abelai in Same, AHI in Aileu, Mahadomi in Manatuto, Saka in Baucau, Sera in Viqueque, Tim Alfa in Lauten and Darah Merah in Ambeno.

The militias were based on pre-existing 'home defence units',[1] which since Indonesia's occupation had been given the task of rooting out anti-integration elements remaining within East Timorese society. In practical terms, these thugs did the dirty work the TNI and the police wished to distance themselves from, as well as creating a sense of an indigenous opposition to the independence movement. By early 1999, however, it was clear that these 'units' were not up to the task of trying to mask or control the rise in openly expressed pro-independence sentiment. The answer was to boost the units and reconstitute them as 'militias' given the task of retaining 'order'.

The domestic basis of the militias was local toughs hired by the senior district official (*bupati*) or his agents. In this sense, the militias and their controlling process was quite feudal, turning a number of local officials into petty warlords. These militias were comprised of some locally born young men, but increasingly men who had either moved to East Timor from elsewhere in the archipelago—especially West Timor—or who were specifically hired in West Timor to work in East Timor for the pre and immediate post-ballot period. Payment for services to these men was either in cash and rice, or in straight cash. The standard payment for the Aitarak militia, for example, was 50,000 rupiah a day (about AU$10, or US$6.50). Other militia received less money, at around 100,000 rupiah a month, along with supplies of government rice. The payments to the militia were already well known, but received a boost in publicity when in July a scandal erupted about counterfeit money being used as payment. Aitarak militia leader Eurico Guterres had been given money to pay his militia members, but instead tried to deposit it into his bank account. The bank refused to accept the money, saying it was counterfeit. Guterres turned to his own paymaster, the TNI, and complained. They explained to him that the 50,000 rupiah notes were to have been given to his men, who would not have known the difference; they were not supposed to contribute to Guterres' personal fortune.

---

[1] Halilintar and Saka had previously existed as militias since 1977 and 1983 respectively. Others began forming in late 1998 and early 1999, drawing on Gardapaksi (Youth Guard for Upholding Integration), a TNI-backed anti-independence youth group.

The militia members were armed with often very crude home-made weapons. Their guns were the firing mechanism of shotguns housed in home-made bodies. In part the idea of these weapons was to show that the militias were somehow self-supporting, and in part to reduce their level of military power compared to the police and the TNI. However, throughout August, as they began to hand in their home-made weapons, the militias were increasingly armed with the TNI's own weapons, including M-16s, G3, SS-1 and AK47 automatic rifles, 9mm pistols and, in the period just before the ballot, hand grenades. By this stage, however, the distinction between the militias and the TNI and the police had become very blurred on the ground.

In Maliana, the local Halilintar militia openly operated out of the local TNI headquarters. The police, mostly from the paramilitary Brimob (Mobile Brigade) group, actively assisted militia members with transport and were reported by eye-witnesses to have shot villagers when militia rampaged through the village of Memo, near Maliana, on 28 August. There were many such reports of close association between the TNI, police and militias on the ground. Militia openly occupied police posts between Batu Gade, on the West Timor border on the northern coast, and the outskirts of Dili. TNI officers and Non-Commissioned Officers were, in some cases, belatedly removed from their posts as a consequence of official and repeated UNAMET complaints about their involvement with the militias.[2]

Despite such superficial acknowledgement of the links between the TNI, police and the militias, the violence continued almost unchecked. The two moments that it seemed to stop were in early August, around the day of the visit to East Timor by Australia's Foreign Minister, Alexander Downer, and during the day of the ballot itself. Apart from that, it escalated in ferocity from July onwards. The killings and kidnappings became more frequent, more homes were burned and more villages ransacked. When faced with the prospect that the pro-integration camp might not win the ballot, one of the key organisers of the pro-integration Forum for Unity, Democracy and Justice, Filomeno Orai, was asked if he would guarantee a peaceful outcome. 'Peace?' he said. 'Why would we want peace? If the vote is for independence we'll just kill—kill everybody' (McBeth 1999c:13).

Aitarak and the other militias were supported and armed by the regional Udayana IX Military Command, based in Bali, and occasionally led in the field by (sometimes former) military intelligence officers, associated with the *Satuan Tugas Intelijen* (Intelligence Duty Unit—SGI) and Kopassus (Special Forces). Through what it called *Operasi Sapu Jagad* (Operation Global Clean

---

[2] For example, in late August the military head of Bobonaro district (around Maliana) and three NCOs were removed from their posts.

Sweep), these gangs were responsible for hundreds of deaths in East Timor between January and July 1999 and caused more than 60,000 people to flee their villages, creating a serious refugee problem. Officials from the key independence organisation, the Timorese National Resistance Council (CNRT), were killed, while its offices in the western part of East Timor were effectively kept closed. A further element of Operation Clean Sweep was to disrupt the UN process in East Timor. This problem escalated into August and had reached radical proportions by early September, with more than 350,000 forced into homelessness and hundreds, probably thousands, tortured and killed.

Requests by Habibie, the nominal supreme commander of TNI, for it to rein in the militias and to impose order in East Timor were contemptuously ignored. By refusing to carry out Habibie's orders to rein in or attempt to rein in his own officers and hence the militias in East Timor, Wiranto showed where real political power in Indonesia, and in East Timor, lay. It was this situation that greeted UNAMET staff when they began to arrive and deploy in East Timor, a situation that was well under way by the time international observers entered the territory.

By July the UNAMET compound in Maliana had already been the subject of several attacks by the Halilintar militia, while Maliana was widely regarded as a town under tight militia control. Halilintar was headed by Joao Tavares, who was also the *panglima* (supreme commander) of all of East Timor's 13 militia, under the banner of the Pasukan Pejuang Integrasi (PPI—Integration Struggle Troops) (Tavares 1999). There has been no doubt about the close links between the militia and the TNI in East Timor, but to underline the obviousness of this claim, Halilintar in Maliana operated directly out of the local military headquarters, situated at the main intersection of the town.

From early on it was clear that the local militias intended to create as much disruption as possible. It was also clear that the militias were intent, at a minimum, on breaking away the three western districts, of Cova Lima, Bobonaro and Liquisa, to try to federate them with West Timor. Beyond this, at a district level meeting of the Persatuan, Demokrasi dan Keadilan (FPDK—Forum for Unity, Democracy and Justice), Barisan Rakyat Timor Timur (BRTT—People's Front for East Timor), and the CNRT, the anti-independence groups demanded that they be given three-quarters of campaign time during the formal campaigning period. And as if their message was not clear, they said that if the CNRT attempted to open an office in Maliana it would be burned and its occupants killed.

Students

Students were a prime target of the militias, because they were active in the cause of independence. Perhaps as importantly, however, students were also targeted because they represented the ability to educate and inform illiterate peasants and to question and challenge the prevailing orthodoxies put about by the Indonesian government and its agents. Attacks against students had become more prevalent during August and many were killed. Eventually, the students went underground, feeling that it was no longer safe to operate in an open and public manner in their own land. For one group of students, however, the decision to go underground came too late.

The small town of Bononaro sits high in the mountains and it is from this old Portuguese settlement that the district around Maliana takes its name. The local priest, a Filipino, had been sheltering students who had come from Dili a month earlier. The students, some of whom were from the district, had come to Bobonaro to encourage people to vote in the ballot. They were clearly pro-independence and, as such, were a prime target of the militias. Having arrived in Bobonaro, the students were trapped by the militia. If they left, they were threatened with death. At this stage churches were still regarded as a safe refuge, even though dozens of people had been killed by the local militia when they sought refuge in the church at Liquisa the April before. By September, the churches had become a place of entrapment, rather than refuge.

They lived in the church, but food was becoming scarce and they had to move. We offered to escort them back to Dili, if we could arrange transport. The students were to meet in Maliana the following morning. Instead of the dozen expected, there were 38 students waiting in the main street. This created a problem in a town where most minbuses would accommodate at most 15 people. Obtaining one vehicle for the students was difficult but manageable. Obtaining two turned out to be impossible, in the circumstances. No sooner had a driver been convinced to take the students back to Dili than a militia member would approach the driver and threaten him. On two occasions the students were in a minibus actually backing out onto the main street when the driver, having been threatened, stopped, got out and walked away.

After three hours of this (and two angry confrontations with militia members), the idea was abandoned. The students went to stay at a community hall. The following night they were attacked there by the local militia. The attack was more for the effect of intimidation than to cause harm, although one student was kidnapped and later killed. The student numbers at the refuge quickly swelled to more than 100, as other students learned of their presence and also sought refuge. But Maliana was too dangerous. The enlarged group of students returned to Bobonaro and to the church there, but after the announcement of the ballot result they were again attacked. This time the death toll was high, although the figure is not precisely known as the priest there fled for his life. The surviving students were scattered into the nearby hills, to face cold and hunger and to be hunted like animals. It was only one story of repression amongst so many, but well illustrated the manner in which these events took place.

On 26 August, militias rampaged through Dili, destroying the CNRT headquarters facing the beach just east of the city centre. Just 11 days before, it had been the festive scene of thousands of people celebrating its opening. Police were not only powerless to stop the militia, they did not even try or in some cases openly supported them. The miltia members who had been trucked into Dili to create havoc on what was the second last day of campaigning for the ballot were then trucked to Maliana. After parading around town for two hours, directed by police, the militias were trucked to the village of Memo, about eight kilometres north of Maliana. Here they attacked the village, burning all 23 houses on one side of a dry creek bed that acted as a barrier against their advance. They also killed two men, one reportedly being shot by a uniformed police officer as he tried to run away. In this case the villagers fought back and one militia member was also killed, while several were injured. Apart from the automatic weapons used by the police, this was an almost feudal battle. Both sides were armed with rudimentary weapons, often just machetes or spears, and the damaged bridge crossing the creek bed was the site at which the tide of the battle had turned. Both the sophistication of the militias' weapons and the ferocity with which they were used increased from this time onwards. Home-made shotguns were replaced by a range of automatic weapons, while machetes were used to decapitate those unlucky enough to have been caught in the catastrophe that was to follow.

The day of the ballot

From before light on 30 August, hundreds of people could be seen streaming down out of the hills, wearing their best Sunday clothing, ballot papers and identification cards clutched firmly in their hands. Many people had begun walking the day before, in order to reach the voting stations by first light, while others arrived by truck and motorcycle. Even before the voting stations opened for public voting at 6.30 am, thousands of people were lined up, smiling, waiting, chatting and laughing. This was their day and nothing could take it away from them. Even the militias kept quiet on this day, while police stood guard, watching helplessly as the people they had so closely controlled were now exercising a choice that could see those very same police removed from this place.

There were some instances of violence on polling day and in many places police, or militia not wearing their t-shirt uniforms, unnecessarily checked voters' identification and generally made their presence known. In the small town and militia stronghold of Balibo, an intelligence agent stood with police and militia members on the verandah of a house directly opposite the polling centre, ostentatiously talking into a two-way radio, which he shared with police. UNAMET staff in Bobonaro district thought that, given the high level of violence and intimidation in preceding days, that at many polling stations they would be lucky to get 50% of registered voters turning out. Even in the village of Memo, which had been attacked just three days previously and in which further threats had been made against villagers if they voted, the voter turn-out rate was 94%. In other polling centres the rate was even higher. If the ballot was to be measured just by the proportion of registered voters who turned out to participate, then it was clearly an overwhelming success. Yet by late that afternoon, some of the sense of euphoria had begun to fade, as people headed back to their villages and waited for the onslaught they all believed would come.

That night the village of Ritabou near Maliana was burned to the ground. The following day, just after the ballot papers were taken by helicopter back to Dili, UNAMET staff began to withdraw. Their work was completed and the environment was increasingly dangerous. The next day, seven local people employed by UNAMET at Maliana were murdered. Many more were killed in the following days. This pattern was repeated throughout the territory.

UNAMET has been criticised by many for leaving these people to the militias, but UNAMET was effectively powerless to stop militia and TNI activity. They were not armed and the maintenance of security was always the responsibility of the Indonesian police. Had the UN insisted on an armed presence, the ballot would not have gone ahead, and even CNRT, which knew there would be reprisals, insisted that it must go ahead. It was, they said, their one chance to secure independence. UNAMET did not fail in its mission. Indeed, it was extraordinarily successful, against the odds and in a most hostile environment.

The result

The total turn-out of registered voters to the poll ended up at an extraordinary 98.6%. In a country where voting is compulsory and there is no political violence or intimidation such as Australia, voting rarely exceeds 92%. Across East Timor, again despite the terror, the trucking-in of many questionable voters from West Timor, and the fact that many voters did not believe their votes were secret, 78.5% of registered voters opted for independence from Indonesia. This result inexorably set in train a process for the establishment of a new state.

But before moves could be made to secure the wishes of the people—within minutes of the ballot result being announced—the violence that had been visited upon ordinary East Timorese people until that time returned in a greater wave of fury. It left huge numbers butchered in an horrific and barbaric manner, and displaced most of the population of a little over 800,000, with many being forcibly removed to West Timor.

The killings were wholesale throughout East Timor, and the heads of pro-independence supporters were stuck on pikes and lined roadways in pro-independence areas. Rape and torture before death was a commonplace. No-one was safe from the slaughter, except for those tens of thousands forced at gunpoint to be shipped to a perilous fate in refugee camps in West Timor (UNHCR 1999). Others were herded in their hundreds onto boats, ostensibly to be sent to other islands. Yet the boats began to return within hours, with no refugees on board. The belief was they had been killed and their bodies dumped at sea. The question has been asked, and at the time of writing not adequately answered: why did this happen? Despite claims by pro-integration groups, the violence was not in response to what they alleged was electoral fraud. The ballot was perhaps the most clean and transparent in Indonesia's history, despite the pre-ballot violence perpetrated by those people who later claimed the vote was somehow rigged. Of all the pro-integration groups' feeble claims, perhaps one stands up to some scrutiny. They claimed that UNAMET employed mostly pro-independence workers for their local staff. Given the overwhelming support for independence amongst ordinary East Timorese, it would have been impossible for a representative grouping employed by UNAMET to be otherwise. This is not to mention the active opposition of the pro-integration groups to the whole idea of a ballot. The other claims, however, were spurious.

At least a part of the attacks on civilians was an attempt to intimidate them into accepting continued Indonesian rule. It was a blunt method, but one that had been used with some success elsewhere in the archipelago in earlier times. In East Timor, it only hardened resistance to the idea. A second reason was to try to provoke Falintil into retaliation, thereby being able to claim a state of civil war and cancel the ballot or annul its result. A third reason was to use East Timor as a lesson to the other provinces of Indonesia considering breaking away: 'this is what happens if to try to leave', it seemed to be saying. The TNI also had problems with the idea that so many of their comrades had been killed in East Timor, and now it seemed to be for nothing. The anger and the sense of betrayal, however misguided, was real for some. And then there was the question of the TNI trying to save face in what was a humiliating defeat, not by force of arms, but at the hands of an unarmed population. It was a rejection not just of Indonesia, but of the idea of 'Indonesia'. The unity of the state was challenged, the concept of nationalism was slapped in the face, the guardians of the state were made to look foolish. The people of East Timor were made to pay for this.

Perhaps finally, there were also some elements of Jakarta's 'palace politics' being played out in East Timor, where a contest of wills between Habibie and Wiranto, or between 'reformists' and 'nationalists', determined policy on the ground. Clearly presidential aspirant Megawati Sukarnoputri had her fingers burned in the tussle, saying in early August that she would respect the outcome of the referendum. Just days later, seemingly at the behest of her ally Wiranto, she made a quick visit to East Timor where, flying by helicopter from town to town, she reversed that call and said she wanted to see East Timor remain a part of Indonesia. It was notable that, during her visit, Megawati failed to call on the head of the UNAMET mission, Ian Martin, or indeed meet any other UNAMET staff.

In most cases the people of East Timor knew there would be some sort of retribution. The information about some sort of post-ballot pro-integration campaign had been too frequent and too varied in its sources not to have some credibility. There was a widespread belief that retribution would come regardless of whether the vote was held or not, or whatever its outcome. The pro-independence people would have to be dealt with. As it turned out, that was more than three-quarters of the population.

Responding belatedly to calls by observers and East Timorese support groups, members of the international community began to coalesce around the idea of sending an armed mission into East Timor. The United States was reluctant but Australia, the population of which was outraged by events there, agreed to head such a mission. By mid-September the UN had given approval to a peace-enforcement mission to East Timor, comprising military from Australia as well as New Zealand, Thailand, Portugal, the Philippines, South Korea, Cambodia, Britain, Ireland, the United States, Singapore and Malaysia (UN 1999a). There were many rhetorical threats made against the force, in particular the Australian contingent, as Australia had been seen by many Indonesians as a driving force behind East Timor's push for independence. But ahead of the landing of the first International Forces to East Timor (InterFET) troops, 'high walled intelligence and interrogation centres were emptied and documents hastily dumped onto bonfires…Two decades of evidence went up in flames' (Murphy and McBeth 1999). As the InterFET troops landed, on 20 September 1999, members of the TNI and the militias had already begun to move across the border into West Timor, taking huge quantities of looted goods with them.

The aftermath

Even before the ballot, Xanana Gusmao had said that the East Timorese needed to look to the future and forget about the past. Rather than blame those East Timorese members of the militias for the violence, Gusmao laid the blame at the feet of the TNI. 'We will do everything to avoid vengeance and hatred between people,' he said. 'Of course we have to focus on reconciliation between East Timorese' (Gusmao 1999a). Gusmao also pointed to the enormous development issues that the new, fledgling state would face: '...we also have to eat,' he said. 'And I can say to you that we have been preparing our development policy since the beginning of April this year.' (Gusmao 1999a). However, the task of developing the half island state was complicated by the TNI's 'scorched earth' policy as it left East Timor. Infrastructure, including communications and water supply, was almost non-existent, most major buildings were destroyed or damaged and industry was non-existent.

— In the years of the Indonesian occupation, most of the disparate peoples of East Timor had been bonded together by a common enemy and by what was increasingly a common religion, Catholicism. The language of Tetun Dili had increasingly become the standard non-Indonesian language of communication, in a similar manner to that of Tagalog in the Philippines. However, most people, and in particular those under 40, also spoke Bahasa Indonesia, while those over 40 often also spoke Portuguese. There were, in short, the identifiable characteristics of a nation, quite distinct from the West Timorese.

In the period after peace was restored to East Timor, the UN was expected to install an interim administration, with the task of rebuilding the basic infrastructure and institutions of state. Apart from the obvious infrastructure requirements, institutions such as a bureaucracy, education system (including rebuilding the university), health service and legal service (including courts and police) would need to be established. In particular, the almost overwhelming health problem presented by malaria needed to be tackled as a matter of urgency, a fact recognised by CNRT. Similarly, a security or law enforcement apparatus needed to be established, both for internal policing and to secure East Timor's border with West Timor. There remained concerns that some militia groups could attempt to conduct cross-border raids against East Timor after the establishment of an independent state.

At one level there were grounds for the establishment of the institutions of state, especially amongst East Timor's diaspora that indicated, in large measure, its desire to return. But it was clear that there would need to be external administrative support for East Timor for several years while these institutions were rebuilt. In this respect, the continuing administrative role of the UN was vital to East Timor's securing a stable future.

East Timor's economy was also a critical issue. As the second poorest province in Indonesia and as an impoverished Portuguese colony, East Timor never had a strong economy. However, it did have some scope for economic development, which perhaps could provide the basis of a viable state. In the first instance, the Timor Gap gas and oil field, which should revert to East Timorese–Australian control after the granting of independence, could provide a reasonable flow of state income. Although not as lucrative as earlier thought, the gas revenues have not been insignificant and could contribute considerably to the fledgling state's coffers. East Timor also has a strong coffee production industry and, while world coffee prices are not high, it is also another source of foreign income.

Despite the damage that has been done to it, East Timor is also in many senses a physically beautiful place and could attract tourism. It has been said that in 1974 East Timor enjoyed the same level of tourism development as Bali. While Bali is perhaps not the best example of tourism development, it has certainly been a major revenue generator. The market for sandalwood, once the reason for foreign interest, is now very small, but it is still a natural resource that could be cultivated. Mineral deposits, especially of decorative stone, are also available for development, while East Timor's coastal region abounds with fish, having the potential to generate income both as exports and from licensed fishing.

But in the final analysis, the international community generally and Australia and Portugal in particular would have to contribute to East Timor's base income for several years. Indonesia, it could have been expected, would not be one of the contributors. It should have been, but such a move was very unpopular in Indonesia, especially given its own economically difficult circumstances and the manner in which it left East Timor. But perhaps as a small measure of redressing the cost to the East Timorese people, to which it added in so many ways, the international community could be expected to bear this cost for several years.

The militia, the military, and the people of Bobonaro district

Peter Bartu

Minister of Defence/Commander of the armed forces, General Wiranto has declared that the Indonesian Armed Forces is not a wild band of men who can be put on trial by anyone. The army always complies with official orders and always acts in conformity with the laws in force and with human rights.

'We have done the best we could in keeping within the law, acting with discipline and basic human rights...' he said.

Suara Pembaruan, Jakarta 3 October 1999

As a political officer with the United Nations Mission in East Timor (UNAMET) I reported on political developments in the volatile western districts, initially from Dili and then from Maliana, the capital of Bobonaro district along the border with West Timor or Nusa Tenggara Timur (NTT) province.

The situation in Bobonaro district was fluid and uncertain for the entire period of the Popular Consultation,[1] during which the beleaguered East Timorese could choose to accept or reject the autonomy package offered by the Indonesian government. The local authorities repeatedly made it clear that they had not signed the 5 May Agreement and they offered begrudging co-operation to UNAMET. Elite members of the District Administration (who stood to lose all if the autonomy option lost) and the Indonesian National Armed Forces (TNI, who would have to withdraw from East Timor) pulled out all stops to improve the chances of an autonomy vote. A parallel track of coercion and violence was pursued through militia proxies. Over the different phases of the UNAMET-run Consultation the militia groups gradually fell apart. The East Timorese people and rank and file militia members passively rejected their instructions and ultimately many left the organisation. By the time of the Consultation on 30 August 1999 the TNI and the Indonesian Police (Polri), including East Timorese in both units, became increasingly responsible for all violence and intimidation. The precision and confidence with which they executed their strategies indicates co-ordination from the highest levels.

Consultation structures

To conduct the Consultation UNAMET divided East Timor into eight regional centres based on population density and logistical considerations. A

---

[1] Hereafter the Consultation.

political officer was assigned to each centre and worked alongside a regional electoral co-ordinator (in charge of technical aspects of the Consultation), a regional UN Civilian Police chief (responsible for advising Polri on their security obligations under the Agreement) and, a small team of military liaison officers who maintained contact with the TNI. Through July and August UNAMET had up to 60 international staff working in at least 22 separate locations throughout Bobonaro district.

To assist with implementing the Agreement the Polri, TNI and the Indonesian Foreign Ministry (DEPLU) each assigned English speaking liaison officers to work alongside UNAMET and the predominantly East Timorese district administration. Typically, Polri liaison officers had served on UN missions before, with Namibia, Cambodia and Bosnia being the common experiences. They worked alongside their local counterparts, many of whom were intimately involved in the pro-integration cause. Other elements of Polri included the 'Kontigen Lorosae', specially formed units which augmented the regular Polri, and the police Brigade Mobile (Brimob) units, including Brimob special forces. DEPLU representatives dealt with the district administration, monitored UNAMET's adherence, or otherwise, to the Agreement and reported to the Indonesian Task Force led by Ambassador Agus Tamizi in Dili. The TNI liaison officers were a bridge between UNAMET and the TNI and in the main reflected a consistently singular and insular view of the process, at odds with the broader perspective of their Polri and DEPLU counterparts who had external experience.

Over time the dynamics between the liaison officers provided unique insights into their respective institutions. Under the Agreement the official elevation of the Polri to central position for all security issues was irksome for the TNI. The military resented being sidelined, but ultimately used their 'diminished role' as an excuse to avoid responsibility for the militia, whom they clearly controlled. While the Polri were formally separated from the TNI on 1 April 1999, they still came under the command of the Defence Minister, General Wiranto, who was also the chief of staff of the armed forces. However, they were never given the power to meet their security obligations. In the circumstances many Polri were frightened of their new role, some were frustrated and others were resigned to the charade in which they had to participate. As one senior officer confessed: 'If we arrest a militiaman, Dili and Jakarta will tell us to let them go. If we shoot one of them, then we know they will attack our [district] headquarters'. On only one occasion in mid-May did Polri attempt to apprehend militia in Maliana—for the theft of cars and motorcycles looted from pro-independence houses. A three hour gunfight ensued when the militia and the TNI fired on the Polri.

Bobonaro district

East Timor is divided into 13 districts, loosely but not exclusively based on the Portuguese administrative structure that cohered the traditional Liurai feudal system, linguistic groupings and often formidable geography into a system of regencies. Bobonaro, the fourth largest district (*kabupaten*) with some 100,000 people, incorporates 6 sub-districts (*kecematan*) stretching from the northern littoral to the southern mountains and dense jungle that define the border with Cova Lima district. The Loes river and a chain of mountains along the east separate Bobonaro from Liquica, the central and coffee—rich district of Ermera, and Ainaro district to the Southeast. The border with NTT is similarly demarcated by a series of hills, towering limestone ridges and waterways. The road network, expanded and improved under Indonesian rule, and constantly under repair due to the impact of the October–February wet season, traverses the northern coastline, ridges and mountains that link the capital Maliana to the outlying sub-districts. Maliana, a sub-district in its own right, is centrally located on a large rice-growing plain. Traditional paths hug the coast, lowland areas and valleys, and rise through mountain passes providing alternate routes, means of escape and refuge for Falintil guerillas and their supporters.

Bobonaro had better road links with Atambua in West Timor than it did with Dili. Each Sunday men would flock from West Timor (where gambling was prohibited) to while away hours at cock fights and gambling games at the border towns of Batugade and Balibo. In general terms Bobonaro was more developed than other parts of East Timor, with good infrastructure. However, commercial activity was concentrated in the hands of a few (notably the Tavares and Monez families) and all imports and exports flowed through West Timor. While bright pupils could one day hope to attend the University of East Timor in Dili, the literacy rate was appalling. Fewer than 30% of the district electorate were able to sign their names on their registration cards.

Security structures

As elsewhere in Indonesia the TNI exercised complete suzerainty over security issues. Structurally the TNI mirrored the civil administration and the Polri. The local military commander (Dandim), Lieutenant Colonel Burhanuddin Siagian, explained that he had responsibilities for issues of 'geography, demography, population, ideology, cultural defence, social issues and external threats'. From his Maliana headquarters (Kodim) Siagian oversaw six sub-district commands (Koramil), below which were the *babinsas*, TNI non-commissioned officers based in each of Bobonaro district's 51 villages. Siagian reported to the Military Sub-Area Command (Korem 164) based in Dili. The commander (Danrem), Colonel Tono

Suratman, was replaced by Colonel Nur Muis on 13 August. Above the Korem/ Danrem level was the Military Area Command (Kodim, Udayana IX) based in Denapasar, Bali. The Commander (Pangdam) Major-General Adam Damiri in turn reported to TNI headquarters in Cilangkap, Jakarta.[2]

Two military figures long associated with East Timor, former military intelligence (BIA) chief Major General Zacky Anwar Makarim and General Gleny Kauripan, were attached to the Indonesian Task Force in Dili. General Anwar had been replaced as BIA chief in January 1999 and served as a special advisor on East Timor to Wiranto before assignment to Dili on 3 June.

Siagian, the local military head, claimed that under his command in Bobonaro district there were 400 East Timorese troops and that they all supported the pro-integration groups. In mid-July Siagian stated on several occasions that there were some 10,000 East Timorese serving within the TNI and the Polri throughout East Timor and that their 'strength had to be noted'. Siagian was clearly disdainful of the East Timorese and the East Timorese National Liberation Army (Forcas Armados de Libertacao Nacional de Timor, Falintil); 'they have no strategy,' he would say. A product of the TNI system, it is difficult to imagine that he had any capacity for independent action. Posted to Bobonaro district on 1 October 1997 he oversaw the creation of the militia system in his district. It is possibly his success in this endeavour that saw him awarded the 'top Kodim' in the whole of Udayana IX command in August 1999.

The importance of Bobonaro district

In early July Falintil members from Sector IV rated Bobonaro district third in terms of violence and intimidation, behind Liquica and Cova Lima districts.[3] By August Bobonaro district had climbed to the number 1 spot, edging out Cova Lima and way ahead of Liquica, where the political fallout after a militia ambush on a UNAMET-led humanitarian convoy on 4 July, in

---

[2] Key officers in Jakarta included: General Wiranto the Armed Forces Commander (Pangab) and also Defence Minister; General Subagyo Hadisiswoyo the Army Chief of Staff (KSAD); his assistant for operations and former East Timor Commander from September 1994 to May 1995 Major General Kiki Syahnakri (who replaced Muis Nur after Martial Law was declared in East Timor on 7 September); Major General Muchdi Purwopranjono, Kopassus Commander; Major General Tiasno Sudarno BIA Commander, and General Ruhsmanhadi, the National Police Chief.

[3] Falintil had divided East Timor into four sectors. The Sector IV commander was Ular Rate. In Bobonaro district Falintil was divided into two companies: North Company commanded by 'Rocke' and the more active South Company commanded by 'Deker'. UNAMET met with Falintil on a number of occasions; however, their lack of military strength and their eventual self cantonment in early August meant that throughout the Consultation, as a group, they had little influence on the course of events.

clear view of the district police station, caused militia activity to go underground. In terms of the organisation of the militia, Bobonaro district appears to have been a model, as indicated by the emergence of documents pertaining to their financing and co-ordination in other districts.

Also, the self-proclaimed head of all militia groups in East Timor, Panglima (supreme commander) Joao Tavares had his nominal base in Maliana. A complex man, at 69 years of age his fighting days were long behind him. Among local residents his name inspired hate, fear and, for some, grudging respect. Several noted that when Tavares had been Bupati of Bobonaro district 'no-one died'. He 'protected East Timorese' and prevented the worst TNI excesses during his time as District Chief in the period 1976–1986. Tavares owned houses in Maliana, Atabai, Atambua, Kupang and Dili and was reported to have an apartment in Jakarta. Of his nine children, eight had successfully completed university courses. One was an Indonesian diplomat and one, aptly nicknamed 'the King', was the village chief of Balibo. Tavares liked to boast that when he was Bupati, the roads were good and the people were happy. His personal influence also extended to other districts. For example the Bupati of Ermera district, Constantino Soares, was a Tavares protégé, having served on Tavares' staff in Bobonaro in the early 1980s.

Tavares claimed to have a working relationship with Xanana Gusmao. Reportedly when the two men were close to striking an accord between the militias and Falintil on 11 April 1999, their talks failed, most likely due to the overnight surge in militia operations, on the same date, which Tavares may or may not have supported.[4] To a certain extent Tavares was but one prop in the TNI's elaborate orchestration of East Timor's political affairs. As the process unfolded Tavares, ill with malaria and often bed-ridden, was frequently unable to explain the structure of his organisation; nor did he have a grasp of militia activities in wider East Timor. On certain days he appeared as what he was, a sick old man at the beck and call of the TNI, accorded minimum respect. TNI controllers followed him everywhere and he never met UNAMET alone. On occasions when he entertained in his Maliana residence he would present guests with a photo of himself from the 1960s. The photo revealed a slim and confident man in his prime, dressed in a traditional

---

[4] The two men also met on 5 May, 18 June, at the end of July and on 4 August. At the June Dare II Reconciliation talks in Jakarta it seemed that the two men were again in sight of a genuine breakthrough. However, at the time it was rumoured that 'someone' walked into Tavares' Dili bank and withdrew millions of rupiah from his account by forging his signature. One close observer with family ties to Tavares explained that the Panglima's biggest problem was 'the money'. The implication is that Tavares was blackmailed or coerced at this point of the process, perhaps because he may have got cold feet or disagreed with instructions from the TNI at the time.

warrior's costume and black framed sunglasses, a symbol of both past and present. In 1999 he seemed conscious of the fact that he was a less impressive figure.

Bobonaro district was important for several reasons. Close to the West Timor border, along with Cova Lima district and the Ambeno enclave, it was always prominently linked in 'secession plans' espoused in public by militia chiefs. That is, in the event that East Timor became independent, the TNI and their proxies hoped to retain this and other western districts as part of Indonesia. The Bupati Guileherme Dos Santos made no secret of his antipathy towards the UN nor his indignation that the Consultation process had been forced upon him. The militia structure in Bobonaro district was the most developed in terms of organisation and funding. It consistently rated among the districts with the highest incidences of political violence and was also the first district evacuated by UNAMET after the 30 August Consultation and before the announcement of the results that catalysed general mayhem across East Timor. The TNI–Militia relationship was anchored in strategies devised as far back as 1994, where home grown East Timorese forces would bear the brunt of field and urban operations against Falintil and pro-independence supporters. Attempts to develop the militia into an institution in their own right, separate from the TNI, ultimately failed during UNAMET's tenure.

Militia activity May 1998–June 1999

When UNAMET's advance team of some ten people arrived in Dili in mid-May the town was still in a state of shock after the 4–6 April massacre of independence supporters in Liquica church and the subsequent 17 April Aitarak (Thorn) rampage in Dili, where as many as 30 people were cut down in Mario Carrascalao's house, including his 17-year-old son, Manuelito. The chiefs of the Conselho Nacional Resistencia Timorense (CNRT) were in hiding (David Diaz Ximenese) or under police protection (Leondro Izaacs).[5] Dili was patrolled by the Aitarak militia under Eurico Guterres and operated without restraint. Information was scant. The East Timorese human rights NGO Yayasan Hak and the Catholic Church had unique and valuable insights into all districts and many East Timorese volunteered information, unsolicited by UNAMET, in circumstances of considerable personal risk. But it was not until the end of May that UNAMET began moving into the field and was in a position to verify many of the allegations concerning the militia. In several visits to the western districts—the Ambeno enclave, Cova Lima, Bobonaro, Ermera and Ainaro district—discussions and interviews with local institutions

---

[5] The CNRT was established in May 1998 as the umbrella organisation for many pro-independence groups including: Ojetil, Renetil, DPP-IMPPETU, Fitun, Opjlatil, Sagrada, Familia, Activist Pro-Independence and the student group DSMTT.

and the population revealed that in a broad sense the formation and expansion of the militia and their activities correlated with the political timetable, often in response to pro-independence initiatives.

For example, several militia members from the Maliana-based Dadurus Merah Putih (Red and White Typhoon) explained that recruitment and plans for their establishment proper commenced in May 1998 as a direct response to the formation of the CNRT—the umbrella organisation for all pro-independence groups in East Timor—in the same month. They claimed that Halilintar was the 'senior' militia group in East Timor. Reportedly in existence since 1973, it had lain dormant from 1976 ('when it was the same as the TNI') before being re-activated, most likely in 1994 in parallel with Kopassus and Prabowo Subianto's 'Gada Paksi' (Gadu Penegak Integrasi, Guards to Uphold Integration) initiative.[6] Halilintar was 'led' by Joao Tavares, but was under the command of Korem164—TNI headquarters—in Dili. It operated in Maliana and Atabai sub-districts, Bobonaro district, but may also have had wider responsibilities for establishing and raising other militia groups. Certainly it had a close relationship with Satgas Intel (Satuan Tugas Intellijen, SGI), the Kopassus intelligence unit that oversaw its re-establishment, tended to its logistic needs, and provided bodyguards to Tavares and training for its senior cadre.[7]

Internal TNI documents smuggled out of Dili in late 1998 noted that Halilintar had a strength of some 121 in August 1998. Press reports from October 1998 gave the same figure, and notably in July 1999 UNAMET was informed by the Halilintar chief in Atabai that it had a strength of 121 hard-core or cadre members, many of whom had been with Joao Tavares since 1975. The consistency in strength of numbers over the period, as reported by three sources, suggests a continuity in the group and, by association, a specific function separate from the other militia groups, which were firmly anchored in precise geographical areas and whose numbers fluctuated as members joined or deserted. Certainly, financial statements for militia funding in Bobonaro district had separate budget lines for Halilintar where the other sub-district militia groups were lumped together. The same statements also

---

[6] The Gada Paksi were established in 1994 by Prabowo as a means of co-opting young East Timorese into the integration cause, in part due to the increasing gains by the pro-independence student groups. Members were assisted into small businesses and given military and intelligence training in Jakarta. Many cadre members of the militias in Bobonaro declared their occupation as 'businessman' before they joined the militia.

[7] In early June 1999 the author witnessed the inauguration of a 'new' militia unit of some 400 youths in Maucola (halfway between Suai and Zumalai) in Cova Lima district. The organising 'team', which included at least one SGI officer, was composed of TNI officers and the chief of the Mahidi (Dead or Alive for Integration) chapter from Zumalai, one Vasco da Cruz. Several people at the site referred to the team collectively as 'Halilintar 612' or 'Battalion 612'.

identified expenditures for the Kopassus chief in Bobonaro district (Dan Satgas Tribuana).

By October 1998 at least eleven militia groups were operational throughout East Timor. Like Halilintar, two other notorious groups were established early and at strategic locations in the western districts. Mahidi (Dead or Alive for Integration) was centred around Cassa in southern Ainaro district, at the crossroads between Manufahi, Ainaro and Cova Lima districts. Besi Merah Putih (Red and White Iron) was based out of Maubara, on the border between Liquica, Ermera and Bobonaro districts. These three 'senior' groups were ideally placed to control the movement of the population in and out of the western districts and also to secede those districts if the need arose. Thus it seems that these militia groups were established on a strategic basis most likely with input from the senior echelons of the TNI with previous experience in East Timor, perhaps as far back as 1975.

These groups continued to recruit and consolidate through 1998, as did the pro-independence groups, creating tension in several districts. According to a church source, in November 1998 pro-independence supporters attacked and burnt 12 houses and demonstrated in front of the Bupati's house in Ainaro district in response to SGI orchestrated intimidation, via Mahidi proxies.

Throughout 1999 politically motivated violence carried out by the TNI and the militia correlated with the negotiation timetable leading to the signing of the 5 May Agreement, the 7 June Indonesian national elections and subsequently with UNAMET's Consultation timetable. In broad terms there were three main periods prior to UNAMET's deployment throughout East Timor:

27 January–Easter

Immediately after B J Habibie's 27 January announcement that he would be prepared to let East Timor separate from Indonesia if the East Timorese rejected autonomy, the CNRT became more active. Emboldened by what was a conferral of legitimacy, independence supporters in some areas drove around town centres waving the outlawed FRETILIN flag. Other CNRT members began preparations for a province-wide campaign. Certainly there was a reinvigoration of nationalist and anti-Indonesian sentiments across the province, which appears to have genuinely worried a significant number of Indonesian administrators and civil functionaries, particularly in the health and education sectors. Suddenly, many of these contract staff felt threatened. One young Javanese doctor in the Ambeno enclave, who had excellent relations with the community in which he lived, described how he was ostracised for several days by a community whose children he helped deliver.

As many as 30,000 such employees, perhaps encouraged by Jakarta, terminated their contracts early or simply left for other provinces. In response the TNI and their militia proteges stepped up their efforts to exact retribution against the independence supporters, many of whom had shown their hand for the first time. Mahidi reportedly commenced operations immediately after 27 January in Ainaro. At the same time TNI–militia operations in Suai reportedly displaced several thousand. On 22 March the 'terror situation' began in Zumalai in eastern Cova Lima district. The former militia leader Tomas Goncalves (in hiding in Macau) stated in September that at a special meeting in Dili on 16 February an SGI officer, Lieutenant Colonel Sudrajud addressed militia chiefs from 12 of the districts and directed them to attack pro-independence supporters from 1 May. Goncalves explained that in fact attacks commenced the next day. He also claimed that at a second meeting on 26 March, allegedly attended by the Governor of East Timor, Abilio Soares, the order was given to attack priests and nuns who sheltered independence supporters.[8] Events in the field suggest that the plan went much further than that. One strand was designed to destroy the CNRT and drive their members underground. Another was to continue with the recruitment and establishment of a province-wide militia consisting of all males over the age of 17, who were to be organised into a 'company' of militia for each of East Timor's 62 sub-districts, with a 'battalion' or senior group based in district centres. A third angle was the province-wide establishment of offices of the political fronts for the integration/autonomy cause, the Forum for Unity, Democracy and Justice (Forum Persatuan, Demokrasi dan Keadilan, FPDK) and the East Timor People's Front (Barisan Rakyat Timor Timur, BRTT).

In two months a comprehensive strategy was implemented to ensure the systematic control of the whole population, while irreversibly altering the political space in favour of the pro-autonomy cause.

Easter–1 June

In this period the TNI and the militia teamed up to drive all independence groups and their supporters underground, beginning with the shocking events in Liquica on 4–6 April, when militia, TNI and the Polri participated in the massacre of independence supporters sheltering in the Liquica church.[9]

---

[8] Tomas Goncalves had been initially recruited by the Indonesian Intelligence Co-ordinating Body (Bakin) in 1975 and trained at Atambua for covert operations under the command of then Kostrad Major Yunus Yosfiah—the officer in charge of the attack on Balibo.

[9] In Maliana in late April several hundred Internally Displaced Persons (IDPs) took refuge in the church grounds. Allegedly the priest was warned in advance by a highly placed TNI NCO that the TNI and the militia would provoke the IDPs with the aim of using their reaction as an excuse for another Liquica style attack. The people remained calm and therefore no attack took place.

Seemingly overnight, militia groups began a systematic and widespread campaign against independence supporters, led by the TNI, who maintained lists of such within their Kodim headquarters across East Timor. Government officials, village chiefs and males over the age of 17 were particularly targeted and forced to declare their support for integration. It was a time of extraordinary pressure on the community at large.

In the west simultaneous operations were carried out in the Ambeno enclave (10 April), Bobonaro (12 April) and Ermera (10–11 April) at precisely the time that Joao Tavares was meeting Xanana Gusmao in Jakarta to discuss reconciliation. In the enclave the militia group Sakunar Merah Putih (Red and White Scorpion) took over the streets with automatic weapons and chased the only overt CNRT member (one of two doctors) out of town. In Bobonaro district the terror began on 12 April when the district finance chief, Manuel Soares Gama, was killed in an ambush on the road to Kailaco. The military commander Siagian and his intelligence chief, Lieutenant Sutrisno, had four people suspected of being Falintil supporters killed on the spot on the grounds that Falintil had been behind the ambush. The weight of evidence suggests that Gama was killed by a combined TNI/SGI/Halilintar team, as a pretext for a district wide crackdown against pro-independence supporters.[10]

No one knows for sure how many people were killed in this period in Bobonaro district. Those who did not flee were forced to 'accept the red and white' and fly the Indonesian flag outside their houses. To not do so was an open invitation to attack. In Bobonaro district CNRT chiefs Manuel Marghalene (believed killed on 4 or 5 September in Maliana) and Jose Andrade da Cruz had their houses burnt and looted and were forced to take refuge in the Police station, where they remained until late July. Another leading CNRT figure, Pedro Gomez, fled to the hills with his seven year-old son, where he hid for nearly two months, in which time his house was destroyed and his car was stolen. On 24 May he was captured by militia from Bobonaro sub-district (Hametin Merah Putih, Red and White Vice) and taken to Maliana. On 1 June he was forced to sign a petition with Jose Andrade, Manuel Marghalene and Francisco Margo at a BRTT rally in Maliana. The four men 'dissolved the CNRT' in Bobonaro district in a bizarre ceremony in front of a large crowd. Original copies of the signed petition were lodged with the district chief of police and would later be produced as evidence that the

---

[10] Most sources stated that Gama was killed by TNI/SGI/Halilintar. Only one source said he was killed by Falintil because he was carrying wages for the militia to Kailaco. Those who suggest it was a TNI operation claim that Gama had been under suspicion for some time because he protested against the TNI's 'treatment' of the people, supported independence and, according to rumour, because he had refused to accept an invitation to Jakarta, where it was suspected he would be asked to form part of the BRTT.

CNRT had ceded its right to campaign in the district. The provincial Chief of the BRTT, Ambassador Lopez da Cruz, used the opportunity to tell all pro-independence supporters to leave the district and warn that the people should 'accept autonomy or face fatal consequences'.

In Suai, 20 members of the CNRT were run out of town in early May and the student office was closed down. By 1 June there were an estimated 3,000 people taking shelter in the surrounding hills. Many were unable to escape to Dili because of militia checkpoints at Zumalai to the east and at Atambua and Batugade along the route to Dili through West Timor.

Other victims in the period were village chiefs who refused to support the 'program'. Many fled to Dili and also lost property and possessions. They were replaced by trusted pro-integrationists, some of whom were TNI 'pensioners'. A small number had dual functions of village chief and militia chief, although this was rare in Bobonaro district.[11] One source stated that Joao Tavares disagreed with Siagian over the plan to recruit all men over the age of 17 into the new militias. Tavares reasoned that the program would drive all the young men away to the forest and to Dili, which it eventually did, after Siagian's instructions prevailed. The scale of the social dislocation caused by this one aspect alone was not fully realised until mid-way through the registration process in late July, when the youths returned to register. In all over 1,000 young men returned: 112 to Atabai, 46 to Balibo, 290 to Maliana, 29 to Kailaco, 494 to Bobonaro and 59 to Lolotoe sub-district. From the figures, Bobonaro would appear to have been the sub-district of greatest repression. One resident described the situation there as the worst it had been since 1975.

The notorious Bupati of Bobonaro district, Guilherme Dos Santos, who described himself as the 'Muhammed Ali of all Bupatis', was reported, at least initially, to have favoured political dialogue with pro-independence student groups. This sentiment was also overturned by Siagian, and Dos Santos became an ardent supporter of the pro-integration side.

In parallel the TNI launched a military campaign in those sub-districts bordering the central mountain spine. The operation was designed to separate Falintil from its support base and to remove any ambiguities in the tacit support offered to the group. As admitted by several Falintil supporters, this may have been in part a reaction to the ongoing collection of the 'revolutionary tax' from villagers.

---

[11] One example was the Mahidi Chief in Zumalai, Cova Lima district, Vasco da Cruz. Vasco was also the village chief (Kepala Desa) of Zumalai, having retired from the police force several years earlier. Vasco was reportedly killed after the Consultation by the TNI or villagers bent on revenge. He was a notorious figure with a reputation for extreme violence.

The combination of militia actions in the urban areas and TNI operations in the interior saw some 40,000 people displaced throughout East Timor. In the hard-hit Kailaco sub-district in Bobonaro for example, some 4,300 people from four villages were brought down from the hills to makeshift camps in the sub-district capital where they were placed under militia 'protection' and were told that they could not return home until after the Consultation. This was done on the pretext that Falintil would attack them. In fact the TNI and the militia burnt many houses and forcibly relocated the villagers. Most of the men had run to Dili or taken refuge in the mountains. Those that remained were co-opted into the sub-district militia Gumtur Merah Putih (Red and White Thunder) under the direction of the intelligence chief Sutrisno.

By mid-May most TNI objectives in Bobonaro district had been met. The CNRT had gone underground, its leaders in hiding or under police protection. Officials in the district administration had sworn allegiance to autonomy. Those who hadn't had been forced to flee. Village chiefs in several areas had been replaced or sidelined, and the youths and men remaining were rapidly being forced into the ranks of the new militia, funding for which had been distributed at the beginning of the month.

In Maliana, Dadurus Merah Putih commenced training with wooden rifles on a daily basis. In the remote and pro-independent sub-districts of Bobonaro and Lolotoe recruitment methods included holding youths hostage in militia chiefs' houses, beatings and generally unfulfilled promises of rice and salaries. In Alberto Leite's, the militia chief of Hametin Merah Putih (Red and White Vice) in Bobonaro sub-district town, some 37 men had been held under effective house arrest until the beginning of June when they were released 'to go and vote for Golkar' in the impending Indonesian national elections.[12]

In early May in Lolotoe, the young men were called into 'peace meetings' where they were forced to swear allegiance to the 'red and white'. After two teachers were killed for refusing to join, a Falintil company under 'Deker' killed three TNI soldiers on 16 May in an ambush where they spared the life of the militia commander, Juni Frewea. It was the only action by Falintil in Bobonaro district—their relative inaction a measure of their own weakness probably more than of adherence to orders from Xanana Gusmao that forbade any reprisal by the guerilla force. Church sources alleged that in response the TNI rounded up 600 and killed an unknown number of people in the villages closest to the ambush site.

New offices were established for the FPDK and the BRTT, led respectively in Bobonaro district by Joao Tavares' brother Jorge Tavares (also the chairman of the District Representative Council, DPRD II) and Francisco

---

[12] This was the same house in which the CNRT leader Pedro Gomez was held.

Soares, aka 'Siko' (also a district official). With all opposition out of the way and before UNAMET's arrival, the militia and the district administration commenced the 'socialisation' process. This involved an extensive series of village, sub-district and district level meetings and 'festivities' across East Timor's 422 villages, 62 sub-districts and 13 districts, paid for from the province's social development fund. This heavy-handed program extolled the virtues of autonomy (the economic benefits of integration, development etc) and for good measure explained that should the autonomy package be rejected, 'the situation would be just like 1975 again'. In Zumalai, Cova Lima district, banners carrying this latter message were still visible in mid-June. Having effectively silenced the CNRT, militia activities re-focussed on further recruitment, military style training for their rank and file delivered by the TNI, and the Indonesian national elections.

1 June–27 June (UNAMET's arrival in Bobonaro district)

By the end of May the militia began a campaign to ensure that all East Timorese participated in the national elections on 7 June. Militia groups visited villages and inspected people's registration cards. Those without them were beaten. All were told that voting was compulsory. The militia and their sponsors wanted to hold credible national elections with maximum turnout, with a view to undermining the UNAMET Consultation since, by participating in the 7 June elections, the East Timorese would have proved their desire to be part of Indonesia. Accordingly, militia violence abated in this period and there was a 'peace' of sorts. At the same time there was a belief in Bobonaro district that the consultation would not necessarily proceed. The Guilherme Dos Santos stated on 3 June that the population was not sure if it wanted the Consultation, and 'there are two ways of casting a ballot. One is to vote and the other is not to vote. It is the people's choice'.

Perhaps the most significant political change involved the harmonisation of all pro-integration and pro-autonomy groups and the security institutions. Specifically, Ambassador Lopez da Cruz, the chief of the BRTT, who had previously advocated a separate, peaceful approach to autonomy, began campaigning with the FPDK and also warned of violence if autonomy were rejected. Generous funding for the socialisation process allowed for the disbursement of significant pay-offs to the district authorities, the Dandim, police chief, Bupati, district Judge and so on. The socialisation funds also bankrolled the militia cadre, providing them with status and an institutional role in what was a 'whole of government approach' by Jakarta in assisting the autonomy cause.

The militia in Bobonaro district

After the Indonesian national elections the militia FPDK chiefs and the militia continued the socialisation process. Pressure was maintained on pro-independence groups, but perhaps because of their absence (they had already fled or gone underground) an uneasy peace reigned in Bobonaro district. UNAMET's gradual deployment into the countryside at this time had an impact as well. By the end of June the militia had been established in all six sub-districts, their status formalised in a ceremony in Dili in June where the militia were given the appellation of PAM Swakarsa (Volunteer Community Security). It was an attempt to place the establishment and organisation of the militia onto a quasi-legal foundation. A member of the Deplu task force benignly described them as a type of 'neighbourhood watch'. A form of paid civilian militia, PAM Swakarsa units first appeared in Jakarta in June 1998 and had been formally established in a special session of the People's Consultative Assembly (MPR) in November 1998 amid much controversy. In East Timor they had first been established in Dili (only) on 19 April 1999 and were financed from the provincial budget.

From 8 July the TNI, Polri and DEPLU liaison officers insisted on use of the term 'PAM Swakarsa' when referring to the militia. However, it did not take hold within the militia. PAM Swakarsa 'posts' were seen in Dili and Liquica but the militia in Bobonaro did not use the title themselves. In fact, the precise role played by the militia in the existing security structures was a source of confusion for many of them. This is perhaps not surprising given the various initiatives with similar structures over the preceding years, such as: Ratih (Rakyat Terlatih, trained people), Hansip (pertahanan sipil, civil defence) and the already mentioned Prabowo initiative, Gada Paksi. The local population used all of the above appellations at one time or another but in essence they referred to the same people.

Further confusion was provided by the other security adjuncts to the TNI (Wanra, People's Resistence, established in 1989) and Polri (Kamra, People's Security, established in February 1999) who were recruited from local communities. Active members of the militia were drawn from both organisations but again the local population saw them as the same people. Prior to June 1999 militia groups throughout Bobonaro district referred to themselves as Besi Merah Putih (Red and White Iron—the name for the Maubara—based group led by Manuel Da Sousa). However, after June they changed to a different nomenclature whereby their new names incorporated Merah Putih as discussed below. In effect all previous structures dovetailed into one and the same 'militia' during the Consultation.

Militia groups in Bobonaro district were organised on a geographical basis with a 'company' at each sub-district forming an overall 'battalion' for the district. As discussed, Joao Tavares' personal force, Halilintar (Lightning/Thunderbolt) was the senior group. Although based in Atabai it had wider responsibilities for co-ordinating the western region or Sector IV of the militia structure, which included Cova Lima district and the Ambeno enclave. Below Halilintar were six sub-district groups as in Table 1.

Table 1: Militia groups in Bobonaro district

sub-district	militia group	name adopted	group commander
Maliana	Dadurus Merah Putih (Red and White Typhoon)	May 1998	Sergeant Domingos Dos Santos (serving TNI soldier)
Balibo/ Batugade	Pemuda Benteng Batugade (Batugade Fortress Youths), also known as FIRMI Merah Putih (unknown acronym)	July 1999	Ruben Tavares (nephew of Panglima Tavares and son of Jorge Tavares).
Atabai	ARMUI Merah Putih (I am ready to die for integration)	July 1999	Jose Amaral Leite (a longtime protégé of Panglima Tavares and also chief of Halilintar in the sub-district).
Kailaco	Gumtur Merah Putih (Red and White Thunder)	April 1999	Adau Abu
Bobonaro	Hametin Merah Putih (Red and White Vice)	June 1999	Alberto Leite (TNI pensioner)
Lolotoe	Kaer Merah Putih (meaning unknown)	June 1999	Juni Frewea (son of sub-district chief, Jose Vicente)

For the rank and file and the population the names were essentially meaningless. More important were the strong men who ran the separate groups.

Trends and discontinuities

Broadly speaking the militia had three levels of command and status. At the bottom of the chain were the rank and file militia who represented males press-ganged into the organisation from April 1999. Their major duty was to report each evening from 6pm until 6am to sentry posts (Pos Jaga/Apel Malam) near their villages where they monitored movement in and out of the villages. In fact the system functioned as a control mechanism whereby on any evening higher level cadres could determine the exact location of all able bodied males over the age of 17. Those who fell asleep, deserted their post or failed to turn up were beaten or punished. One punishment involved being tipped upside down in an oil drum full of water from which the person had to extricate themselves. The duty was hated by the men as it meant they were exhausted during the day and often unable to tend their farms and gardens.

Training obligations included weapons drill with mock rifles, physical exercise, how to deal with UNAMET and instruction in the benefits of autonomy. Each Saturday muster parades were conducted at sub-district KORAMILS where the new 'line' and the latest news was disseminated. Each night in Maliana the Pos Jagas would ring cowbells on the hour. By the end of July and before the end of the registration process the cowbells were silent because of wholesale desertions by the rank and file. Faced with such large scale 'civil disobedience' the TNI and the militia could do little. The focus changed when the rank and file were summoned to attend specific pro-autonomy campaign activities or events like the Indonesian National Day celebrations on 17 August. Again, beatings were handed out for those who did not attend.

The second level militia were the 'cadre' staff selected from more trusted East Timorese, some of whom had graduated from the Gada Paksi program. These cadre were allocated resources such as radios and motorbikes and were given command positions. They were responsible for mobilising manpower in their areas and also for collecting and disseminating information. One platoon commander from Dadurus Merah Putih stated that his other responsibilities included monitoring all the villages in his area for Falintil and pro-independence supporters, checking on fund-raising activities for Falintil and the CNRT, and checking on 'corruption'—thrice monthly.

The highest tier in the militia comprised the sub-district chiefs and their lieutenants. Their backgrounds varied considerably. Some were East Timorese serving within the TNI, others were TNI pensioners. Several were next of kin to high ranking district officials. One was a lecturer from the University of East Timor (UNTIM) and doubled as deputy head of the FPDK. A few had been with Joao Tavares since 1975. Background did not determine how vindictive, murderous or harsh a militia chief would be. Top tier commanders were privileged, with extra resources and funding, and attended key meetings in Dili until just after the registration period, when co-ordination of militia activities shifted to Atambua. District activities until then were co-ordinated from the bupati's office, through which funding passed, or the Kodim.

As the TNI's need for plausible denial grew, the FPDK and the BRTT picked up the responsibility for the tactical co-ordination of district operations in concert with the Bupati. However, these operations were always overseen by TNI and SGI, often with career officers from other provinces.

By the end of the registration period (16 July–6 August) many of the tier one militia had already left their organisations. By mid-August TNI–militia designs for the post-consultation period became evident; they planned to eject UNAMET, seal the district, cut the power, evacuate communities to West Timor, carry out retribution attacks on pro-independence supporters and destroy all facilities. In Bobonaro district these actions began before the announcement of results on 4 September. All the evidence suggests that in early August the assessment that the pro-autonomy camp would lose had already been made. Militia leaders from throughout East Timor were briefed at meetings in Dili in this period and told what to do.

Several second level militia commanders sought accommodation with the CNRT on the basis that they did not want to participate in such plans and also because they did not want to live in Atambua after the Consultation. It shows they accurately anticipated the results of the Consultation and that they comprehended what was in store, at least to a certain extent. In any event the CNRT refused reconciliation to several low level leaders, with clear reason. Throughout the Consultation the CNRT had been denied any political space whatsoever and never opened an office in the district. On the one day that they campaigned, all of their supporters were subject to house visits by militia, TNI and in some cases SGI. Throughout the Campaign period (14–27 August) the TNI and the militia stepped up their activities, which included several murders, house burnings, widespread intimidation and the indiscriminate terrorising of whole communities. The Polri never once intervened and in several cases were accessories to the fact through either their prior knowledge or inaction. In the week preceding the Consultation up to 40 militia members from Dadurus Merah Putih decided to take their chances in the hills and left the group, following the majority of the population.

On 27 August, the last day of the campaign, the militia rampaged through Memo, a village in Maliana sub-district. Three villagers were killed and twenty houses were razed; TNI liaison officers initially described the incident as a 'Falintil attack'. Many of the pro-autonomy participants were believed to be from West Timor, to make up the numbers in the increasing absence of militia from Bobonaro district. That night militia members fired automatic weapons for two hours over Maliana town to further intimidate the community and UNAMET staff. On 28 August Maliana emptied of people and became a ghost town.

At dawn on 30 August the sun rose over thousands of voters who had emerged from hiding to cast their ballots. By 2pm the town had emptied again, with pro-independence supporters returning to the hills and pro-autonomy supporters to Atambua. On 2 September two UNAMET local staff were shot dead by a TNI sergeant who doubled as the militia chief of a Maliana suburb. The killings capped weeks of intimidation against UNAMET's local staff. On at least two occasions the Dandim, Lieutenant Colonel Siagian had personally told local staff that they would be killed after the Consultation. That night the militia began to burn Maliana. On 3 September UNAMET left the district while observing members of the TNI direct remaining militia members to burn and destroy specific houses and buildings in the town associated with UNAMET and pro-independence groups. The Polri remained in their police station, singing songs.

Conclusion

The TNI were heavily involved in all aspects of militia activity in Bobonaro district aimed at ensuring a pro-autonomy vote in the Popular Consultation. At the higher levels the sub-district militia leaders were co-ordinated and directed by the Dandim and his intelligence chief from the Kodim and from the Bupati's office. At the sub-district level the militia were either directly commanded by TNI personnel or directly supported by Koramil staff. At the village level the militia worked hand in hand with military posts and Babinsas.

In early August, after the successful registration of some 450,000 East Timorese (well above the 380,000 registered for the 7 June national elections), it was clear that the autonomy package would be rejected. The pro-autonomy camp and its TNI backbone shifted their headquarters to Atambua and began preparations for the post-Consultation period. Alarmed at the impending carnage, the lower and mid-level order of the militia began to fragment. In the days following the Consultation the TNI emerged as primary architects of the plan to destroy Bobonaro district—a plan they implemented with confidence and precision.

A reporter's view

Hidayat Djajamihardja

Decades of limitations

People in Indonesia tend to have doubts when they read reports about some new development happening in the country. If the report is not in the government's favour, the doubts centre on the accuracy or fairness of the report. An example would be a report about a successful operation by the anti-narcotic unit of the Jakarta police, when a big quantity of heroin was confiscated and more than ten people arrested, two of whom were related to Indonesia's political elite.

During a press conference at the Jakarta Metropolitan Headquarters, the police chief said that the operation would reduce significantly the heroin supply in the capital. He said police had also seized two leather bags containing cash understood to be worth hundreds of millions of rupiahs.

If one asked people in the street what they think about the report, I am sure that they would give different answers. Some would believe it, and some wouldn't. But the bottom line would be that people are getting more and more sceptical about official announcements. Their scepticism was formed through a very long process. This is the result of the limitations imposed on the media for the past three decades.

The Indonesian media during the Suharto era became accustomed to the word 'limitations'. In the era of the New Order's 'Pancasila Democracy' the Indonesian media were asked to impose 'self censorship'—to refrain from criticising the government.

This policy in many ways still leaves its mark on the Indonesian media of today in an era of reform. The burgeoning number of newspapers and magazines, it does not mean that self-censorship does not still exist in Indonesia, especially when reporting on East Timor. Some journalists from local television channels commented that they had to check their footage of the East Timor carnage very thoroughly before transmitting it to Jakarta. They did not want 'awful things' to be screened, for such a display might embarrass or discredit the authorities, especially the military.

Western media did not have such limitations reporting East Timor. Western journalists could report anything and everything taking place there. The only hindrance facing the Western media was perhaps the language barrier. Not many low and middle ranking officers in the Indonesian armed forces (TNI), or police force speak English. Many foreign journalists relied on their local stringers and interpreters for their information.

Many weeks prior to East Timor's popular consultation, it was hard to find interpreters who were trilingual, being able to speak Indonesian, English and Tetun. Most of the interpreters were either East Timorese university students from Jakarta or local East Timorese studying at the University of East Timor in Dili. The majority of university students in Dili supported independence. At some stage, doubts must have existed as to whether those students were really translating what was being said or interpreting it.

The role of the national media in Indonesia during the East Timor crisis was vital, even though it faced the self-imposed censorship. During the Suharto era such an arrangement was a necessity for survival. The end result of this formula is rather frightening. During the East Timor crisis, this type of self censorship resulted in Indonesian television viewers having a different picture about what was really taking place in the province, especially in Dili.

Indeed, they did report all the clashes and casualties. But they refrained from reporting about the mass destruction and the scorched earth campaign in Dili and other major centres. Given that fact, it was not surprising that Indonesian people, especially some of the highly politicised students and youths movement in Jakarta, thought that Australia, which reacted to such destruction, had interfered in Indonesia's internal affairs.

The term 'internal affairs' must be stressed here because those students and youths were the product of the post-1976 era—the year when East Timor was integrated into the Republic of Indonesia. The Indonesian government, in this case, had succeeded in making the issue of 'annexation of East Timor' an issue of 'salvaging the oppressed East Timorese from the chains of Portuguese colonization'.

The word 'integration' (*integrasi*) has entered Indonesia's political and journalistic vocabulary. The New Order government managed to change the history of Indonesian involvement in East Timor. And for a few weeks after the Popular Consultation, hundreds of students and youths staged demonstrations against Australia's participation in the multinational Interfet forces.

Since such policy is an official line, it is only logical if the national media, especially electronic media, apply this 'self censorship'. Consequently, the general population has a different picture about the East Timor tragedy from the view of other countries. The fact that the affluent middle class could see what was really happening in East Timor through cable networks such as the BBC or CNN does not change the situation.

On the issue of East Timor, we can see there is a differing stand between the national newspapers in Indonesian and that of the English language papers. If one reads the *Jakarta Post*, which is popular among foreign diplomats and guests at Jakarta's five star hotels, one can only assume that Indonesian newspapers are free and fair and objective, like newspapers in most of the Western world. The fact that the *Jakarta Post* is printed in English has saved it from most official reprimand and even closure.

The *Jakarta Post* editorial of 17 September 1999 started with a biting opening:

> Thanks to the leadership of President Habibie and the Indonesian Military Commander, General Wiranto, we Indonesians as a nation have suffered one international indignity after another these past two weeks. The decision to accept on Sunday a United Nations peacekeeping force in East Timor—diplomatically worded as an invitation—came in the face of strong international pressure. Then on Wednesday, the Security Council unanimously voted to establish a multinational force and gave it a full mandate to restore peace. This means the use of military force if necessary. Rubbing salt into the wound, the UN Secretary General Kofi Annan ignored Indonesia's objections and named Australia to head the force.

I cannot imagine an Indonesian language newspaper printing such an editorial, especially during the Suharto era. Since its independence in 1945, Indonesia has never suffered such an international blow to its dignity. Its first two presidents, although they were often targets of international criticism, were adept at steering away from this kind of humiliation.

If the East Timor crisis had taken place in the 1960s, President Sukarno would probably have told the Secretary General of the United Nations, Kofi Annan, to go to hell. The fact that President Habibie has invited the multinational forces has been regarded by most Indonesians as a humiliating defeat in tackling the East Timor issue. There is no denying that the entire nation suffered as a result. According to the *Jakarta Post*, no matter how much Indonesia tried to explain it and come up with plenty of excuses about the situation in East Timor, the bottom line was that Indonesia was responsible for everything that happened there. 'The killings, the forced evacuation of people from their homes, and the destruction resulting from the scorched-earth campaign took place when the territory was under Indonesia's charge,' said the paper.

It is interesting to note the stark difference between the way the issue of East Timor has been handled by the Indonesian and Australian media. If we look at the history of their inception, the media in both countries came into existence through different processes. The Australian press developed like any other media in the Western world. It is an information necessity as well as an economic enterprise. However, the Indonesian press came into existence hand-in-hand with the nation's independence, at least in its early days.

In their reporting, the issue of East Timor has been handled rather differently by the Indonesian and Australian media. The latter have been perceived to be concentrating more on the pro-independence movement and their activities. Every single rally, no matter how small, would get coverage. It is only logical, I suppose, because for the past 25 years East Timor had not witnessed such activities. The fact that there are more pro-independence leaders who speak English than their pro-autonomy opposition also made a difference.

However, their Indonesian have concentrated more on the official line. Statements given by the governor, the police chief or the military authorities would get wide coverage in the Indonesian media in addition to their own journalist's reports about certain incidents or clashes between pro-autonomy and pro-independence groups. The national media tended to print accounts given by the authorities in more detailed format than their Australian counterparts. There are, of course, some newspapers, such as *Kompas*, that report everything in detail, in such a way that sometimes annoys the military authorities.

Unlike reports by foreign correspondents in English, which can only be enjoyed by Indonesia's elite political circles, reports about East Timor by Indonesian journalists, be they in print or electronic media, can be read almost immediately by most people in Indonesia. This fact might also have influenced, to a certain extent, the objectivity of Indonesian reporters. Unfavourable reports could result in unfortunate events. One example from personal experience: I received some veiled threats from official circles. One day, a police officer in plain clothes casually approached me during a pro-autonomy political rally in Dili just to remind me that I should have been more nationalistic in my reports. 'You're still holding a green passport,' he said, indicating he knew that I was still an Indonesian citizen. On the other hand, many local ordinary people congratulated me for what they described as good and fair reports on East Timor.

East Timor as I remember

After 11 years of direct coverage of East Timor, I have received many veiled threats. I first went to the territory in April 1988, when East Timor was officially closed to foreign journalists. I got the idea of going to the province while attending the swearing-in ceremony at the State Palace of General Try Sutrisno as Commander of the Indonesian Armed Forces in late February 1993. He was replacing General LB Murdani, who had been named Minister of Defence and Security.

In such a ceremony, it is customary for everyone to congratulate the guests of honour, this time the new commander of the Armed Forces. When we, local and foreign journalists, were allowed to join the line-up, I whispered to the General that I would like to visit East Timor to see for myself what was happening in the territory. He nodded his head and said that I should see his aide, a Colonel Sudrajat. Arrangements were made and I met him at the Armed Forces Headquarters at Merdeka Barat. I thought I would have received the permit right there and then. But I was wrong.

I was sent to BAIS (Badan Intelijen dan Strategi) Headquarters, in the eastern sector of Jakarta. BAIS is the intelligence and strategy body of the armed forces. Such a requirement was not unusual because East Timor was under military administration, even though the province was officially headed by Governor Mario Viegas Carrascalao, an East Timorese agriculture graduate from Portugal.

The man in charge of giving permission to anyone wishing to visit East Timor then was Tony Sumarjo, a colonel from the army's elite red beret Kopassus (Komando Pasukan Khusus – Special Force Command). I was interviewed on two occasions, during which Colonel Tony Sumarjo asked about my professional and family background. He also asked why I wanted to go to East Timor when I knew that the province was officially closed to foreign journalists. I said to him that the media coverage of East Timor in Australia was wide and in detail. I also showed him a newspaper clipping from Melbourne newspaper the *Age* showing a group of Indonesian soldiers in the jungle. One of them was holding a trophy in the form of a severed head of a long haired man with his eyes still open. I tried to assure him that my trip, if approved, would be beneficial because I would see the province for myself.

Colonel Tony Sumarjo rejected the authenticity of the photograph and accused foreign media of slandering the Indonesian armed forces. Such a picture, he said, must have been an engineered effort to discredit Indonesia. 'We are not like that,' said the colonel, adding that with the state ideology of Pancasila the armed forces were waging a war of persuasion. 'One of the five pillars of the state ideology is humanity, so it is impossible that the armed forces would do gruesome things like chopping off someone's head,' he said. 'That is against the pillar of humanity in our Pancasila.'

After two sessions of thorough interview, I was permitted to visit East Timor, although not until I had introduced myself at two civilian institutions, the Centre For Strategic and International Studies (CSIS), and the Jakarta office of the Governor of East Timor. In both visits I had to sit for further interviews. I was also briefed about the dos and don'ts while in East Timor. It was becoming more obvious at this stage that my trip to East Timor would be a sanitised one and not much could be expected from it.

This suspicion turned out to be correct. Two middle ranking government officials met me at the Komoro Airport of Dili in a government car. I was given a pre-arranged itinerary and a military helicopter had been allocated to me.

My original plan of seeing East Timor and having a chat with local people was dashed the moment I arrived in Dili. Wherever I went a young Major Tony, no relation to Colonel Tony Sumarjo from the BAIS Headquarters in Jakarta, would be standing next to me. He was a member of Kopassus. He said he was a good friend of Lieutenant Colonel Prabowo Subianto, President Suharto's son-in-law, who would later would take over as the Commandant General of Kopassus.

I was taken to many interesting places, always in the company of officials. Major Tony even showed me the estimated area of East Timor jungle where the Fretilin were said to be operating. I was allowed to take some pictures of it from the helicopter. My journalistic spirit rose when I was told that Major Tony had to go to Jakarta for an urgent assignment. I said to myself that I would be able to wander around East Timor looking for good newsy reports. I had no such luck. Another middle-ranking officer was assigned to 'assist' me. This time it was Lieutenant Colonel Bimo from the green beret Kostrad.

Colonel Bimo was the head of the intelligence unit of the Kolakops Timor Timur or Komando Pelaksana Operasi Timor Timur, the Operational Command of East Timor. He was a devout Catholic. One day he took me in a Navy helicopter to Atauro (or Pulau Kambing), the island allocated for ex-Fretilin members who had 'returned to the fold of the motherland', meaning that they had surrendered.

When we were flying over the sea separating mainland Timor and Atauro Island, Colonel Bimo said that the shark infested Straits of Wetar were very useful for 'milking' military secrets from many Fretilin prisoners. 'They normally would tell you anything you wanted to know as long as you don't drop them into the water,' he once told me.

Atauro Island is peaceful, with sandy soil and rows and rows of palm and banana trees. I was introduced to a former Fretilin member who had become a fisherman. He said he was grateful to the Indonesian government, who had given him a motor engine for his boat to catch fish, which he then sold to Dili.

One of the military officials I had to meet was the commander of the Wira Dharma Regional Command, a full colonel. When I asked if I could interview him for Radio Australia, he did not say yes but instead looked at Lieutenant Colonel Bimo to see whether it was okay for him to grant me an interview. The commander was not a good speaker. He struggled to find answers to my standard questions, such as one about the Army's civic mission project, a road not far from the capital. He also wasn't sure, he said, if he could answer my question regarding some generals who owned coffee plantations in the province.

The role of Radio Australia in East Timor

I found that the position of Radio Australia in the province was important. The East Timorese listened to the station for the latest reports about the territory. But at the same time these people risked their lives. Apparently, unofficially, it was an offence to listen to Radio Australia when the territory was under military rule.

I only found out during my recent trip to the territory that in 1980s and the 1990s, until the downfall of President Suharto, the people of East Timor had to lower the volume of their transistor radios while listening to Radio Australia news bulletins. A bellboy in my hotel told me that in spite of the risk people did listen to Radio Australia news, especially during critical times, such as the period following the massacre at the Santa Cruz cemetery in Dili.

During my trip in 1988, I was officially a guest of the Governor, who granted me two interviews. Even at that time, Governor Carrascalao was regarded as a brave man, as he never feared criticising the central government or the armed forces. In one of the interviews he said he had complained to the central government that his policy of developing the province had been sabotaged by the local military.

I could sense fear of the military among the local population, especially in Dili. One afternoon I went to a photo studio to have my film developed. Having introduced myself as a Radio Australia reporter I was received with handshakes and pats on the back from the owner and his staff. I explained how broadcasters worked in our Melbourne studio and they, some six of them, listened with great interest. They dispersed and went to their corners quietly when they saw Major Tony enter the shop. The young officer tried to break the ice by cracking a joke to two female staff, but their faces clearly showed that they didn't want to have anything to do with him, an officer of the red beret Kopassus.

Dili in 1988 was a small town in both area and population. There were new schools and a cathedral was being built. The Indonesian government was clearly trying to show to the world that it was planning to change East Timor into a developed province. A big city market was being built then. However, security was still the main concern. The city was practically dead after sunset.

One evening I asked Major Tony if we could go to a local restaurant for dinner. I thought it was a good idea to entertain him after had taken me to many different places. But instead he introduced me to a Colonel Adang, the intelligence chief for the whole military command cover chain of islands stretching from Bali in the west to Timor in the east. We went to a relatively good restaurant, just like a local bistro in any good-sized country town of Australia.

Colonel Adang was a pleasant person, coming from West Javanese city of Bandung, my home town. Every now and then we spoke about politics and national leadership. He boasted about the military's role in helping the East Timorese and in building East Timor from its backwardness in 1976. He told me that after years of living in different parts of Indonesia he now believed the theory he said he learned at school, that dark skinned people were inferior to brown skinned people. He said he had proved it during his military postings in Irian Jaya and now in East Timor. He mentioned that people in those areas were lazy, slow and stupid.

That evening we stayed until almost midnight. Gradually, the number of people swelled, and eventually there were about a dozen of us. Almost all of them were young officers in their late 20s or early 30s. They were all from Kopassus. When we were about to leave I approached the owner, a Chinese from the Central Java capital of Semarang, with the intention of settling the bill for the whole party. 'It won't make me broke, after all my travelling allowance from the ABC is quite generous,' I said to myself. But he politely declined. On the way back to the hotel, Major Tony told me that most businesses in Dili were grateful to the military for making the city a peaceful place. He said he didn't have to bother paying the bill in any restaurant because the owner would not take the money anyway. I did try to get this confirmed by the owners but to no avail. Perhaps they didn't want the hassle that might follow. But I just could not accept that a restaurant owner entertained a dozen people for nothing.

The elite regiment Kopassus had been based semi-permanently in East Timor since 1987. The red beret commando unit had been held in high regard among Indonesians. They were said to be a good fighting regiment. However, its prestige dissipated after the Kopassus command was placed under Major General Prabowo Subianto. The red beret regiment became a notorious unit specialising in kidnapping pro-democracy activists and student leaders during the last days of Suharto's presidency.

In East Timor, Kopassus quickly became an oppressive force. The year was 1987 and the man who had that idea was (then) Colonel Prabowo. The intention was to provide Kopassus with a training ground to 'blood' its members in counter-insurgency activities. The fate of East Timor would have been different had the President's son-in-law not suggested that Kopassus open a base in East Timor.

In one of the interviews I had with Manuel Carrascalao, the pro-independence leader told me that Prabowo had changed East Timor into a hunting ground and torture chamber. Oppression and torture had become Kopassus code of conduct. The so-called 'Ninja' unit, people dressed in the black martial arts costume, had been active in kidnapping pro-independence activists. According to Manuel Carrascalao, during the mid-1980s the people of East Timor were nearly convinced that integration with Indonesia was the best option for the future of their children. 'Schools had been built, roads were open and so were hospitals and so on,' said the CNRT elder statesman. The East Timorese leaders were almost in agreement in accepting that fact until Prabowo and the Kopassus decided to make East Timor one of its bases. From that year onward the people of East Timor became more determined to become independent.

Military operations were waged in East Timor almost on a continual basis. Soldiers in fatigue were seen throughout the city. Not many journalists were allowed to visit the territory. The Garuda or Merpati Nusantara flights to the territory had to stop at Denpasar where all passengers had to go to the transit lounge. When they went back to the plane, passengers heading for Dili would have to show their permits to enter East Timor.

The Indonesian army made East Timor its own playground. They protected it from unflattering reports religiously. Each report about East Timor had to be vetted very thoroughly. During my one-week stay in Dili, I managed to send only one voice report to our Melbourne studio. The official reason was poor telephone communication. Another reason was, of course, army control. As an official guest, I had to play by their rules. I had to hand my short report about East Timor in to be checked by Lieutenant. Colonel Bimo, the intelligence officer. He didn't change a single word, but the fact that he had to read my report before I even read it over the telephone made me feel annoyed and angry.

One free evening I was meaning to read some books about development in East Timor given to me by Governor Carrascalao. While in Dili, I was given accommodation at Hotel Resende, one of two good hotels in town at that time (the other being Hotel Turismo, which stands next to the beach). Hotel Resende is a stone's throw away from the governor's office and less than 100 metres from the military command headquarters. Around 9pm there was a knock on the door. A bellboy told me that an army major was waiting to see me at the lobby.

He introduced himself and said that he wanted to pay a courtesy call. He told me that he could recognise me because, he said, I have a uniquely deep and heavy voice. We were chatting about radio stations in East Timor when he asked me a question I didn't expect. The major asked me if I could help him to sort out a problem. I told him that I would try to help if I could.

The major asked to remain anonymous. He said that as an officer of the A1 section, meaning intelligence section, he had been puzzled by the accuracy and immediacy of our news bulletins. He told me in total confidence that he had two suspicions. Firstly, there might be a mole in my department, and secondly, that Radio Australia had used hi-tech equipment in order to get information on East Timor. Now it was my turn to be puzzled. I didn't know why he came to me with such a question. When I asked him to elaborate, the major, who looked to be mid-40s and was therefore probably not a military academy graduate, begged me not to broadcast his assessment.

He said he had been wondering how Radio Australia obtained reports about what was happening in East Timor. 'Did you use military satellites over East Timor to gain your information?' I was stunned by the question, not knowing whether I should feel flattered on behalf of Radio Australia or burst into laughter by the silliest question I've ever heard in my entire professional life as a journalist. I tried to explain to him that we are not in the spy business. 'Radio Australia is a broadcasting organisation which gets its news and information from its correspondents around the world who send their reports through normal channels, the telephone,' I told him.

He couldn't help wondering how Radio Australia managed to broadcast something that took place in Dili in the morning; sometimes a planned operation was already broadcast before it had been executed. I tried to explain to him that there was nothing special about it. 'This is modern journalism, we use telecommunications to the maximum,' I said to the major. I explained that a journalist was just like any other person. 'What we do is just correlate all the information we have with statements given by some officials or military officers,' I explained to him that a journalist might have got information from one of his men who inadvertantly mentioned a planned operation. That would then be reported by Radio Australia.

I didn't know how I should feel when I left East Timor. Perhaps the trip was more an assisted and guided tour of the province. Lieutenant Colonel Bimo drove me to the airport in his Kostrad uniform with green beret. One thing that made the trip to East Timor unique was that I was contacted at my aunt's residence in South Jakarta by an officer from the BAIS. I was told to see Colonel Tony Sumarjo again for another interview. I was also asked to give him any copies of reports sent to Radio Australia from Dili.

I obliged half-heartedly, and only because the powerful BAIS was in a position to stop me from leaving the country if it wanted to. At that time any Indonesian citizen leaving the country had to get a so-called 'exit permit' from the Immigration Office. The BAIS and other intelligence bodies had used this measure to prevent any anti-government element from leaving Indonesia.

My 'get together' session with Colonel Tony Sumarjo, surprisingly, went very well. In all he received three reports, which included my so-called assessment about the general situation in East Timor. I explained to him that the situation in Dili needed improvement and there were too many troops on the road. He explained that the measure was needed to deter the Fretilin rebels from entering the city.

Tony Sumarjo was a military academy graduate of the mid-1960s. Some of his classmates were already brigadiers or major generals. His serious looking face changed that morning. He was rather friendly. He started his story by telling me that he had first entered East Timor in late 1974. That was well before the invasion in December 1975. His dark skin helped him disguise himself as one of the local population. 'When a Porto officer came to our village we would all sit on the ground,' he said. 'We wouldn't even dare look up.' He said that that was the life of East Timorese under the Portuguese.

He tried to explain to me that as soldiers he and his men had suffered much in liberating East Timor from colonisation. 'That's why we keep fighting this GPK mob,' he said, referring to Fretilin as the peace-disturbing mob. 'They're not many; we'll clean the province very soon from this mob,' he said convincingly. Fretilin's advantage, said Colonel Tony Sumarjo, was that their number was small and that they could slip in and out of villages very easily. Many of them were also good shots, he added.

'We were walking...some officers...casually in the bush, then suddenly one of the group fell to the ground with blood running from his mouth, his eyes still open but he's already dead,' said the colonel. 'Who wouldn't be angry? Our good friend is dead. His wife and our wives are just like sisters. So when we caught the man who shot him...his friends would just WHACK.' The colonel ran five fingers across his neck. 'We couldn't blame a young officer like him,' he said pointing to his assistant Lieutenant Colonel Ali Musa. 'A young man like him would be very angry with such a killing...and demand revenge.'

That morning Colonel Tony Sumarjo failed to remember the most important point he had quoted a few weeks earlier when I showed him the clipping from the Melbourne *Age* of a severed head being held as a trophy by a Kopassus unit in the bush in East Timor. They had forgotten one of the five pillars of the state ideology of Pancasila—'humanity'.

I didn't know if I could take that account of his as an accusation, but when I confronted Lieutenant Ali Musa on the way to the carpark, he denied it.

'Bullshit, I never did such a thing. Perhaps, he was talking about his own experience,' the young officer said, defending himself.

The militia—a new problem for East Timor

Following the downfall of President Suharto in May 1998, the popularity of Kopassus[1] dissipated and some people even said it has sunk to the lowest level within the Indonesian armed forces. Its association with the kidnappings of the pro-democracy activists in the preceding months made the red beret unit a notorious group. The trial and the conviction of some of its members known as Tim Mawar (Rose Team) made Kopassus almost a laughing stock among pro-democracy student movements in Jakarta.

However, in East Timor it was a different matter altogether. Before I left the province, Kopassus was still the dominant force. The activities of Kopassus became more and more evident after President Habibie gave the East Timorese two options either to accept autonomy under Indonesia or to become independent. The formation of so-called militia groups in East Timor was closely linked with Kopassus elements in the province. In every one of East Timor's 13 districts (*kabupaten*) there formed a militia group. Their duty was to 'salvage' the integration of the territory within Indonesia.

From the announcement of the plan to hold a referendum, East Timor became a more open territory to the NGOs, international observers and of course foreign journalists. Their assessment that Kopassus was active in creating various militia groups was almost unanimous. The elite force was understood to have played a major role in arming and training the militia. People knew that; so did the local authorities. For journalists, it did not make much difference. Either way, we had to cover the preparation for the campaign period and the conduct of the Popular Consultation itself. Newsagencies had been carrying reports about pro-independence activists who went missing in Dili and other centres.

I went to East Timor exactly one week before the Popular Consultation. I did not have many contacts in Dili at that time. Highest on the short list were the ABC journalists in the city. There were also some people in East Timor whom I contacted from time to time for telephone interviews, such as Bishop Carlos Belo and some journalists from East Timor's only newspaper, the *Voice of East Timor* (*Suara Timor Timur*).

When the plane stopped in Denpasar, I recognised someone with whom I kept in touch. He was a former member of parliament from East Timor. Salvador Ximenes Soares was returning to Dili after attending a secret meeting in Jakarta with the UN representatives and the pro-independence

---

[1] Such as it was with ordinary Indonesians. (Ed)

group. I asked him for a brief interview for Radio Australia's afternoon transmission and he obliged. He also introduced me to someone I had always wanted to meet, Eurico Guterres, the leader of the Aitarak (Thorn) militia group that dominated Dili. Eurico was, to my amazement, soft spoken and polite. He agreed to be interviewed.

My first impression about the Aitarak leader proved to be inaccurate. When speaking to his men, Eurico Guterres was completely different. He loathed UNAMET, the United Nations Assistance For East Timor, which organised the Popular Consultation. His fiery speech the following day offered no compromise to the pro-independence groups and the United Nations.

In my first interview with Eurico Guterres, I asked the Aitarak leader what he would do should the pro-autonomy side lose the election. His answer was straightforward, almost given instantaneously, that whatever the outcome of the referendum, he and his militia group would not leave East Timor. I was a little puzzled by the answer because he stressed that the pro-autonomy groups were going to demand the partition of East Timor. He mentioned that at least 40% of the East Timorese wanted their territory to remain part of Indonesia. He even urged the UN to send a peace-keeping force to areas along the western sector of East Timor which, he said, was going to eventually be claimed by the pro-autonomy side.

His extreme political stand matched the attitude of his organisation. The members of his militia group regularly 'patrolled' Dili. They would roam the city and terrorise its population. Wearing the uniform of black t-shirt with the word Aitarak written on the back, they attacked pro-independence supporters and on some occasions settled old scores with them. When they were in action, terrorising the people, it was wise to stay off Dili's streets.

If that sounds rather alarmist I can say it in all honesty because I have been terrorised by this militia group myself. It was Thursday 26 August, a little after 3.45pm. I was with Mark Bowling, ABC Jakarta correspondent, when our car was stopped and we found ourselves surrounded by some 50 Aitarak members. Many of them were wielding machetes and some brandishing home-made guns. We were told to reverse but couldn't because our way was blocked by about half a dozen militia members. We couldn't go forward either as three or four of them were standing and threatening us with machetes. So our local driver just stayed put while some of the militia members kicked the back door of our hardtop Toyota four wheel drive. Suddenly came a big noise; a marble rock about the size of an adult's fist was thrown into the back of the car where I was sitting. Fortunately the rock only hit my back and not my head; but still I could feel the pain. Pieces of broken glass showered my left elbow and some even got into my runners where my poor feet were not wearing socks.

I could hear the militia members kicking the car and screaming: 'Out,out,out'. I came out limping and holding my microphone and the mini disk shouting, 'Wait, wait, okay I'm out'. Before I realised it, a pistol was directed at me and was about one metre away from my head. A man dressed in black t-shirt was holding it; I could see the barrel very clearly. The man was in his late 20s. His face looked lifeless but his eyeballs were almost popping out. I could remember some people from both sides of the street were shouting and screaming 'kill him, kill him'. I froze in the middle of the road. Then I heard someone shout 'Go, go, go'. I limped back into the car and the driver sped off, zigzagging under the shower of rocks toward Lecidere beach.

The Aitarak mob had just attacked the CNRT's newly opened headquarters nearby. We dashed to the beach looking for cover near palm trees there. We always had the fear of being hit by a sniper or of becoming victim to a stray bullet. The situation at that time was hectic and full of excitement. A military helicopter with some troops at the ready had just landed. Then came another military truck followed by two green four wheel drives speeding toward an intersection. Not long after, there were about two truckloads of police stopped in front of the badly damaged CNRT office. About half a dozen motorcycles were damaged too, presumably belonging to some pro-independence activists who had been guarding the office. They now had gone into hiding, perhaps by climbing the high fence at the back of the office into some houses.

Mark Bowling ran towards a tree with his mobile phone close to his head. He was reporting the incident we had just experienced. Abel, the local driver, and the interpreter nursed my injury and to stop the blood I asked him to cover it with a hand towel I always keep in my equipment bag to wrap the valuable disk. In the meantime, after some attempts, I managed to send a live report to Melbourne while our afternoon transmission was still on air. At least our listeners would know what was happening that very minute in Dili.

Rumour was rife in East Timor, especially Dili, as it was here that the militia, the Indonesian military (TNI), UNAMET and the provincial government all had their headquarters. One leaked document from UNAMET said that the militia were going to attack Maliana on 27 August to purge the township of pro-independence supporters. It was almost becoming a closely practised tradition among journalists in Dili that we ask other journalists about the situation in a certain place. And the news about Maliana was not good.[2]

Maliana is a district capital and is situated about 150 kilometres southwest of Dili. It was also the centre of an extreme militia group called Halilintar

---

[2] The main incident in Maliana at this time occurred on the night on 27–28 August. (Ed)

(Thunderbolt) whose territory expanded south of Bobonaro almost to Liquica, less than 50 kilometres west of Dili. So the group controlled quite a wide area. That Saturday morning, two days before the popular consultation, four of us decided to make a day trip to Maliana to find out for ourselves what had been happening there. Tim Lester, ABC correspondent in Bangkok, Di Martin of Radio Australia's Asia–Pacific program and me plus a local driver used the four wheel drive while cameraman David Anderson and another Timorese driver used another car.

The road to Maliana is narrow and has lots and lots of potholes. The traffic seemed to be all one way—cars and trucks were leaving the town. We were told there was one checkpoint, near Balibo, and the militia would check all sorts of passes and official papers. Given the fact that Australia is not popular among the militia, Tim Lester and Di Martin devised a plan that if asked about their citizenship, the driver would tell the militia that they were British. I made my own plan that I was a government official from Jakarta escorting them. As supporting evidence I had a permanent press card from my friends at the Department of Information in Jakarta, and the part stating my occupation as Radio ABC Reporter was covered by the department stamp. We had to peel off ABC and Radio Australia stickers and official signs on our recorders and microphones. It turned out to be an overcautious effort. The militia guarding the checkpoint did not ask for our papers. They only looked at us and asked where we were going and for what purpose.

The expected militia attack on Maliana did not eventuate. But we arrived that midday at a tense moment. Even the UNAMET officials were unusually quiet and gave no interviews. A member of CivPol (UN Civilian Police) from Australia briefed us about the situation. The night before, the house where he and some other CivPol members lived was terrorised by a militia unit. They were pinned down there while some of the militia members attacked pro-independence activists at a nearby village.[3] When we arrived at the village, Memo, we saw some of the houses were still on fire; most of them had been gutted. About two dozen pro-independence supporters, most of them in their 20s, assembled near a bridge already blocked with logs. Many of them were wielding machetes and spears and some of them carried bows and arrows. They looked ready to fight.

The UN CivPol team and a group of local police officers from Maliana and Dili who inspected the gutted village returned to the capital in a helicopter. 'All we can do is collect some information about the incident and the number

---

[3] In this attack, two villagers and one militia member were killed, and several people were seriously injured. (Ed)

of casualties. Whatever the UN can do to help,' said the Australian CivPol chief, Commissioner Alan Mills.

One day before the Popular Consultation, the pro-independence and the pro-autonomy groups signed an agreement that they would ban their respective military wings from leaving their cantonments carrying firearms. Falintil had already placed itself in cantonment by this stage, and had been militarily inactive for some weeks. However, the agreement, signed in the presence of UNAMET officials, did not last long. Militia attacks took place, this time, in the western Dili suburb of Comoro, near Dili Airport.

The East Timorese had been waiting for 30 August 1999. It was the day they would decide their own future—whether to accept broad autonomy under Indonesia or be independent. They chose independence. From the very beginning, pro-Indonesian supporters might have suspected that the pro-independence side would win. As early as July, official documents had been leaked to the media showing that the Jakarta government had been arranging a contingency plan in anticipation of a loss in the August ballot. The plan was said to include massive evacuation of civil servants and migrants from East Timor before the poll results were announced. In spite of Jakarta's denial of the document's legitimacy, what happened in East Timor immediately after the referendum supported the existence of contingency plan. Massive and forced evacuation of East Timorese took place almost immediately after the poll.

What perhaps was not expected was the scorched earth campaign by the militia with, according to reports and evidence available, the support of the TNI. As we were representatives of the Australian media, our position in Dili was getting more precarious. One day, two or three militia members were said to be looking for journalists at Hotel Turismo. Having failed to find any, one of them roughed up a Canadian female observer. Later that day, not one journalist was seen on the Dili streets. Australian journalists were said to be high on the militia hit list.

Almost every night we held what we called a 'security meeting', which meant discussing contingency plans should our hotel be attacked by the militia. We asked for police protection, but they declined. According to a spokesman, the force did not have enough men. So we had to find a way out. The situation was already so critical for the seven of us that we had to sleep fully clothed, just in case the Aitarak members paid us a visit in the middle of the night. As a precaution, we blocked the front door with the hotel's big refrigerator. At least there was only one door to mind.

We were determined to escape from the militia should they attack us. One of the places we had been advised to go to was the police station or the

military post. Neither gave us peace of mind. So we decided that we would
escape using the high concrete wall from the upper level of the Dili ABC
office. We planned to follow this four metre high wall to the next house and to
hide there until daybreak. That was our first and most reliable contingency
plan; the other option was to drive all the way to the airport by following an
unused path and crossing a creek. Once we were at the airport, we would be
safe...we hoped!

As it turned out, we did not have to follow this plan. The militia were
thinking of bigger things. Not only did they drive out all the journalists, but
also the international observers and UNAMET eventually had to leave Dili.
That Friday, on the eve of the announcement of the poll result, the eastern
sector of Dili was already being torched. We could see some of it from about
a 2,000 metre altitude. I was one of the passengers in a chartered flight
leaving Dili around midday. Earlier in the day, the head of ABC International
News and Current Affairs in Sydney suggested that there were two vacant
seats in a chartered flight to Denpasar and that I should take one of them. I
reluctantly accepted the suggestion, even though it meant that I had to leave
Dili before the announcement of the result of the Popular Consultation, the
reason I had come to East Timor.

The United Nations in East Timor: Comparisons with Cambodia

Sue Downie

Introduction

Two nights before the 30 August vote, the militia rampaged through the district capital of Maliana, terrorising residents, attacking a group of students and kidnapping one young man. Hours later, we went to the village of Memo and walked around houses still smoldering from the attack by the militia, and were shown what was left after a man was cut to death with machetes. This was typical of militia activity in most districts. Their aim was to intimidate people into believing that if they rejected Jakarta's offer of autonomy there would be bloodshed. This kind of thuggery had been seen in other UN mission areas, in Bosnia, Somalia and Rwanda. Despite this, on the morning of the vote we walked down the main street of Maliana at 5.30 and saw hundreds of people queuing outside the polling centre, all dressed in their best clothes. Given the intimidation, kidnappings, torture and burnings in the preceding weeks, it was a spectacular and very moving sight. For me, it was a flashback to 23 May 1993, when thousands of Cambodians, dressed in their best clothes, queued outside polling centres at dawn, despite intimidation, kidnappings, torture and burnings in preceding weeks. During three weeks in East Timor and in the time since returning, I have been continuously struck by East Timor–Cambodia comparisons and lessons for peace-keeping, balloting and state-building.

It is estimated that during the Khmer Rouge's 'killing fields' era (1974–79) up to one-third of all Cambodians were killed or died and virtually the entire population was displaced—internally or across the border to Thailand. During the earlier period of the Indonesian occupation of East Timor, an estimated 200,000–220,000 East Timorese—equal to one-third of the population—were killed or died. Immediately after the ballot the killing resumed and virtually the entire population was displaced—internally, or by force across the border to West Timor or taken by boat to other islands. Cambodia is almost landlocked, with a tiny coastline; East Timor is half an island. Every year large parts of Cambodia are under water; East Timor is one of the driest of the more than 13,000 islands then claimed by Indonesia. At the beginning of their respective UN missions, Cambodia had a population of more than nine million, East Timor had approximately 850,000. Yet, despite such differences, for 20 years both suffered significant social and physical dislocation and destruction, the consequences of invasion and civil conflict;

and both are in the process of being reconstructed by the United Nations and its various agencies.

The only UN peace-keeping missions in Southeast Asia in the past 35 years have been in Cambodia (1991–93) and East Timor, hence this comparative study. It was written in the period between the two East Timor missions—while the assistance mission (UNAMET) was being wound-up and the transitional administration (UNTAET) was being prepared. Nevertheless, it is a reminder that the problems, reactions and requirements in East Timor are not unique, and that lessons—positive and negative—can be learned from similar UN attempts to facilitate peace and encourage good governance. The UN will be creating a state for the second time in history, Israel being the first, and will be in a position to implement or reject the accumulated lessons of the past 50 years—and the Cambodia mission offers many.

The UN's involvement in peace-keeping, balloting and state-building

The United Nations' primary function (as defined in Chapter 1, article 1, paragraph 1 of the UN Charter) is to maintain international peace and security. To achieve this, the UN can use Chapter VI of the Charter, which calls for dispute resolution 'by negotiation, enquiry, mediation, conciliation, arbitration, judicial settlement', termed *peace-keeping*. If these measures fail, the UN can invoke Chapter VII. which allows for the use of economic embargoes, blockades and 'air, sea, or land forces' (UN Charter:Art.33, 41, 42), generally regarded as *peace-enforcing*. The term 'peace-keeping' was not employed by those who wrote the 1945 Charter, however the UN has subsequently defined peace-keeping as 'politico-military activity aimed at conflict control' whereby the UN is in the field, with the consent of the parties, to (a) implement or monitor the implementation of agreements, and/or (b) protect the delivery of humanitarian relief (UN DPKO).

Peace-keeping missions are authorised by the UN's 15-member Security Council and are implemented by the Secretary General, whose office daily receives mission reports and issues directions to those in the field. UN member countries volunteer to contribute troops, as well as police and medical contingents where required.

The number of peace-keeping operations has increased significantly in recent years. In its first 40 years, the UN initiated 17 peace-keeping missions, and 18 in the next six years (1988–93) (Heininger 1994:3). Over the first 50 years, 49 peace-keeping operations were created, 36 of them in the 1988–98 (UN DPIa), hence the number of peace-keepers has increased almost sevenfold scince 1992–93 (Heininger 1994:3). At its peak in 1993, the UN spent US$3.29 billion on 17 missions, deploying more than 80,000 troops (Heininger 1994:3) from 77 countries (UN DPIb).

The nature of peace-keeping has also changed in recent years and has been extended beyond its original task of monitoring cease-fires and troop withdrawals, to include balloting, policing, administration and human rights investigation. Of the 13 missions that began between 1988 and 1992, nine involved the UN successfully facilitating resolution of domestic conflicts and the establishment of democratic regimes. Balloting and the emergence of new regimes, as part of peace-keeping operations, are the two aspects of UN missions discussed in this chapter.

Since 1945, the UN has been assisting states and territories to undertake elections and referenda, by (a) developing international standards of state behaviour, which involves developing the principle of the right to self-determination; and (b) strengthening international human rights law, especially the principle that governments should be chosen through genuine and periodic elections according to universal suffrage (UN DPAa).

With an increase in the number and complexity of requests for assistance, in 1992 the UN established the Electoral Assistance Division (EAD), which has since provided assistance to more than 70 states and territories. The UN offers two forms of assistance.

1. Technical assistance: the most common, whereby the UN assists the state's own electoral authorities with administration, budgets, planning, logistics, training election officials, assessing electoral laws/regulations, voter registration, voter education, co-ordinating international donor assistance, co-ordinating international observers, procuring election materials, balloting and counting. The only countries in the region to have received EAD assistance are the Philippines (1992–3), Fiji (1995) and Cambodia (1998).

2. Major electoral activities: these involve the UN's verifying or supervising or organising and conducting the ballot, and normally form part of a comprehensive peace-keeping operation (UN DPAb).

Electoral work was included in peace-keeping for the first time in Namibia, where the UN observed the election (November 1989), and in 11 subsequent missions. The UN's first attempt at conducting an election was in Cambodia (May 1993), followed by Eastern Slavonia (April 1997) (UN DPAc). The autonomy vote in East Timor was the UN's third experience at conducting a ballot, but this was an assistance mission, not a peace-keeping mission. Therefore, the forthcoming election in East Timor will be only the fourth time the UN has organised a ballot and the third time this has been done as part of a peace-keeping mission.

The peace-keeping mission (UNTAET) was only the fourth time in history that the UN gave itself the authority to assume complete responsibility for the administration of a territory/state. The first was, ironically, West Papua (now Irian Jaya), also a half-island territory of Indonesia, to the east of East Timor; the second time was Cambodia (1992–93); the third Eastern Slavonia (1997). In West Papua, the UN Temporary Executive Authority (UNTEA) ran the administration during the transition from Dutch to Indonesian control, October 1962 to May 1963, and was supported by a 1500-strong peace-keeping force (UN Security Force, UNSF). At the end of the mission, under an agreement between the governments of the Netherlands and Indonesia, the territory would come under Indonesian administration (Agreement 1962:Art. XII). It was later agreed that the people of West Papua would vote to either join Indonesia or become independent. Peace-keeping historians regard the West Papua operation as one of the UN's most successful, especially as the mandate was completed in time, there were no fatalities and the cost was not borne by the UN but split between the Netherlands and Indonesia (Harbottle 1971:89–94; Rikhye 1984:42–45; Whittaker 1995:193–203). However, the 'freeness' of the 1969 'Act of Free Choice'—which was organised by Indonesia and opposed by the Free Papua Movement (*OPM, Organisasi Papua Merdaka*)—has since been the subject of considerable debate and is the reason for OPM's ongoing struggle for West Papua independence (Cribb and Brown 1995:122; Drake 1989:56; Grant 1996:214; Rikhye 1984:45; Whittaker 1995:201).

UNTEA was mandated to replace top Netherlands officials with non-Netherlands, non-Indonesian officials and to put West Papuans in administrative and technical positions (Agreement 1962:Art.IX). UNTEA also brought in specialists—building surveyors, telephone engineers, medical personnel, engineers and agriculture experts—from other countries to rehabilitate the local government system as well as the most important physical infrastructures (Harbottle 1971:93; Whittaker 1995:199). Although limited by time, this might have been the beginning of a state-building process, had the 1969 vote been for independence.

The UN and its agencies have been for many years undertaking state-building activities in various forms. These include electoral assistance and peace-keeping mandates that have involved restoration of democracy and the protection of human rights, and helping states draft constitutions, create independent judicial systems, de-politicise military establishments, build police forces that respect and enforce the rule of law, establish national institutions for the promotion and protection of human rights and encourage public participation in political processes (UN 1996). In 1992 the Secretary-General, Boutros Boutros-Ghali, issued 'An Agenda for Peace', which called for a comprehensive approach to peace, incorporating preventive diplomacy, peace-making, peace-keeping and peace-building (UN 1992b). In 1994, he produced 'An Agenda for Development' in which he said development is multidimensional, involving not just economic growth but also democracy as good governance (UN 1994). In 1996, Boutros-Ghali presented his 'An Agenda for Democratization', saying peace, development and democracy are inextricably linked (UN 1996).

In Cambodia, the UN could have laid the foundations for developing a state, as a follow-on from—if not part of—the peace-keeping mission. However, the mission regarded the election as the end-point rather than one part of the process and therefore did not give sufficient consideration to the post-election state-building phase, departing before the foundations were laid. In East Timor, the UN had the opportunity to plan and implement strong state-building measures.

Comparisons between the UN missions in East Timor and Cambodia are numerous, but can be placed in three broad categories:

1. the procedure of the UN's missions;
2. the reaction of the parties and the population, and the refusal of losing parties to accept the democratic process;
3. reconciliation, rehabilitation and state-building.

The United Nations' missions in Cambodia and East Timor

No two UN missions are the same. Each is shaped by regional politics and recent history, as well as the political, social and cultural features of the mission area. However, some aspects of the procedure are similar, and some lessons—of what to do and what not to do—can be incorporated in subsequent missions. For this reason, some features of the UN's procedure in East Timor and Cambodia are worth comparison. While the size of the two missions is different, the composition, deployment and *modus operandi* are similar.

The mandate

The UN mission in Cambodia was two-phased, where the advance mission (UNAMIC, the UN Advance Mission in Cambodia) of November 1991 expanded in March 1992 into a much larger peace-keeping operation (UNTAC, the UN Transitional Authority in Cambodia) which comprised seven components including administration, electoral, repatriation and rehabilitation. The June–September 1999 mission in East Timor began as an assistance mission (UNAMET, the UN Assistance Mission in East Timor), to be followed by a peace-keeping operation (UNTAET, the UN Transitional

Administration in East Timor), also with administration, electoral, repatriation and rehabilitation tasks. While UNTAET and the two missions in Cambodia are peace-keeping operations, UNAMET was an electoral assistance mission preceding a peace-keeping operation. The International Force in East Timor (InterFET) is a peace-enforcement operation, mandated to restore peace and security, to protect UNAMET, and facilitate humanitarian assistance before the arrival of the peace-keeping force, UNTAET (UNSC 1999).

While the primary task of both UNTAC and UNAMET was to organise and conduct a ballot, the main differences were in security arrangements and size: UNAMET registered 450,000 voters for a referendum with two protagonists—the pro-autonomy and pro-independence groups—while UNTAC ran an election contested by 20 parties, with almost 4.7 million voters. Although the voting population in East Timor was less than one-tenth that of Cambodia, UNAMET's budget ($51 million) and number of personnel (988) was far less than one-tenth that of UNTAC ($1.6 billion, 22,000 personnel).

UNTAC, which began in March 1992, was the largest, most ambitious and most intrusive peace-keeping mission the UN had ever undertaken. The UN had to disarm 200,000 soldiers and 250,000 militia, repatriate 360,000 refugees, help resettle 700,000 refugees, internally displaced people and demobilised soldiers, register 4.7 million voters, organise and conduct the election, and begin the slow process of rehabilitation and rebuilding. The UN was also given the unprecedented task of controlling the country's administration during the transitional period in the lead-up to national elections, in May 1993.

The Transitional Administration in East Timor also disarmed repatriated, rebuilt and controlled. As was the case in Cambodia, this required:

- disarming the soldiers and militia of the rival factions and demobilising all or a portion of them, and retraining some;
- repatriating and resettling the refugees and internally displaced people (IDPs);
- preparing and conducting the election: writing an electoral law, facilitating the establishment of political parties, conducting voter education, supervising an election campaign, monitoring the media, and conducting the ballot and count;
- maintaining law and order, training police, controlling the administration, and rehabilitating the essential infrastructures, while planning for state-building and long-term restoration.

UNTAET is the temporary authority as East Timor moves from Indonesian control to independence, and UNTAET is extremely powerful—mandated to 'exercise all legislative and executive authority' in East Timor for up to three years (UN 1999e). Under the Peace Agreement in October 1991, the UN was the authority in Cambodia. All civil police were to operate under UNTAC control and UNTAC would supervise other law enforcement and judicial processes 'to the extent necessary'. In theory, UNTAC personnel had unrestricted access to all administrative operations and information, and had the power to reassign or remove personnel from any office. UNTAC had the right to control the administration of the incumbent State of Cambodia (SOC) and the three resistance factions. This meant the 'five key areas' areas most likely to influence the election—foreign affairs, national defence, finance, public security and information—were placed under the direct control of UNTAC, although these administrative bodies were to continue functioning day to day. Any other area could also come under UNTAC's direct supervision or control (UN 1992a:18–19). This was the mandate given to UNTAC by the Security Council; the fact that UNTAC failed to fulfill parts of the mandate to the extent envisaged has been documented elsewhere (Doyle 1995; Doyle and Suzuki 1995; Heder and Ledgerwood 1996; Heininger 1994; Hughes 1996; Carney and Tan 1993; Berry 1997).

In the context of lessons for East Timor, there are two reasons for that failure. First, UNTAC did not fully understand the workings of the Vietnamese-installed SOC administration and the extent to which SOC controlled the entire country's administrative apparatus, from the State Council to the village level. This may be relevant to UNTAET in rebuilding the remnants of the Indonesian-installed administration. Secondly, UNTAC had a policy to control the administration, but no strategy. Consequently, UNTAC's Civil Administration personnel were deployed to the provinces without sufficient briefings (therefore understanding) and without a plan of how to approach the problem of controlling the SOC administration. Indeed, Boutros Boutros-Ghali, the Secretary-General responsible for UNTAC, later admitted that the Civil Administration component's task of direct supervision 'turned out to be nearly impossible to achieve because of language problems, lack of enforcement measures and inadequate experience on the part of UNTAC personnel with the kind of bureaucratic structures and procedures employed by the SOC' (UN 1995:55). It can only be hoped that the current Secretary-General and his staff took these comments into consideration when planning and implementing UNTAET.

Two shortcomings of the UNTAC mandate may be relevant to UNTAET. First, UNTAC did not have the power to implement its authority; so, for example, when the UNTAC chief, Yasushi Akashi, asked SOC to remove the obstructive governor of Battambang Province, Prime Minister Hun Sen refused, leaving Akashi unable to act on this or, more importantly, on any subsequent cases. Second, part-way through the mission, the Security Council gave UNTAC the authority to 'arrest, detain and prosecute persons accused of politically motivated criminal acts and human rights violations' (UN 1995:270). However, SOC's politically controlled courts refused to try the first four suspects arrested by UNTAC. Consequently, UNTAC was put in the unprecedented position of having to detain those arrested, and in the embarrassing position of holding untried prisoners longer than permitted in its own rules.

Planning

The decision to create a peace-keeping or peace-enforcement mission rests with the Security Council, which is influenced largely by the foreign relations and economic interests of its members, especially the five permanent members, who can veto any Council resolution. The international community's response to complex emergencies has varied. For example, more than one million people died in Rwanda before UN member states committed troops to the peace-keeping mission (UNAMIR); fighting continued in Bosnia for three years before the international community (through NATO) took measures to stop the killings, but only three months in Kosovo (again through NATO), and in less than two weeks in East Timor (MacLeod 1999). Just 11 days after East Timor's post-announcement violence began, the Security Council passed resolution 1264 to establish the multinational force under Chapter VII of the UN Charter, and authorised the force to 'take all necessary measures to fulfil [its] mandate' (UNSC 1999)—an extraordinarily authorisation agreed to in an extraordinary short time. Four days later, the first InterFET troops were on the ground in Dili.

Peace-keeping missions are planned and managed on a day-to-day basis in the UN's Department of Peace-Keeping Operations (DPKO), which has expanded significantly in recent years, reflecting the increase in number, size and complexity of missions. At its peak in 1993, DPkO was handling 17 missions concurrently, the largest being the UN Protection Force (UNPROFOR) in the former Yugoslavia, with 38,000 troops. In theory, mission planning cannot begin until the mission's mandate and budget are approved by the General Assembly. However, survey missions—comprising UN and non-UN military and civilian personnel—may be sent to the mission area to gather information and make recommendations to the Secretary-General, who then submits a mission proposal to the Security Council. This process typically takes months rather than weeks.

To prepare for the 1991 advance mission in Cambodia (UNAMIC), a military survey mission was sent to the region from 19 August to 4 September and the Secretary-General submitted their report (which detailed tasks, budget and personnel required) to the Security Council on 30 September (UN 1995:125). On 16 October, the Council agreed that UNAMIC could be established immediately after the signing of the peace agreement on 23 October (UN 1995:131). Although the date for the signing had been set well in advance, officially DPKO could not begin planning for the mission until a week before the mission was to begin. Nevertheless, two Australian Army officers were in New York preparing for the mission in September and in Cambodia two weeks before the signing. Consequently, Australian troops were on the ground in Cambodia 19 days after the signing (UN 1995:150).

Australia made a significant contribution to behind-the-scenes preparations for the peace-keeping operations in both Cambodia and East Timor. In an unprecedented move, in the lead-up to deployment in Cambodia the UNTAC military commander-designate, General John Sanderson, and three of his Army officers spent several weeks at UN headquarters in New York working on the military preparations for UNTAC. And in 1999, the Australian Defence Department (ADF) began preparing for a peace-keeping mission in East Timor immediately after President Habibie announced in February that the referendum would take place (ADF 1999). Subsequently, one senior Defence peace-keeping planner was seconded to New York from September to help prepare for UNTAET.

The military is only one of several components in today's multifaceted peace-keeping missions; survey missions for electoral and repatriation tasks were also deployed to Cambodia to prepare for UNTAC, and presumably will be, deployed to East Timor to prepare for UNTAET. While Sanderson and his officers were in New York planning Cambodia's military operation, members of the electoral survey team gathered in New York in January 1992 to draft an electoral law to cover the rules for the Cambodia election. They also had to establish the computer system that would be needed to register more than 4 million Khmer names transliterated to English—a mammoth task that UNTAET will not have to confront.

Some countries—and contingents within countries—are better than others at preparing for missions. The Canadians selected for Cambodia underwent almost three months' military and diplomatic training on the history of the UN and UNTAC, and the history, culture and religion of Cambodia (Bourne 1993). This level of preparation was exceptional. Most international staff attended two to three days of briefings after arriving in Cambodia, but in the following months the actions of many proved that this was not sufficient. It is impossible for a newcomer to the region to acclimatise physically and culturally in such a short time, and simultaneously find accommodation, identify service points, hire local staff and fully understand the mission mandate, their component's roles and responsibilities, and how their own work fits into that mandate. They also need to develop a thorough understanding of recent political history, especially the workings of the government and administration, and the political links, know who is whom and be able to recognise different military uniforms and ranks. It can only be hoped that all UNTAET personnel—military and civilian—are familiar with East Timor's history, politics, culture and society, and not only recognise names and faces but know their political affiliations and past activities.

Deployment

As mentioned above, UNAMIC soldiers were on the ground in Cambodia 19 days after the peace signing, and InterFET troops were in Dili four days after the Security Council authorised the multinational force. Obviously, this required considerable advance preparation. In the case of InterFET, this was helped by the fact that Australia had an SAS regiment and two battalions on standby.

Before a mission begins, country representatives to the UN in New York are called to a troop contributors' conference to be briefed on what troops will be needed and to ask what their representative governments can contribute to the mission. This would normally be followed by a troop commanders' conference to brief the military commanders chosen to lead the battalions and service units during the mission. Even though the Security Council authorised UNTAC on 28 February 1992, the UNTAC contributors' conference was not held until 6 March—nine days before UNTAC was to begin—and the commanders' conference was held on 6 April—three weeks after Akashi and Sanderson arrived in Cambodia. Funding for deployment was not authorised until 10 April, almost a month after UNTAC began. This lag in time can be attributed to UN bureaucracy, the slowness of countries to contribute personnel, and a lack of co-ordination between UN departments and between the UN and contributing countries. The preparation and deployment for UNTAET demonstrated to what extent the UN has taken on board lessons from Cambodia and subsequent missions.

Deploying a battalion is a major logistical operation, especially when it is required to be self-sufficient, as is often the case in conflict areas where infrastructure and supply lines have been damaged. Those going into Cambodia were told to take everything from generators to notepads. UNTAC's 12 infantry battalions each comprised on average 850 soldiers and enough equipment and supplies for at least two months. They had to be shipped and flown from Bangladesh, Bulgaria, France, Ghana, India,

Indonesia, the Netherlands, Malaysia, Pakistan, Tunisia and Uruguay. The UN also had to bring engineering units from China, Japan, France, Poland and Thailand; medical units from Germany and India; logistics units from Canada, Pakistan and Poland; marines from the Philippines and Uruguay; a communications unit from Australia and an air support unit from France.

Composition

As can be seen from the above, UN peace-keeping missions, by definition, are multinational, and generally have an even mix of personnel from the five continents. (Peace-enforcement missions are usually led and dominated by one country, for example the US in Somalia and Australia in East Timor.) The civilian staff is also multinational. In UNAMET, for example, the head of mission (Ian Martin) was from the UK, his deputy (Francesc Vendrell) from Spain, the chief of civilian police (Alan Mills) from Australia, the chief military liaison officer (Rezaqul Haider) from Bangladesh and a chief electoral officer (Jeff Fischer) from the US. Given that the UN was in Cambodia as a consequence of Vietnam's occupation, Vietnam did not contribute any personnel to the mission there. For the same reasons, it would be inappropriate for Indonesia to be part of UNTAET, except perhaps to provide background information on the workings of the administration they installed.

The structure of UNTAET was similar to UNTAC's, reflecting their similar tasks. UNTAC had seven components: military, civilian police, electoral, civil administration, human rights, repatriation and rehabilitation, plus an information and education division. UNTAET has three components: governance and public administration; humanitarian assistance and emergency rehabilitation; and military. The governance and public administration component will oversee the restructuring of the judiciary and public services, handle economic, financial and development affairs, take charge of the 13 districts, pay the salaries of local civil servants, run the electoral operations and oversee the rebuilding of the civilian police force. The humanitarian and rehabilitation component will work with UN agencies and non-government organisations (NGOs) to re-establish social and physical infrastructures. The military component was expected to comprise an 8,950-strong UN force and 200 military observers (UN 1999f).

UNTAET could also have benefitted from an active information unit with control and analysis functions. UNTAC's Information-Education Division was formed to (a) control the Cambodian media (checking for disinformation and political bias); (b) disseminate UNTAC information to the Cambodian public (mainly on disarmament, human rights and the election); and (c) gather information from Cambodian sources and analyse it for UNTAC. The last was extremely important for assessing political trends and public opinion of UNTAC, and its analysis was the basis for some of UNTAC's most important decisions. The analysis unit was directed by Steve Heder, a long-term Cambodia researcher, and his contribution highlighted the need for missions to include people of this calibre who understand and can analyse the local political, military, social, cultural and economic scene.

Balloting

For both the election in Cambodia and the referendum in East Timor, the constituency was largely a poor, peasant, illiterate population experiencing their first democratic vote. Hence, in both cases, the UN undertook voter education campaigns to inform the public of the UN's mandate and the process for the forthcoming vote, to ensure the public knew who was eligible to vote, and to encourage voters to register and vote. The campaign consisted of printed material, radio broadcasts and voting demonstrations in villages, and daily media briefings. UN electoral workers in both East Timor and Cambodia were UN Volunteers (UNVs). They travelled to villages in the remotest parts (in Cambodia, by helicopter, boat and elephant, in East Timor by four-wheel drive) to distribute posters, broadcast tapes and videos and to address village meetings, often simulating a polling centre. As vehicles and electricity were not always available, some UNVs in Cambodia hired ox carts to carry around the audio-visual equipment that ran off truck batteries.

Many villagers in East Timor heard UNAMET's broadcasts on radio sets donated from Japan.These radios were distributed all over Cambodia and were highly sought after. UNTAC produced radio and television programs to be broadcast on Cambodian stations, then half-way through the mission established its own radio station, Radio UNTAC, which was able to broadcast continuously and independently. The importance of this was highlighted when the election results were announced. Members of the government did not like what they were hearing, so they sent a tank and truck load of soldiers to Radio UNTAC. The UN countered by reinforcing the radio station with troops and heavy weapons, and Radio UNTAC continued to broadcast. While most attention was focussed on the expectation that the Khmer Rouge would disrupt the election, this threat came from the government and was a harsh reminder that broadcast stations are a prime political target and that mission planners need to cover all contingencies.

One lesson, or resource, from Cambodia not recognised in East Timor was the electoral guidelines that detailed the rights and responsibilities of the parties during the lead-up to the vote. The Code of Conduct for Participants was drafted by UNAMET's legal officer, who, when asked if he had taken many examples from the Cambodian electoral law, admitted he did not know it existed. This was one of many examples where institutional memory was lacking in the UN, and the UN was not utilising material or examples from previous missions, even though in 1995 the DPKO established a Lessons Learned Unit.

In East Timor, pro-autonomy and pro-independence leaders signed the Code of Conduct, which stipulated 'intimidation, in any form, is unacceptable, and is expressly forbidden. No participant shall kill, torture, injure, apply violence to intimidate or threaten any other person in connection with that person's political beliefs' (UN 1999b:Art 14–15). However, the two-week campaign period was marked by intimidation and violence, which included killings, kidnappings, tortures and burning of houses. As UNTAET prepared for East Timor's post-independence vote, the general election, it might have kept in mind that sometimes codes of conduct are not worth the paper they are written on.

In spite of the campaign violence, remarkably, polling day was calm compared with the preceding weeks. The few incidents on polling day, if nothing else, showed that the military could control the militia when they wanted to. This also happened in Cambodia in the 1998 election, where the lead-up to the vote had been marred by intimidation and violence, but polling day was virtually incident-free. The voter turnout of 98% in East Timor, higher than the 90% in Cambodia in 1993 and 1998, was remarkable.

Security

A major difference between UNTAC and UNAMET was the provision of security. While the UN in Cambodia had 12 armed battalions, UNAMET personnel were unarmed and relied on the Indonesian police to provide security. Under the 5 May 1999 tripartite agreement—between the UN, Indonesia and Portugal—during the UNAMET period, June–September, the Indonesian security forces were responsible for maintaining 'a secure environment devoid of violence or other forms of intimidation'—which on numerous occasions they failed to do, or did belatedly.

In both East Timor and Cambodia, the high level of fear that permeated the environment was such that a single shot or incident could spark terror. The militia in East Timor and the Khmer Rouge in Cambodia worked at maintaining this fear, so that it only required a small incident for people, including the UN, to run. In both Cambodia and East Timor, the consequence of the UN's withdrawal was the peoples' loss of confidence in the peace and electoral processes. UNAMET had assured the East Timorese it would not leave after the vote but, apart from the 12 commendable people who remained in Dili at the peak of the violence in September, UNAMET did leave.

The militias in East Timor were very different to the Khmer Rouge, except that their common aim was to disrupt polling, and their technique was fear and rumour. Whereas Khmer Rouge foot soldiers carried grenade launchers, anti-tank mines and AK47 assault rifles, in the lead-up to the ballot the militias often attacked with home-made guns and machetes, although automatic weapons and grenades were increasingly made available to them through the TNI. In 1992–3, the UN and the Cambodian government confronted a long-established, well-armed, jungle-hardened Khmer Rouge army, led by committed ideologues who had been fighting for up to 25 years. The militia leaders were more concerned with economic interests than ideology, and an estimated 80% of the rank and file were non-East Timorese, many of whom had been recently recruited and paid to wear militia T-shirts.

The reaction of the parties and population

The people and the leaders of institutions often react dramatically, and sometimes unexpectedly, in the face of adversity, and this occurred in both East Timor and Cambodia with similar patterns.

The people's reaction

The high voter registration in East Timor and the subsequent 98% voter turnout demonstrated the population's determination to exercise their right to vote, in spite of threats and possible repercussions. Given pre-vote intimidation and violence, the UN was under pressure to postpone (which it did twice) or cancel the referendum. In light of the post-vote violence, UNAMET was criticised for not having cancelled the ballot. However, this would have meant discarding the small window of opportunity that existed while Habibie was President and, consequently, denying the East Timorese the chance to determine their future. As the UN said later:

> The agreed time frame for the consultation was very tight. The prospect of achieving greater security through delaying the process—or halting it—had to be weighed carefully against the risk of depriving the people of East Timor of a historic opportunity which might never be repeated. The desire of the East Timorese to continue was evident. Despite violence and intimidation, they had shown their determination to go on with the process by turning out in massive numbers to register. In their contacts with UNAMET and other UN representatives, East Timorese leaders and people in communities indicated their support for continuing the process. (UN 1999d)

East Timorese leader Xanana Gusmao supported the UN's decision to proceed with the referendum, and said that for 23 years the people of East Timor had lived in danger and suffered a huge death toll to gain the right to self-determination. They took the risk, and they were determined to continue in order to achieve their sacred goal (Gusmao 1999b).

The UN in Cambodia had faced a similar quandary. In the weeks leading to the election, senior staff meetings were dominated by discussions on whether or not to proceed, with some mission leaders asking, 'how many more people have to die before we call it off?' In the end, the Khmer Rouge did not attack polling centres or disrupt the six-day voting process.

The campaign period in both East Timor and Cambodia saw an exodus of non-indigenous populations. Ethnic Vietnamese fled Cambodia following massacres and further threats against them from the Khmer Rouge. In the week before the vote, many non-East Timorese closed businesses, loaded household goods onto trucks, buses and utes and headed across the border to West Timor.

The losers' reaction

In both East Timor and Cambodia, there was a refusal of the losers to accept the democratic process, and a tendency for the losers to retreat to their old bases. When the Cambodian People's Party, which had been in power for 13 years, lost the election to the royalist Funcinpec party, elements of CPP reacted in two ways: one group began harassing and killing Funcinpec members; a second group (not necessarily unrelated) attempted to take control of the six provinces bordering Vietnam, the birthplace of what became CPP. The secessionists also attempted to push the UN out of those provinces. The secessionist movement failed, but the attempt and the killings forced Prince Ranariddh to form a coalition government with CPP. Immediately after the UN announced on 4 September that 78.5% of East Timorese voters had rejected autonomy, the militia began killing and burning. Ten days later, militia leaders threatened to take control of, and bar UNAMET from, the three districts bordering West Timor, using as their base Atambua, from where the Indonesia armed forces (ABRI, renamed TNI) had launched the takeover of East Timor in 1975.

The refusal of the losing parties to accept the result highlighted the political immaturity of the parties' leaders. Those in CPP had no experience of democracy, pluralism or a parliamentary opposition, and could not accept the possibility of relinquishing power. Equally, Indonesia was undergoing a process of democratisation, but some generals, referred to as the incumbent and the old guard (Budiman 1999), were resisting change and were reluctant to surrender control of East Timor.

Although the timing and motive were different, the militia and TNI's campaign of destruction and displacement in September can be compared with the Khmer Rouge's 'Year Zero' campaign (1975–79), during which temples, schools and banks were destroyed, monks and intellectuals executed, and almost the entire population displaced. Their aim was to wipe the slate clean—remove all undesirable elements of former regimes—so that Cambodia could begin again, from Year Zero. While the Khmer Rouge destroyed what they considered luxury items, including office equipment, cars, motorbikes, refrigerators and generators, the TNI took such items for their personal use or sale. The militia and TNI's aim in destroying and displacing was also to wipe the slate clean, as punishment to those who voted for change and to make it difficult for the new state to become established.

Reconciliation, rehabilitation and state-building

The most important stage of the UN mission is not the election, but reconciliation, rehabilitation and state building. The planning of this should be an integral part of the peace-keeping plan and should be implemented concurrently with all other aspects of the peace-keeping operation, not merely placed at the end as a separate task.

Reconciliation

East Timorese leaders, who won popular support, faced the same quandary their Cambodian colleagues did after the 1993 election: whether and, if so, how, to reconcile and integrate those who voted against them. The Khmer Rouge had removed themselves from the UN peace process and taken up arms against the new government, so the royalist Funcinpec party—who for 13 years had fought in unison with the Khmer Rouge against CPP—joined CPP to form a coalition government that then passed a law banning the Khmer Rouge. In early October 1999, Gusmao said he would accommodate the militia, and appealed to them to join in rebuilding East Timor.

One aspect of UNTAET's mandate was to establish appropriate advisory bodies at all levels to ensure East Timorese participation in the governance and administration of the territory. In this context it is worth looking at the Cambodian experience, not so much for lessons to follow, but perhaps for what not to do. At the instigation of the UN and ASEAN, prior to the Peace Agreement, the four Cambodian factions formed the Supreme National Council (SNC), with six seats allocated to SOC and two to each of the three 'resistance' factions who had been opposing the incumbent, politically and militarily, for 13 years. The SNC had three main functions: (a) to represent Cambodia externally and occupy the Cambodia seat at the UN; (b) to collectively make decisions on national issues, such as the electoral law, a moratorium on the export of logs and gems, and the issuing of passports during the UN transitional period; and (c) to advise and liaise with UNTAC.

The SNC did not fully function as intended, for perhaps two reasons that may have been relevant to UNTAET: (a) it did not meet regularly, nor often enough; and (b) the composition—the SNC had only 12 members (representing nine million people), they were the most senior people in the country and they were all leaders of political parties. An alternative might have been regular meetings of a larger, more diverse membership, for example a council of national reconciliation comprising 35–40 members drawn from political, administrative, technical, legal, academic and business backgrounds. It would not be inappropriate for East Timor to have a transitional national council comprising members of CNRT (the National Council for Timorese Resistance), expatriate East Timorese and pro-Indonesianists who want to be part of the new administration or government.

It should be remembered that CNRT comprises members of a number of parties who share the common goal of an independent East Timor but who have differing backgrounds and philosophies, and who may wish to stand against each other in the forthcoming election. Without successful reconciliation, the possibility of hostile competition cannot be ruled out.

Rebuilding, capacity-building and state-building

Rebuilding East Timor, or building the state of East Timor, will be similar to the rehabilitation of Cambodia following more than 20 years of physical and social destruction. The priority should be to establish rule of law, which will involve setting up a police force and a judicial and prison system with appropriately-trained lawyers, prosecutors, court officials and prison officers. In addition to rebuilding physical infrastructure, it will be necessary to establish a political system, undertake administrative reform, revamp the financial and tax system, formulate foreign policy, and draft laws, as well as train teachers, health workers, independent journalists and so on.

If East Timor's new leaders follow the democratic process, they will have to consider public consultation and participation, the drafting of a constitution, the establishment of a multiparty system, and the role and function of an effective opposition. They will also have to face three of the most difficult issues that Cambodian leaders have failed to address: impunity, nepotism and corruption.

One of the lessons that should be learned from Cambodia is that the UN mission should not end with the election of a new parliament. The ultimate goal of UNTAC was the election. Once that was accomplished, 'Untacists' patted themselves on the back and went home (except those working on Operation Paymaster, which involved paying the civil servants and armed forces in order to maintain civil order). UNTAC's mandate ended three months after the election, when the resulting constituent assembly passed a new constitution and transformed itself into a legislative assembly (UN 1992a:9; UN 1995:333). Virtually no consideration was given to what would happen the next day, let alone for the next months or years. There was no plan and therefore no mechanism for the UN mission to assist the new government. What was to happen in the new parliament? What were the new MPs to do, some of whom previously had been farmers, taxi drivers and restaurateurs? How would they perform? They had little experience or understanding of the parliamentary process. Cambodia had never had an effective legislative opposition. What would be an opposition's role, rights and responsibilities, and how was the government going to act towards and react to an opposition? This post-UNTAC phase was not adequately taken into account by the mission planners. But it should be incorporated in the UNTAET mandate as part of the state-building process.

UNTAC undertook a massive civic education and human rights awareness program during the mission, and unofficially offered guidance in writing the constitution at the end. Although rehabilitation was one of UNTAC's seven components, it did not function as intended. Consequently, after UNTAC departed, the sourcing and allocation of funds was left to the UN Development Program (UNDP) and the International Committee on the Reconstruction of Cambodia (ICORC), which met annually to pledge funding for Cambodia's on-going rehabilitation.

Conclusion

In spite of intimidation and violence, the East Timorese in August 1999 demonstrated their desire for change. Given the international community's inaction over East Timor in the preceding 24 years there were compelling reasons for it to not only act but to also get it right. With the people of East Timor, the UN will be creating a new state, and it is in a unique position to show it has the will and ability to implement or reject lessons accumulated over the past 50 years. The UN can do this by combining its skills in peace keeping, balloting and state-building to develop solid foundations for sustainable political, social and economic development. As Boutros-Ghali said, peace, development and democracy are inextricably linked. An election does not equal democracy, and peace-keeping is not an isolated activity. It is part of the whole democratisation and state-building process. Peace-keeping is not one component, and rehabilitation simply another that follows. They should be intertwined, and the linkage should be defined in the planning phase.

The process does not occur overnight. The rebuilding of Cambodia was continuing six years after the UN mission ended and some aspects of Cambodia's political, social, cultural and economic systems have still not reached the level they were in the 1960s. The rebuilding of East Timor could have been expected to raise many similar problems to those in Cambodia, which were similarly difficult to resolve or reconcile.

Accountability for human rights abuses in East Timor

Annemarie Devereux

International lawyers, like many in the general community, have watched recent events in East Timor with both hope and despair. Given their concern in the past with analysing the implications of Indonesia's invasion in 1975 for the recognition of Indonesia's territorial sovereignty, and the content and significance of the East Timorese people's right to self-determination (see for instance Franck and Hoffman 1975–6; Elliot 1978; Clark 1980; Suter 1982; Cassese 1995), the 30 August 1999 Popular Consultation was interpreted by international lawyers as an opportunity for the East Timorese to decide their own fate. That the United Nations had brokered the deal between Portugal and Indonesia was seen as a positive step and an affirmation of the role for the community of nations in upholding the right of all peoples to self-determination. Yet with the recent violence, intimidation, and forcible transfer of East Timorese and the widespread destruction of personal and public property by members of pro-Jakarta militia,[1] seemingly supported by members of the TNI, there has been horror and an ongoing debate on the best means for the international community to address the 'crimes against humanity' and other egregious human rights violations.

The calls immediately after the well-publicised atrocities that took place in the aftermath of the Popular Consultation were for an international war crimes tribunal to be established. At a specially convened meeting in late September 1999, the United Nations Commission on Human Rights resolved to establish a Commission of Inquiry. The UN Commission was empowered to gather and compile information on possible violations of human rights that might constitute breaches of international humanitarian law committed in East Timor since January 1999.[2] Immediately prior to this step, Indonesia announced its own Commission of Inquiry into Human Rights Violations in East Timor (KPP-HAM). Both the Indonesian and the UN Commission of

---

[1] This comment is not to suggest that the human rights abuses have occurred only since the vote took place. Indeed a case could be made that the violence, intimidation and property destruction represent the culmination of an existing pattern of violence suffered by East Timorese for many years. However, the magnitude (and visibility) of the occurrences and unilateral nature of the violence have gained the attention of the international community.

[2] The mandate of the UN Commission of Inquiry, see the website of the Commission on Human Rights.

Inquiry have now issued their reports.[3] Importantly, both bodies have concluded there to be strong evidence of both the commission of human rights abuses and the involvement of the Indonesian military, the TNI. An as yet unresolved issue is the method for further investigation and redress. Whilst the UN Commission of Inquiry has called for the establishment of an international human rights tribunal and recommended that the UN Transitional Authority in East Timor (UNTAET) be empowered to undertake ongoing human rights investigations, Indonesia insists that it is for Indonesia to deal with the matters arising from activities that occurred on Indonesian soil and involved Indonesian citizens. By failing to endorse the recommendation for an international body in his address to the General Assembly, the UN Secretary General, Kofi Annan, seems to have given his implicit support to Indonesia's position whilst at the same time encouraging UNTAET to co-operate in the investigation of abuses.

No doubt a number of factors have played a role in determining the Secretary-General's current position. The Secretary-General might be desirous of supporting the movement within Indonesia to democratise and move toward a system firmly supportive of human rights. Permitting Indonesia to exercise sole jurisdiction over perpetrators would thus give it the opportunity to demonstrate its commitment to justice. Financial and pragmatic incentives might also be influential. An Indonesian investigation would use local Indonesian resources. It would also have the advantage of more easily being able to exercise personal jurisdiction over its officials than either an international body or an UNTAET-organised tribunal.[4] It is also possible to view the Secretary-General's position, however, as reflecting the international community's more profound conservativeness of approach in dealing with intervention in 'human rights' matters. In contrast to the international community's preparedness to establish bodies in the aftermath of war to consider breaches of 'humanitarian law',[5] the international community has

---

[3] The UN Commission of Inquiry's report was made public by the Secretary-General on 31 January 2000. For the full text seethe UN website (UNCI). The author has not had access to the text of the KPP-HAM report, but its findings have been widely reported in the media.

[4] The possibility of the establishment of an UNTAET organised tribunal has not been widely canvassed. However, there are certainly precedents for a UN transitional authority to undertake the investigations and prosecutions of human rights abuses as the power in authority in a territory: note for example, the establishment of the Special Prosecutor's Office in Cambodia during the UNTAC period of administration. In such a case, the body would be regarded as 'local' rather than 'international' in character.

[5] As discussed below, not all humanitarian norms apply only in times of war. In particular, crimes against humanity are recognised as a category of humanitarian law, but can be committed in times of peace or war.

tended to await consent from the sovereign state before taking international action against perpetrators of abuse.

For non-lawyers, the distinction between the international community establishing a war crimes tribunal to deal with breaches of humanitarian law (such as those established in Rwanda and Yugoslavia[6]) and its establishing an international human rights tribunal might seem elusive. Whether a group of persons is slaughtered during a period of war or peace does not seem a particularly compelling reason to make a distinction in terms of mechanisms for accountability. Yet, the centrality of notions of state sovereignty and non-interference in matters of 'domestic jurisdiction' has impeded the development of non-consent based international systems of accountability for human rights abuses in a way that has not hindered war crimes tribunals. In such circumstances, it is tempting to support the establishment of an international war crimes tribunal for East Timor. What this chapter attempts to demonstrate, however, is that a war crimes tribunal would not have the jurisdiction necessary to consider the range of abuses that have occurred within East Timor without distortion of the historical experience of East Timor. It thus appears preferable, if the international community is to establish a body, for its mandate to include both humanitarian and human rights norms.

Ultimately, the question of what body is set up to investigate the atrocities in East Timor should be informed by the desires of the East Timorese through their representatives. Ideally, it is a decision which should be made on a tripartite basis—between East Timor, Indonesia and the United Nations. Given the separation of East Timor and Indonesia, it cannot be accepted that the Indonesian Government will necessarily adopt a position in the best long term interests of both it and East Timor. Thus the debate and further consultation must continue. Hopefully, this chapter assists the debate by placing the issues within their international law framework: highlighting some of the challenges facing proponents of an international human rights tribunal and suggesting some strategies for overcoming the jurisdictional hurdles.

The lead up to the Popular Consultation

It is impossible to consider recent events in East Timor in isolation. East Timor's troubled history has included conflict with Indonesia ever since

---

[6] The International Tribunal for the Prosecution of Persons Responsible for Serious Violations of International Humanitarian Law in the Territory of the Former Yugoslavia (ICTY) was established by Security Council Resolution 808 (1993). The International Tribunal for the Prosecution of Persons Responsible for Serious Violations of International Humanitarian Law in the Territory of Rwanda and Rwandan Citizens responsible for Such Violations Committed in the Territory of Neighbouring States (ICTR) was established by UN Doc S/RES/955 (1994)

Indonesia's invasion of East Timor in late 1975. To briefly recap on East Timor's history, East Timor became a Portuguese colony in the 16th century. In 1960 it was listed as a non-self-governing territory under Chapter XI of the UN Charter, with Portugal recognised as the administering power. This categorisation was a clear indication that the international community recognised the right of the peoples of East Timor's to self-determination. The 'right to self-determination' recognised in the UN Charter (Article 1[2]) and in various General Assembly declarations[7] was given its most expansive articulation in the international human rights covenants. Article 1 of the International Covenant on Civil and Political Rights, for example, proclaims:

1. All peoples have the right of self-determination. By virtue of that right they freely determine their political status and freely pursue their economic, social and cultural development.

2. All peoples may, for their own ends, freely dispose of their natural wealth and resources without prejudice to any obligations arising out of international economic co-operation, based upon the principle of mutual benefit, and international law. In no case may a people be deprived of its own means of subsistence.[8]

Whilst the East Timorese, by virtue of this right, were not compelled to choose independence and the creation of a new state rather than integration or association with another state, it was and remained a right of the East Timorese people.

Although Portugal initially resisted the characterisation of East Timor as a non-self-governing territory, after a change of government in Portugal in 1974 a change in East Timor policy was announced. In July 1975, the Portuguese Parliament enacted a law stipulating that the political future of East Timor would be determined in accordance with the wishes of the East Timorese, after free elections (Chinkin 1992; Delaney and Langford 1996). During 1975, however, Portugal admitted its inability to maintain control in East Timor in the face of armed conflict between Fretlin (who later proclaimed the independence of East Timor and their status as the provisional government) and groups whose preference was for integration with Indonesia. In August 1975, Portugal withdrew to Atauro Island. Indonesia invaded East Timor on 7

---

[7] Declaration on the Granting of Independence to Colonial Countries and Peoples, UN Doc GAOR 1514 (XV) 1960, Declaration on Principles of International Law Concerning Friendly Relations and Cooperation Among States in Accordance with the Charter of the United Nations, UN Doc GAOR 2625 (XXV) 1970.

[8] The right of self-determination has been recognised by the International Court of Justice as a peremptory norm of international law (that is, an obligation that cannot be derogated from by any nation) (see *Advisory Opinion on Namibia* [1971] ICJ at 31 quoted in *Advisory Opinion on Western Sahara* [1975] ICJ at 31-5; Chen 1976).

December 1975 and proceeded to annex East Timor. The actions of Indonesia met with an immediate condemnatory reaction from the international community—with resolutions of the Security Council and the General Assembly deploring the use of force and calling upon Indonesia to permit the East Timorese to exercise their right of self-determination in peace.[9]

Whilst recognising that the East Timorese had a 'right to self-determination', Indonesia justified its use of force in 1975 as being necessary to preserve regional stability. It interpreted the results of voting in 1976 by the East Timor Regional Popular Assembly as indicative that the East Timorese exercised their right of self-determination in favour of integration with Indonesia. The (appointed) Regional Popular Assembly established in East Timor did pass a resolution in favour of integration with East Timor. However, as later commentators such as Cassese (1995:224-6) and Pomerance (1982) have emphasised, the acceptance of Indonesian authority in 1976 bore none of the usual hallmarks of 'free and genuine expression' of the East Timorese political will.[10] Firstly, the majority of East Timorese were not involved in the choice made since the Assembly was not democratically chosen nor did it seek to ascertain the views of East Timorese in a democratic referendum.[11] Secondly, the election for integration was made at a time when the Indonesian military force was still overwhelmingly present—thus undermining the capacity for political leaders, let alone the East Timorese people, to make a free and voluntary choice. Certainly, the United Nations did not interpret the events of 1976 as representing an act of self-determination, with their disapproval being explicit in resolutions and implicit in turning down invitations to visit East Timor to witness the process.[12]

Despite ongoing opposition from within East Timor, in particular from the Falantil (the armed independence movement) and trenchant criticism by Portugal and human rights advocates, Indonesia maintained that it had rightful authority over East Timor until 29 October 1999. The consistency with which Indonesia defended its position and challenged the right of the international community to interfere in what it regarded as an issue of 'national

---

[9] UN Docs GAOR 3485 (XXX), 1975; S/RES/ 384 (1975); S/RES/389 (1976)

[10] This was the language used by the ICJ to describe an exercise of the right to self determination in *Advisory Opinion on Western Sahara*.

[11] Pomerance (1982) has outlined the non-democratic nature of the process established in East Timor: whilst Act No 1/AD 1976 recognised the right of self-determination according to the principles of democracy as inalienable and indisputable (Article 1), this right was said to be implemented in accordance with the traditions of the people of East Timor. This permitted rejection of a general rule of one vote per person (see Report of the Secretary-General, S/121066, June 1976, appendix; Pomerance 1982:99 fn 193).

[12] The UN Special Committee of 24 and the President of the Security Council rejected invitations to visit missions of East Timor (Pomerance 1982:101).

sovereignty' even led some international law commentators to doubt whether the East Timorese would be regarded as having an ongoing right to 'external' self-determination (ie secession).[13] East Timor was frequently regarded as one of the 'forgotten' human rights issues (See for instance, Simpson 1997:833). However, with the ascension to power of President Habibie and his support for a referendum to determine the future of East Timor, the prospects for an East Timorese exercise of the right of self-determination suddenly improved. As a result of negotiations with Portugal and the United Nations, a process was agreed upon to lead up to a 'Popular Consultation' with the people of East Timor as to whether they desired an 'autonomy' proposal within Indonesia—or conversely, independence. On 30 August 1999, the East Timorese overwhelmingly voted (78.5%) for independence from Indonesia.

Reported human rights abuses in the period surrounding the Popular Consultation

The reports of the UN and Indonesian Commission of Inquiries confirm widespread commission of atrocities in the lead up to and the wake of the Popular Consultation. No doubt, as investigations continue there will be fuller accounts of the events that occurred. Rather than their being the isolated acts of a 'splinter group' in East Timor, Indonesia and the UN have accepted that there the Indonesian military force collaborated, if not organised, the activities committed by pro-Jakarta militia.[14] Even had the military merely failed to protect East Timorese, there would be concern given that the military had a responsibility under the 5 May Agreement to ensure the security of participants in the Popular Consultation process. However, the evidence that members of the TNI actively participated in or controlled activities of the militia is mounting. From information gathered by UN-accredited observers during the Popular Consultation (including the author and her AETIVP colleagues[15]) and the testimony provided to the UN Commission of Inquiry, the human rights abuses reported fall into the following general categories:

- Threats to individuals (verbal threats of personal and property damage, shooting of guns to intimidate) should they vote in favour of independence;

---

[13] See Cassese's lamentations about international law commentaries (1995:206).

[14] The connection between militia activity and TNI command was commented on by the UN High Commissioner for Human Rights before the UN Commission of Inquiry was established (see for instance, Robinson 1999). The UN Commission of Inquiry and the KPP-HAM confirm this connection.

[15] The Australian East Timor International Volunteers Project was organised by a coalition of Australian NGOs to provide international observers for the Popular Consultation. Observers reported incidents representing breaches of the Code of Conduct for Participants in the Process. The Report of Incidents (to be published) is on file with the author.

- Burning of houses and institutions;
- Kidnapping of individuals, in particular those associated with the pro-independence movement such as CNRT officials and students;
- Sexual assaults of women;
- Injuring and killing of individuals, in particular those associated with the popular consultation process and those perceived as pro-independence;
- Forced transportation of people within East Timor and to West Timor;[16]
- Establishment of roadblocks to limit people's movements in East Timor;
- Blocking of food, water and medical supplies to displaced persons in temporary camps in East Timor.
- Sieges.

Each of these categories of incident raises significant human rights issues. If one were to examine them in the light of guarantees within the 'International Bill of Rights' (that is, the Universal Declaration of Human Rights, the International Covenant on Civil and Political Rights and the International Covenant on Economic, Social and Cultural Rights) one would note breaches of, *inter alia*, the right to life (Article 6, ICCPR), the right to liberty and security of person (Article 9 ICCPR), the right to freedom of movement (Article 12 ICCPR), the right not to be arbitrarily deprived of property (Article 17, UDHR), the right not to be subjected to arbitrary or unlawful interference with one's privacy, family, home or correspondence (Article 17 ICCPR), the right to hold opinions (Article 19 ICCPR) and to freedom of expression (Article 19(2) ICCPR), the right to equality before the law (Article 26 ICCPR), the right to an adequate standard of living (Article 11 ICESCR) and the right not to be tortured (Article 7 ICCPR). In the circumstances of the disrupted lives of so many East Timorese men, women and children, it is also possible to perceive consequential breaches of the right to work (Article 6 ICESCR), the right to education (Article 13 ICESCR) and the right to health (Article 12 ICESCR). Given that these incidents were explicitly designed to influence votes in the Popular Consultation , and later as a reprisal for the vote, effectively delaying the transition of East Timor to an independent state, the activities more broadly represent a breach of the East Timorese right to self-determination (Article 1 ICCPR, ICESCR). If, as present indications suggest, the violations can be demonstrated to have occurred on a widespread and/or systematic basis, the incidents also constitute 'crimes against humanity' for which international criminal responsibility

---

[16] The UN Commission of Inquiry found that about 200,000 people were moved from East Timor to West Timor (para 93). As at the time of writing this article, approximately 110,000 East Timorese were reported to still be in West Timor.

attaches to the direct and indirect perpetrators. Depending on the view taken of the nature of the background conflict in East Timor, the incidents might also represent 'war crimes'.[17]

Even if the direct perpetrators of the abuses were 'private' militia members, this fact alone does not shield the Indonesian military or the Indonesian State[18] from being ascribed responsibility under international law. The *ad hoc* International Criminal Tribunal for the former Yugoslavia (the ICTY) has recently considered the tests for imputing responsibility to public officials for *inter alia* private individuals in the *Tadic* case. The ICTY confirmed that the test is whether the public official exercises 'overall control' over the actions of individuals and that when dealing with paramilitary groups, there would be a need to demonstrate such control through the equipping and financing of operations together with the coordination and/or assistance with the general planning of the activities. In reaching the conclusion in the Tadic decision (*Prosecutor v Tadic*, 15 July 1999, ICTY Appeals Chamber) that the armed forces of the Republika Srpksa could be regarded as acting within the overall control of and on behalf of the Yugoslav Government, the ICTY followed the general trend of other international tribunals who have looked behind formal demarcations of government/non government personnel to hold responsible those in positions of power. In addition to being potentially responsible for the actions of the militia, the Indonesian military's direct actions might also be made the subject of investigation—insofar as they positively omitted to provide sufficient protection for the East Timorese people and so contributed to the atrocities.[19] Provided officials of Indonesia bear responsibility for the atrocities, the State of Indonesia will itself also be regarded as responsible.[20] Such responsibility

---

[17] The difficulties in classifying incidents as 'war crimes' are discussed later in this chapter.

[18] Individuals and the State may, however, be treated differently in terms of consequences—whether civil or criminal for breaches of international law—this will be dealt with more fully in the latter section of this chapter.

[19] See for instance the *Teheran Hostages Case*, [Case Concerning US Diplomatic and Consular Staff in Teheran (USA v Iran) 1988] ICJ Rep 3, in which Iran was regarded by the International Court of Justice as bearing some responsibility for the ongoing siege, given their *ex post facto* endorsement of the actions of the direct perpetrators and their failure to provide the level of protection they were required to give pursuant to their treaty obligations. Note too that in the *Rodriguez-Velasquez* case (Inter-Am Ct Human Rights (Ser C), No 4 P174 1988), the Inter American Court of Human Rights held the Honduras Government responsible for the killing of a man by terrorists where the Government not only knew of the activities of the terrorist groups but actively encouraged them. In *Yeager v Iran* (1987), 17 Iran-USCTR 92, the Iran–US Claims Tribunal held Iran responsible for the acts of 'revolutionary guards' who acted as local security forces in the immediate aftermath of the revolution, despite their lack of formal recognition under Iranian law and despite their lack of formal status.

[20] States are responsible for the acts of their organs, agents and officials: *Nicaragua (Merits)* case 1986 ICJ Rep 4 even where such organs, agents or officials exceed their competence or

would be the case notwithstanding arguments that 'rogue' members of the military acted against any political commands, ie were acting outside their actual authority.[21]

In speaking of breaches of human rights and humanitarian norms, we are discussing breaches of international law—for which the international community ascribes responsibility and consequences. Behind the promptness with which NGOs, UN personnel, individual government spokespersons and East Timorese leaders called for a 'War Crimes Tribunal' is the expectation that perpetrators of gross abuses will be held individually accountable by the international community; that their behaviour offends not simply the individual victim but the international community. International bodies are seen as important for affirming and upholding the 'rule of international law', for providing adjudication in a manner less influenced by local politics or prejudices and for facilitating the dispensation of impartial, informed justice.[22] Gaining international consensus on the desirability of the establishment of an international body is complicated by perceptions not only of whether 'local remedies' are more effective, cathartic, empowering and cost-effective, but whether the international role has a proper role in relation to the specific events which have taken place. Given that the events in East Timor were a direct challenge to the process organised by the Security Council, it may be that members of the international community are prepared to accept responsibility for ensuring redress of the violations. However, it will not be surprising if opponents of international action call upon 'domestic jurisdiction' arguments to undermine the basis for an international body.

Basis for United Nations establishment of an international body and its limitations

As was explicit in the debates within the Commission on Human Rights on the establishment of the UN Commission of Inquiry, the issue that dogs the establishment of international accountability bodies[23] is the extent to which the establishment of such a body constitutes an interference with the 'national

---

contravene instructions (see too Article 10 of the ILC Draft Articles on State Responsibility, GAOR 51st Session, Supp 10, 125).

[21] In the *Youman's claim* case (US v Mexico) (1926) 4 RIAA 110, for example, Mexico was held liable for the death of some Americans in circumstances where soldiers who were sent to quell a riot outside the house of the US citizens in fact joined in the riot and fired into the house.

[22] For a powerful analysis of these justifications, see Alvarez (1999:377).

[23] Throughout this article, the term acccountability is used in its broadest sense—in terms of holding responsible those persons and institutions responsible for human rights abuses. Others have used the term in a more limited fashion to refer to notions of individual responsibility alone (see Ratner 1999).

sovereignty' Indonesia. Whilst the UN Charter clearly recognises the right of Member States to exercise without interference 'domestic jurisdiction',[24] this right of Member States would not seem to prevent the establishment of an international body. Firstly, it is possible to argue that gross human rights and humanitarian abuses fall outside the realm of 'domestic jurisdiction'. The ICTR and ICTY, for instance, have been granted jurisdiction over crimes such as systematic murders and rapes which represent breaches of both international humanitarian and human rights laws. Greater challenges could be expected in relation to human rights norms. Under existing human rights treaty law, acceptance of the right of international committees to hear the complaints of individuals remains a matter of state consent. The more common method of establishing jurisdiction is reliance upon the UN's exceptional powers under Chapter VII of the UN Charter. Once the Security Council has determined that a threat to international peace and security exists under Chapter VII, it has clear power to take action to combat the threat to international peace, even where such action would normally constitute an interference with domestic sovereignty. This power, for instance, was used in relation to the setting up of tribunals in Yugoslavia and Rwanda and could be used in East Timor given that the Security Council has already determined that a threat to the peace existed in East Timor.[25] Whether the Security Council accedes to demands to create an international body is likely to be determined by political factors rather than legal ones; suffice it to say that there are sufficient precedents for Security Council action in this respect.

At the same time, the source of the power to create the international body serves as a limitation on the form of international body that can be created. Firstly, the Security Council's powers relate to the maintenance of peace rather than a more general function of 'maintaining the rule of law' or 'punishing perpetrators of human rights abuses'. In practice in Rwanda and Yugoslavia this has not proved a particularly limiting factor in establishing bodies since the Security Council has concluded that infringement of the rule of (international) law is a factor which contributes to a threat to the peace. Secondly, the Security Council has no power to 'legislate' for the international community. Any body it establishes can only deal with breaches of international law norms that are accepted as binding on the relevant states. Furthermore, the body can only take the sort of civil or criminal action in

---

[24] Article 2(7) of the UN Charter states: 'Nothing contained in the present Charter shall authorize the United Nations to intervene in matters which are essentially within the domestic jurisdiction of any State or shall require the Members to submit such matters to settlement under the present Charter; but this principle shall not prejudice the application of enforcement measures under Chapter VII'.

[25] UN Doc S/RES/1264 (1999).

relation to those breaches that are accepted in international law as applying to those norms. Hence, for instance the emphasis in the Secretary-General's Report concerning the proposed statute for the ICTY that the body would be limited to applying international humanitarian law.[26] Of particular sensitivity in the criminal law (given the expectation that criminal laws will not be applied retrospectively), it applies with equal force to the field of international 'civil' law. A state could not be held to have breached international law and responsible to pay reparations according to a rule of international law developed after the commission of the activity. Thus, in considering the 'substantive law' applied (ie prohibitions of conduct) and the means of accountability/redress (whether they be criminal sanctions or civil compensation), the provisions of the document giving power to an international body must reflect rather than transcend binding international law as of the date of the activity.

Breadth of an international tribunal's jurisdiction

As was noted above, the initial calls from supporters of international action was for the establishment of an international war crimes tribunal, that is a body to consider breaches of international humanitarian law. It was also the focal point of the UN Commission of Inquiry's mandate. With the temporal proximity of the tribunals for Yugoslavia and Rwanda and the General Assembly's adoption of the Statute for the International Criminal Court,[27] this call is not surprising. It also reflects the dominant view that international criminal law offers a superior method of ensuring accountability than traditional state (civil) responsibility on the basis that prosecuting the individuals responsible leads to tangible outcomes and highlights the seriousness of the events by removing them from the ordinary course of state-to-state discourse. Yet, the movement of the discourse towards calls for an International Human Rights Tribunal, though more ambitious, are to be welcomed. The historic position of East Timor and the seemingly 'unilateral nature' of the atrocities that occurred in 1999 highlight the inappropriateness of merely cloning the jurisdiction given to the ICTR and ICTY. Instead, any international body established should be given a broader mandate to investigate human rights and humanitarian violations and consider both criminal and civil penalties.

---

[26] UN Doc S/25704 para 29.

[27] In 1998, the Rome Statute of the International Criminal Court was finalised and opened for signature and ratification. It will not come into force until 60 States ratify it (with only 6 ratifications to date). Furthermore, the ICC will not have retrospective jurisdiction, meaning that it will not in the future be able to look at recent events in East Timor.

Difficulties in the solitary application of international humanitarian law norms to the case of East Timor.

Under both the ICTR and ICTY statutes, the international bodies established have jurisdiction over four primary areas: grave breaches of the Geneva Conventions, breaches of the laws and customs of war, genocide and crimes against humanity. Although the latter two categories of international humanitarian law could be applied in the context of East Timor without conceptual difficulties, application of those offences relating to 'war crimes' are somewhat more problematic, primarily because they are predicated upon the existence of either an international or non-international (civil) armed conflict.

Armed conflict—specific crimes

Despite the fact that many of the abuses which took place in East Timor represent crimes of a similar nature to those prohibited by the Geneva Conventions and the laws and customs of war, many would not fall within these humanitarian prohibitions if they occurred outside the context of war. The Geneva Convention prohibitions are restricted to times of international armed conflict, whilst the 'laws and customs of war' are said to apply in times of international and non-international armed conflict. In relation to East Timor, it is not self-evident that there was an 'armed conflict' as of August 1999, or if there was, whether it would be classified as 'international' or 'non-international'.

For an 'armed conflict' to exist, there needs to be a resort to armed forces between states, protracted armed violence between governmental authorities and organised armed groups or such violence between armed groups within the state.[28] It is apparent in such a definition that the use of arms has to be mutual. Depending upon what timeframe is used by the international body, it may be difficult to establish that an armed conflict was occurring in East Timor at or around the time of the 'Popular Consultation' atrocities. To date, the evidence that has emerged supports the view that the violence was unilateral—that is, that militia groups used violence against unarmed East Timorese. Whilst the independence movement in East Timor certainly has an armed element, the Falantil, most of the accounts indicate that by the time of the Popular Consultation the Falantil had ceased armed activities such that the violence around the time of the vote could not be classed as 'armed conflict'. If, however, a longer term perspective was adopted that located the current

---

[28] See *Prosecutor v Tadic*, 2 October 1995, 35 ILM 32, para 70. Note that a number of commentators have recognised the need to develop humanitarian norms which apply in peace and war (see for instance Meron, 1983; Petrasek 1998).

violence within the broader context of the recent history of East Timor, it is possible that an international body could come to the conclusion that an armed conflict was occurring in East Timor.

There would remain a further controversy over whether any such armed conflict would be properly classified as 'international' or 'civil'. This in turn relates to the question of whether Indonesia would be regarded as a 'foreign country' *vis-à-vis* East Timor or the sovereign authority of East Timor. Despite Indonesia's effective control of East Timor since 1976, there has never been an unambiguous international acceptance of Indonesia's sovereignty over East Timor. On the one hand there has been the view expressed that despite the manner in which Indonesia gained control of East Timor, a process of historical consolidation confirmed Indonesian control over East Timor. Support for this view has relied on analogies with the international community's acceptance of India's control over Goa (which it invaded in 1961) or Indonesia's control over West Papua. Advocates of this view have also pointed to the level of acquiescence by members of the international community concerning Indonesia's control over East Timor and the cessation of condemnatory resolutions in the General Assembly in 1982 (see Pomerance1982:20). The United Nations' acceptance that Indonesia was the appropriate state to provide the security services for the Popular Consultation and that its consent was sought to the intervention of a peace-keeping or peace-enforcement force might also be used in support of this view.

The major alternate argument is that Indonesia's illegal use of force and repression of a people's right to self-determination served as a permanent bar to Indonesia's ever gaining sovereignty over East Timor and that sovereignty remained with Portugal up until the Popular Consultation and its aftermath. Advocates of this view have noted that East Timor's listing as a non-self-governing territory under the administration of Portugal was continuous and that Portugal maintained its right of proper administration over East Timor both in its general dealings with the United Nations[29] and in taking action against countries who have failed to recognise its sovereignty—eg its action against Australia before the International Court of Justice.[30] Furthermore, they

---

[29] Portugal, for instance, in reporting to the Human Rights Committee has maintained its ongoing responsibility for the human rights of East Timorese while indicating regret that it has not been able to exercise control over East Timor: for the details of Portugal's second periodic report to the Human Rights Committee (see Cassese 1995:225).

[30] Portugal in 1991 instituted action against Australia before the International Court of Justice claiming that Australia's entry into the Timor Gap Treaty with Indonesia breached Portugal's rights in relation to East Timor and the East Timorese right to self-determination. A majority of the International Court of Justice, whilst affirming the East Timorese right to self-determination, decided that they were unable to consider the merits of the case given that

have pointed to the very limited recognition of Indonesia's sovereignty over East Timor by other countries.[31] The strength of any implication from Indonesia's role as the security force for the Popular Consultation process is discounted given that the United Nations involved both Portugal and Indonesia in the negotiations leading up to the 5 May Agreement.

A further possible argument which might be raised if this jurisdictional issue arose was that Indonesia was indeed a 'foreign country' *vis-à-vis* East Timor as sovereignty resided in the East Timorese people. Although an attractive argument for East Timorese who wish to characterise Indonesia's military activity as the use of force against a sovereign people, it seems unlikely that East Timor would be regarded as a separate state prior to the Popular Consultation, given the lack of a government in effective control of the territory.[32]

Although the International Court of Justice was asked in part to determine the issue of Portugal versus Indonesian sovereignty of East Timor in the *Timor Gap* case, its refusal to do so leaves the international community without an 'agreed position' on whether any conflict between Indonesia and East Timorese would be characterised as 'civil' or 'international' conflict. In the light of this uncertainty, and with the lack of clarity concerning whether an 'armed conflict' was in fact in existence as of the date of the Popular Consultation, primary reliance on 'war crimes' offences would seem an unreliable method of providing accountability for the atrocities that have occurred.

Indonesia was not a party to the proceedings: *Portugal v Australia* (Timor Gap case) (1995) ICJ Rep 90.

[31] For a good analysis of the reactions of States to Indonesian authority over East Timor, see Cassese(1995:226). Australia is the only country to have unequivocally recognised Indonesia's sovereignty over East Timor (in 1979). India and the United States have indicated some level of recognition whilst others have entered into treaties with Indonesia that by virtue of their territorial clause, extend to East Timor. This, with the speeches given by some delegations in explaining votes in the General Assembly, has been used by Australia to respond to attacks on Australia's isolated stance (see Senator Evans, *Senate Debates* 1994:2958).

[32] Under Article 1 of the Montevideo Convention on the Rights and Duties of States 1933, the four traditional criteria for recognition of Statehood are a defined territory, a permanent population, a government in control of the territory and the capacity to enter into relations with other countries. More recently these criteria have been augmented by notions of consistency with the right of self-determination, constitutional government, and respect for human rights—particularly the right of minorities, as was evidenced in the European Union Guidelines on Recognition of New States in Eastern Europe and the USSR (1992).

Non-armed conflict dependent norms— genocide and crimes against humanity)

More promising would appear to be use of norms against 'genocide' and 'crimes against humanity', though even these norms will not serve to provide the international body with jurisdiction over the range of human rights abuses committed in East Timor. Both 'genocide' and 'crimes against humanity' are freestanding humanitarian norms—they can be committed outside the context of armed conflict. Yet the definitions remain stringent. For genocide to exist, one not only needs to show the primary destructive act (such as killing members of a group, causing serious bodily or mental harm to the group[33]) but also that the act was motivated by an intention to destroy in whole or in part 'a national, ethnical, racial or religious group'. If evidence displays the intention to destroy the East Timorese as such, the prospects of a successful genocide case are reasonable. However, should the evidence reflect a political motive alone (eg an intention of killing all independence supporters), the destructive acts would fall outside the scope of 'genocide'. 'Crimes against humanity' have the benefit of including acts perpetrated for a political motive. As defined in Article 3 of the Statute of the ICTR, 'crimes against humanity' include murder, extermination, enslavement, deportation, imprisonment, torture, rape, persecutions on political, racial and religious grounds, and 'other inhumane acts' when committed as part of a widespread or systematic attack against any civilian population.[34] The inclusion of the terms 'persecution' and 'other inhumane acts' is also advantageous in that it opens the way for consideration of a wider range of acts—including for example, the deprivation of basic supplies to displaced persons.[35] Whether it would extend as far as crimes against property (eg burning villages or community infrastructure) is unclear. The limitation with 'crimes against humanity' is that they must be demonstrably part of a 'widespread or systematic attack'. Thus, if the evidence established that certain forms of activity were carried out on a sporadic basis (eg killings or rapes), they may not constitute crimes against humanity despite being serious violations of rights.

---

[33]The various 'primary' acts mentioned in the definition of genocide are: killing members of the group; causing serious bodily or mental harm to members of the group; deliberately inflicting on the group conditions of life calculated to bring about its physical destruction in whole or in part; imposing measures intended to prevent births within the group and forcibly transferring children of the group to another group.

[34] Note that members of the Falantil armed resistance movement may not constitute civilians.

[35] In the trial chamber decision of *Prosecutor v Tadic*, the court considered that persecution might include deprivation of food supply or paid employment: Judgment of 7 May 1997, at para 703–7.

In light of these limitations of international humanitarian law in the circumstances of East Timor, any international body should be given jurisdiction in relation to violations of human rights: norms which apply in times of peace and war. Furthermore, using human rights norms to broaden the jurisdiction of the body has the advantage of avoiding the question of Indonesia's status in relation to East Timor since states (and thus public officials and the military) have a responsibility for respecting the rights of all those subject to the state's jurisdiction[36].

Additional human rights bases

If an international body were to be established by the Security Council using its Chapter VII, it would be necessary for the body to be able to justify its mandate according to binding international norms. Unfortunately, there has been far less consideration of the extent to which human rights guarantees[37] and international individual/state responsibility[38] for abuses form part of binding international law (outside a specific treaty context) than in relation to humanitarian law.

In a chapter of this length it is not possible to traverse all available evidence to ascertain which of the norms from the International Bill of Rights would meet the threshold test for inclusion in the mandate of an international body. However, three norms look particularly promising for further consideration insofar as there would be (comparatively) little debate about their status as norms of customary international law.[39] These three norms are: the right of self-determination, the prohibition on torture and the prohibition on systematic or mass violations of human rights.

1. The right of self-determination has been recognised as both a peremptory norm of international law (thus is non-derogable) and an obligation owed to the entire international community (an obligation *erga omnes*) by the

---

[36] Note for instance, Article 2 of the ICCPR, which states that 'Each State Party to the present Covenant undertakes to respect and to ensure to all individuals within its territory and subject to its jurisdiction the rights recognized in the present Covenant...'. Although there is an argument that it is only individuals both within a State's territory and subject to its jurisdiction who are covered by a State's obligation, this would seem to be inconsistent with the 'universalist' nature of human rights recognised elsewhere—see for instance the Preamble to the Universal Declaration of Human Rights.

[37] Notable exceptions are Meron (1989); Symposium (1995).

[38] The issue of the lack of accountability options (in terms of individual criminality norms) for human rights breaches has generated much writing (see for example Morris 1996; Ratner 1998; Bassiouni 1996; Joyner 1998).

[39] Choosing three norms is a modest act given the number of human rights guarantees that individually would not be recognised in this list. However, in the opinion of the author, these norms would provide a good 'hook' for consideration of a range of human rights issues and would enable more focussed research by any commission of experts.

International Court of Justice (ICJ 1971:31; *Portugal v Australia* [Timor Gap] case: 1995 ICJ Rep 90 at para 29).

2. Prohibition on torture: In addition to being the subject of a specific, widely ratified treaty (the Convention against Torture and other Cruel, Inhuman and Degrading Treatment 1984—a treaty that Indonesia has ratified), it was regarded by the House of Lords in the Pinochet case as a part of customary international law and an international crime that attracted universal jurisdiction.[40] It has also been recognised as part of customary international law in the Restatement of Foreign Relations Law of the United States (s 702).[41]

3. Systematic or mass violations of human rights: This category of human rights is drawn from the 1991 ILC Draft of Crimes Against the Peace and Security of Mankind and has also been recognised as part of customary international law in the Restatement of Foreign Relations Law of the United States. In most senses it is the same as the category of 'crimes against humanity', though it is not qualified by application to civilian persons alone. What would particularly useful is an explicit cross-reference to human rights guarantees within the international bill of rights so that any international body could consider breaches of economic and social rights, which often suffer neglect from international scrutiny. If further evidence of the status of this norm is required (ie outside the evidence for the category of 'crimes against humanity'), recourse could be had to consideration of the number of ratifications of the specialised international human rights covenants, the recognition of human rights norms in the UN Charter (Article 55, 56) and the way in which human rights have been recognised in humanitarian intervention pronouncements.[42]

---

[40] *R v Bow Street Magistrate; ex p Pinochet* [1999] 2 WLR 827 (HL); Bradley and Goldsmith 1999; see too *Filartiga v Pena-Irala* 630 F 2d (1980); (1980) 19 ILM 966. Note though the alternative view that because torture is so widely practised, it cannot be established that there is sufficient State practice to support a prohibition on torture (see for instance Sunga 1992).

[41] Section 702 of the Restatement states: 'A State violates international law if, as a matter of State policy, it practices, encourages or condones (a) genocide, (b) slavery or slave trade, (c) the murder or causing the disappearance of individuals, (d) torture or other cruel, inhuman or degrading treatment or punishment, (e) prolonged arbitrary detention, (f) systematic racial discrimination, or (g) consistent patterns of gross violations of internationally recognized human rights'.

[42] The conclusion that these norms form part of customary international law if the UN resolutions and practice were accepted as evidence of State practice as well as opinio juris: for commentary upon this approach (Simma and Alston 1992; Lillich 1995–6).

The usual criticism made of the application of international human rights law to internal disturbances is that too many derogations are permitted in times of war or emergency.[43] Applying this argument to avoid inclusion of a 'human rights' mandate for the international body would seem to overstate and distort the objection. Firstly, a number of the relevant rights recognised in international human rights law are not subject to derogation (such as the right to life, the prohibition on torture, the prohibition on slavery, the prohibition on retrospective criminal laws and the right to recognition before the law). Secondly, it is questionable whether an alleged state/military inspired spate of violence would constitute a 'state of emergency' such as to bring into play the realm of 'permissible derogations'. Thirdly, derogations are only possible 'to the extent strictly required by the exigencies of the situation': whilst freedom of movement may be a 'derogable right', restricting persons' freedom of movement through forcible transfers or roadblocks as in East Timor would not seem to fulfil a test of necessity, even allowing a state a 'margin of appreciation'.

It would also be necessary to establish that international law attaches consequences to the breaches of human rights norms, of a type which can be encapsulated in criminal and civil functions for the tribunal. From general international law principles, a state is responsible for its international law wrongs.[44] Traditionally this has been in the context of one state being responsible to another state for such wrongs, rather than a state being 'accountable' to make reparations to individuals subject to its jurisdiction. More recently, however, there has been greater consideration of the issue of a state's responsibility to make reparations for human rights violations within its own territory.[45] Certainly the mechanisms incorporated within the

---

[43] Article 4 of the ICCPR, for instance states: 'In time of public emergency which threatens the life of the nation and the existence of which is officially proclaimed, the States Parties to the present Covenant may take measures derogating from their obligations under the present Covenant to the extent strictly required by the exigencies of the situation, provided that such measures are not inconsistent with their other obligations under international law and do not involve discrimination solely on the ground of race, colour, sex, language, religion or social origin.'

[44] The Permanent Court in the *Chorzow Factory* case stated 'It is a principle of international law and even a general conception of law, that any breach of an engagement involves an obligation to make reparation': 1928 PCIJ, Ser A, no 17, 29 (see Brownlie 1991:135).

[45] A Study of the right to restitution, compensation and rehabilitation for victims of gross violations of human rights and fundamental freedoms was carried out by a Special Rapporteur of the Commission on Human Rights, Mr Theodore van Boven: UN Doc E/CN.4/Sub 2/1993/8. See too views of the Human Rights Committee in CCPR/C/55/D/563/1993, para 8(6); and the Basic Principles and Guidelines on the Right to Reparation for Victims of Gross Violations of Human Rights and Humanitarian Law, E/CN.4/Sub2/1996/17 annex. The International Bill of Rights also requires States to provide a remedy for human rights violations: Art 8, UDHR, Art 2(3) ICCPR.

international human rights treaties incorporate an underlying belief in this form of accountability (though the treaties condition the application of this principle upon state consent to the process).[46] It could be argued that despite the fact that most international bodies gain jurisdiction through 'state consent', the underlying rule is that states are responsible to make reparations to the victims of their human rights violations.[47]

In relation to the likely 'individual criminal jurisdiction' of the international body, it is certainly arguable that breaches of these human rights norms represent 'international crimes' to which individual culpability attaches. Certainly the Security Council in considering recent events in East Timor articulated a broad view of the individual criminality of human rights abuses. In its Resolution 1264 of 15 September 1999, for instance, the Security Council stressed that persons committing violations of international humanitarian and human rights laws bear individual responsibility and called upon Member States to demand that those responsible for acts of violence be brought to justice. Particularised evidence might also be offered in relation to the specific human rights norms isolated above. In relation to torture, one is encouraged by the persuasive authority of the recent *Pinochet* decision.[48] The case for criminal consequences attaching to breach of the right of self-determination could be strengthened by recourse to the inclusion of the crime of colonial/alien domination (breaching the right of self-determination) in the. ILC's Draft Code of Crimes Against the Peace and Security of Mankind.[49] In relation to the third norm listed above, that of the systematic violation of human rights, much of the evidence would be that which supported application of the 'crime against humanity' prohibition to contexts outside of armed conflict. Human rights lawyers could be called upon to compile evidence of domestic practices concerning the criminalisation of human rights abuses.

---

[46] See the Optional Protocol to the ICCPR. There are also individual complaints procedures under CAT and CERD. An optional protocol for CEDAW has also been finalised by the General Assembly.

[47] The separate issue of individual civil responsibility is not considered here. Note though Morris' (1996) argument that successor governments giving reparations in fact serves to give impunity to individual perpetrators.

[48] *Pinochet*—see above.

[49] The Human Rights Committee has determined that it has no capacity to consider breaches of this right since it is a collective rather than an individual human right: see *Mikmaq Tribal Society v Canada*, UN Doc CCPR/C/43/D205/1986. This, however, would not seem to make the right non-justiciable or be a relevant factor in considering the criminality of violations of this right.

A body with criminal and/or civil jurisdiction

Although the emphasis in much of the early debate related to ensuring individual criminal responsibility, it is important that the issue of civil (compensation) hearings should not be ignored. Whilst criminal prosecutions no doubt serve an important purpose, there is the risk in focussing upon criminal accountability alone that the responsibility of the state is minimised. Furthermore, criminal prosecutions do nothing to redress the material disadvantage of those who have suffered the human rights abuses—whether they take the form of destroyed property and livelihoods, psychological trauma, physical injury or death (Lutz 1989). In East Timor specifically it is easy to envisage the devastation for individuals, families and communities as a result of the policies undertaken—whether one is considering individuals who have been injured and will not be able to make the same level of provision to their families for physical or psychological reasons, those communities and families whose means of subsistence and means of living (in terms of housing) has been destroyed, or those individuals who will re-live the nightmare of experiencing or witnessing human rights atrocities. It is thus relevant to ask what response the international community will make to ensure that victims receive appropriate compensation.[50]

Although the situation is somewhat complicated in East Timor given that the government and state that is in the process of becoming (East Timor) will be distinct from the entity in power during the atrocities (Indonesia), targeted research needs to be undertaken on the ability of the international community to establish a body with complementary civil and criminal jurisdiction.[51] Obviously obtaining the agreement of Indonesia is desirable for pragmatic reasons—so that any judgments by an international body could be enforced. If research demonstrates the impracticality of giving the body compulsory civil jurisdiction, political pressure should be maintained for a 'political solution'—eg the granting of moneys to East Timor upon independence, which might be distributed to victims of the atrocities.

---

[50] In Chile, the United Nations provided supervision of a compensation process following the holding of the Truth Commission.

[51] I would note that the ICTR has been given limited powers to order reparations—it has the power to order the return of any property and proceeds acquired by criminal conduct, including by means of duress to their rightful owners': Article 23, Statute of the ICTR. What would seem more useful in the East Timorese conduct would be the inclusion of a general power to order compensation for those affected by the commission of the international crimes, or as result of breaches by the State of international law.

Addressing the failure to respect Security Council resolutions

Within the UN Commission of Inquiry's Report there is an appreciable emphasis on the fact that the atrocities which occurred within East Timor not only represented offences against the East Timorese people, but were contrary to Security Council directives. Repeated references can be found to Indonesia's responsibility to maintain peace and security during the Popular Consultation process.[52] Furthermore Indonesia, as with all members of the United Nations, is under a continuing obligation to follow the Security Council's Chapter VII directive to bring those responsible for acts of violence in East Timor.[53] Even if initially the United Nations defers to Indonesia's proposal to permit Indonesia to exercise primary jurisdiction over the perpetrators of abuse, the scene is set for the Security Council to take the view that it is not fulfilling its responsibilities pursuant to Resolution 1264 and to proceed with establishing an international human rights tribunal.

Conclusion

If the international community opts for the establishment of an international tribunal in relation to East Timor, considerable care will have to be taken to ensure that the mandate of the body is appropriate and duly reflects the historical experience of East Timorese. This chapter recommends that any body be given authority to look at both humanitarian and human rights abuses and possess both criminal and civil jurisdiction. Whilst current indications appear to be against the establishment of such a body, the international community needs to remain vigilant to ensure justice for the victims of the abuse.

---

[52] See for instance, UN Docs S/RES/1236 (1999), 7 May 1999; S/RES/1246 (1999), 11 June 1999

[53] UN Doc S/RES 1264 (1999), 15 September 1999 stated that the Security Council 'condemns all acts of violence in East Timor, calls for their immediate end and demands that those responsible for such acts be brought to justice'.

Big states and little secessionist movements

Gerry van Klinken[1]

On 20 August 1999, 15,000–20,000 East Timorese mountain villagers held a huge party in the Region II resistance base near Ermera. Amidst all-night dancing, lubricated with many litres of palm wine, they celebrated the anniversary of the founding of Falintil, the resistance army that had fought for them but that most of the villagers had never seen till now. Similar festivities took place in three other regions across the territory. For 24 years the world press had mocked them as a 'rag-tag rebel band'. Now they smelled victory over the army of the world's fourth largest nation.

What does the sudden independence of East Timor from Indonesia, won not just by Falintil but by a combination of globalising and localising forces, tell us about the future of the big, post-colonial state of Indonesia? For that matter, we might ask what it tells us about the future of any big post-colonial state (such as Sudan, Nigeria, Congo), or of imperial states such as the Soviet Union. Indeed, since the fall of the Berlin Wall a flood of literature has asked whether the dominance of the big modern state in general these last two centuries will turn out to have been merely a blip on the long-term pattern of a multitude of much smaller units. However, the future of Indonesia is already a big enough question for this essay.

States can be centralist or federalist, or something in between. They can also be democratic or non-democratic, or something in between. These two simple axes mark out a field upon which we can plot all the states in the world. Rudolph Rummel has shown that one corner of this field, namely the centralist, non-democratic state, is highly dangerous to its own citizens (eg Rummel 1997). The concentrated but unaccountable power that the elites of such states possess has led to death on a scale that far exceeds all the casualties of war, whether domestic or foreign, in the 20th century.

For historical reasons, Indonesia became precisely such a centralist, non-democratic state. But I will argue that East Timor 1999 is a sign that Indonesia may be about to move (or be moved by forces beyond its control) out of that dangerous corner towards a constellation of dispersed power. The move along the democratic axis has been widely discussed; the move away from centralism much less so. Our enquiry into this latter shift will be fraught with difficulties, but it should start from the realisation that the centralist, non-democratic state is failing Indonesia's people.

---

[1] Profuse thanks to Richard Tanter, Mark Selden and Steve Shalom for helpful criticism of earlier drafts.

The colonial legacy

Like all post-colonial countries, Indonesia was a state before it was a nation. On 27 December 1949, the newly ascendant Indonesian elite won full control over a state whose territory had been carved out by the imperialist Dutch in the last half of the nineteenth century. Unlike say China, Japan or Korea, which have long traditions of rule, that Indonesian state had no historical legitimation of any depth. Much as Sukarno tried to invent a legitimation for it drawn from geography, from shared hopes, or sometimes from the problematic precedent of the pre-modern trading empires of Majapahit and Sriwijaya, the Indonesian state remained uncomfortably tied to the alien project of extraction and imperial competition that gave rise to it.

Until late in the 19th century, the Netherlands Indies colonial state had been an *ad hoc* affair consisting of numerous agreements with local rulers, who retained many of their powers (Resink 1968). But by the early 20th century, those local powers had practically vanished before the omnipotence of the central bureaucratic state. With them vanished a level of political order that had to some extent shielded individual Indonesians from the influence of the central state.

Dutch colonial officials did make some efforts to establish a federal structure during the late colonial years. They often explained their efforts in the democratising language that suited the new 'ethical' policy towards the natives. But in reality they intended to seize the opportunity to extend the bureaucracy into the remotest region.[2] When the Japanese intervened in 1942, the Netherlands Indies was still a centralised, non-democratic state.

Meanwhile, most pre-independence Indonesian nationalists felt more attracted to the possibilities of centralised power than to the 'parochialism' of power in the regions. They found allies among liberal Dutch critics of colonialism, who resisted colonial federal proposals as merely a strategy to divide and rule nationwide Indonesian public opinion.

Those few Indonesians, all from outside the central island of Java, who did support federalist ideas did so in the conviction that political movements achieve their greatest power not from the 'artificial' constructs of socialism or Indonesian nationalism but from backward-looking identity markers—ethnicity, religion and tradition.

---

[2] Local municipal councils were established by a 1903 law on decentralisation, but rather than empowering local communities they became vehicles to facilitate the tasks of the central government more effectively. Similarly, the 1922 Administrative Reform Law provided for the creation of provinces, but it was backed by conservative figures mainly interested in improving government control in the regions while keeping popular demands in check.

The 1945 constitution establishes the 'unitary' nature of the Republic of Indonesia in its first clause. A late Dutch attempt to impose a federative form on the embryonic republic only made those Indonesians with the greatest say even more determined to defend the unitary form (Schiller 1955).

Nevertheless, many regional elites had supported the Dutch federal idea in 1949. Arthur Schiller even called the short-lived federal constitution 'wholly an Indonesian document' (Schiller 1955:62). Moreover, the regional revolts of 1956–57 led to a law in 1957 that granted extensive autonomy to restive regions, albeit within the context of the unitary state. An autonomy deal in 1959 did much to ameliorate demands in Aceh, and it still provides the model today for how to deal with provincial unrest. Regional autonomy, and for that matter federalism, were bold experiments. But as central power regrouped in subsequent years, the concessions were gradually withdrawn (Legge 1961).

Indonesians in the 1950s not only challenged the centralist aspect of the state they inherited from their colonial masters, but also its non-democratic aspect. The 1945 constitution had been drafted under a fascist Japanese regime experiencing its death throes, but the 1950 constitution was a liberal document that consciously aimed to move the state away from its Dutch and Japanese colonial origins. Full parliamentary accountability was its central feature. A remarkably free election was held in 1955. However, this experiment failed as well. In 1959, with approval from a military growing impatient with the slow pace of democratic negotiation, President Sukarno restored the 'revolutionary' 1945 constitution. Herbert Feith disconsolately summed up the period by entitling his classic study *The decline of constitutional democracy in Indonesia* (Feith 1962).

Making concessions to the regions was depicted in the national discourse as a regretable administrative convenience, in conflict with the centralising task of 'nation-building'. While stimulating loyalty to the new state, nation-building completed the colonial emasculation of the once independent social orders between the central state and the individual. It systematically discouraged regional languages. Throughout the archipelago it co-opted community and religious leaders for the central state. If this was true in the 1950s, it became even more so thereafter.

Late in 1965 the military began actively to seek allies for a short cut to 'stability'. From this point on, state terror took the place of debate. State-backed militias slaughtered perhaps half a million people on the grounds that the victims had 'betrayed' the state by allegedly backing a supposedly communist coup attempt on 30 September 1965. One and a half million others were arrested, tens of thousands of them with the intention that they never be released. Another 200,000 died as part of the purely imperial project of annexing East Timor. Life in the capital, meanwhile, went on as if nothing untoward had occurred.

The final proof, if more was needed, of the callous violence of which the centralist non-democratic state is capable was the expulsion from their homes by state-backed militias in September 1999 of half a million East Timorese, over half the population, because the Timorese wanted out from the state.

Such mass slaughter, imprisonment and terror ought to cast a shadow, not so much over Indonesian society for being fractious, but over the centralist, non-democratic state that is its ultimate perpetrator. It fits into a long list of horrors committed by such states in the 20th century.

The creators of Suharto's regime hoped that growth produced by a command economy would reduce the need for both debate and state terror. They were right, because it did for several decades. But when the growth suddenly plummeted below zero in early 1998, a political crisis ensued that soon brought down Suharto as well. As a political environment suddenly thawed that had been frozen for over three decades, Indonesia fell into a turmoil that remains far from resolved.

Today the country resembles the Indonesia of 1957, when disempowered regions also confronted a centralising state after a much-anticipated election. As then, so today many hope to reconstruct a democratic culture that is open to negotiation even on the possibility of radically new state arrangements. But others—including the military men who planned the scorched earth destruction of East Timor after the UN ballot—find only confirmation of their deepest fears in this talk of popular empowerment.

We should place East Timor in the context of an Indonesian state that is colonially tainted and democratically challenged, and which is now in crisis.

East Timor as a case of secession

In a moment I shall argue that East Timor gives us an 'insider' view of the Indonesian state and therefore has some characteristics of a secessionist movement. But of course legally it never belonged to Indonesia at all, and resistance is more properly described as a nationalist reaction to an illegal occupation. International law, and the United Nations consensus, understands East Timor in these 'outsider' terms, and this has formed the basis for a strong international campaign for independence. Belatedly, even governments that had welcomed the 'integration' of East Timor into Indonesia and asked the UN to recognise it too, are assuming this view.[3] No matter how belated, every

---

[3] When asked what made East Timor different from other independence movements around Indonesia, Australian Foreign Minister Alexander Downer told ABC Radio on 29 September 1999: 'Back in 1975 Indonesia invaded East Timor. The East Timorese people wanted their

government that agrees to uphold the resolutions of the UN deserves a round of applause. Indeed, the UN has been East Timor's saviour.

However, the fact that the multinational force went into East Timor only after receiving an 'invitation' from the Indonesian government reminds us of an important blind spot in the UN worldview. The organisation is predicated on the sovereignty of its member states, no matter how cruel those states may be towards their own citizens. The UN therefore (notwithstanding Chapter VII of its charter) has great difficulty tracing problems to a crisis within the state itself.

Even the decolonisation agenda, as important for the UN as it was for the League of Nations, and which benefitted East Timor because it was a European colony, is hedged about by state-centred limitations. The most important of these is the successor state principle, in which borders once established by the Western colonial powers can never be changed, no matter how reasonable the case for change.

Legally therefore, East Timor is not a case of secession, and has nothing to say about the Indonesian state because it never belonged to Indonesia. But sociologically, it in fact shares some characteristics with secessionist movements of the kind seen in several places around Indonesia (Van Klinken 1995). If East Timorese had improved their lives following the 1975 invasion then, in spite of the many dead, we may have seen the resistance decay slowly as the horrors receded into historical memory. Far from fading, however, the resistance in recent years grew ever stronger. This demonstrates that much of its energy had contemporary roots.

Prominent among the constantly-refreshed contemporary grievances channelled into the resistance movement was frustration with the (largely unplanned) inundation by aggressive small entrepreneurs from southern Sulawesi, not just in Dili but throughout East Timor. Another was the difficulty educated young East Timorese experienced gaining access to jobs in the civil service, the major employer in this impoverished territory.

---

independence. The United Nations had never acknowledged East Timor's incorporation into Indonesia. Circumstances in other parts of Indonesia are entirely different. They go back to the Dutch colonial rule and the creation of modern Indonesia out of that.' Australian recognition of integration had been emphatic and bipartisan for over 20 years. President Habibie himself told journalists that he woke up one morning and thought: 'Hey, why the hell is East Timor with us...it doesn't belong to our declared territory as of independence' (*Sydney Morning Herald* 1999).

An important reason for Indonesian military anger over Australia's leading the multinational force in East Timor is its sense of betrayal over this long-standing recognition. The pressing question in Indonesia's armed forces headquarters could well be: Which province will they target next?

One reason for the Indonesian decision to 'open up' East Timor early in 1989, for the first time since the invasion, was to attract private investors. Few came in. East Timor always remained the poorest province in Indonesia on many social indicators. Jakarta did throw bucket-loads of 'development' money at East Timor, but much of it fell into the hands of newcomer contractors, who bounced it straight back to their head offices in Surabaya and Jakarta. Oil exploration activity in the Timor Sea benefitted West Timor but not East Timor.

The Carrascalao family are substantial landowners. They have a history of collaboration with Jakarta. Mario Carrascalao was the governor between 1982 and 1992. His brother Manuel was a provincial parliamentarian. Both had assisted the Indonesian invasion force in 1975. But when both began to show increasingly open sympathies with the independence cause from about the mid-1990s, Jakarta should have seen it as a threatening omen. By 1999, with the national economy in tatters, almost no elite East Timorese still believed they could get a better deal with Indonesia.

Such grievances are not unique to East Timor. They are widely shared around the periphery of the Indonesian archipelago, where economies often have an extractive, frontier-colonial character.

Aceh at the western tip of the archipelago also has a lively secessionist movement. It is legitimated by the argument that the Dutch should not have annexed the Acehnese sultanate by their 1873 invasion, but fuelled by the economic inequalities flaunted by Mobil's gigantic liquid natural gas plant at Lhokseumawe since it opened in the 1970s (Kell 1995). At the eastern end, West Papua has a movement legitimated by complaints that the 1969 UN ballot integrating it with Indonesia was unfair, but fuelled by the way non-Papuans dominate every aspect of the economy (Osborne 1985). In both areas the military have multiplied popular anger by the brutality they practise with complete impunity.

In Riau province in Sumatra, another major oil-producing area, students have launched an entirely peaceful campaign for a vastly increased slice of the royalties (Colombijn 1999:19). Two other major arenas of conflict are not essentially secessionist, but can also be traced to failures on the part of the state. In West Kalimantan violence within society may be related to state-protected land grabs by large plantation companies (HRWA 1997). In Ambon (Maluku) it can be traced to state-protected corruption in making civil service appointments (HRWA 1999; Van Klinken 1996:15–16).

One notable feature of the 7 June 1999 election result is that the protest vote against the Suharto-era establishment party Golkar was strong in the heartlands, but that Golkar retained areas of dominance in the outer regions

(Van Klinken 1999a). This result reflected a pattern long understood by the colonial Dutch and Japanese, who often felt compelled to make political concessions to the populism of densely populated Java but were able to run an unencumbered autocratic regime in the resource-rich outer islands.

Of such considerations are 'domino theory' and 'balkanisation' fears born. They are the result of a state that concentrates unaccountable power in the hands of a privileged elite in the capital city.

National elites are part of the problem

Not only the military treat people as subjects rather than as citizens. Key non-military elites in Jakarta too illustrate the failure of the centralist, non-democratic state in the way they responded to unrest in East Timor. The most striking difference between the Indonesian Foreign Minister's and international observers' views on East Timor lies in the explanation each gave for the violence on the ground. The international community was moved by the view that the East Timorese were united in a legitimate nationalist rejection of a brutal, alien regime. Foreign Minister Ali Alatas, on the contrary, refused to dignify the East Timorese with such unity and insisted that this was a fractious society pretty evenly divided between those who favoured integration with Indonesia and those who rejected it. This distrustful image of a primitive society, where life is nasty, brutish and short, often includes a racial element too. The East Timorese resistance, Jakarta's policy makers often say, is led by a *mestizo* elite that had it good under the Portuguese, whereas indigenous Timorese felt liberated by joining Indonesia.[4]

The Jakartan view that the natives need (not empowerment but) a firm guiding hand is not directed only at East Timor. The rash of unrest around the archipelago that has accompanied the weakening of central government authority since late 1996, but especially the resurgence of regional demands following the resignation of President Suharto in May 1998, has elicited an anxious discourse of *disintegrasi* in the mainstream national discourse.

No-one has yet written a good account of this disintegration discourse. Rather than ascribe it to any failing of the state, establishment commentary takes the view (drawn from Durkheim) that collective violence is a sign of anomie, of a sickness in society's soul. Its origin is often traced to a weakening of religious faith. Other commentary ascribing it to mysterious 'provocateurs' is reminiscent of the well-known Suharto-era fear-mongering

---

[4] For example, one strain in the campaign against former Indonesian governor of East Timor Mario Carrascalao, when he declared his support for an independent East Timor early in 1999, was that he was an opportunist because his mixed blood left him without attachment to any land (*Ummat* 1999).

about 'communists'. The discourse reflects deep anxiety about the anarchic forces that lie ever dormant within society.

Another, somewhat contradictory feature of the elite analysis of social unrest is a conspiratorial aspect. Just as, under Suharto, the authorities claimed that diabolical communist elements threatened to 'infiltrate' the very organs of the state itself, so today 'provocateurs' are routinely supposed to be moved by shadowy elite figures who 'only think of their own advantage'. Society, on this view, is a kind of bubbling but essentially inanimate cauldron that merely reacts to whatever stimulus is mixed into it by the only sentient beings in this world, namely the elite, who are perpetually locked in an Olympean competition.

Students of the French Revolution are familiar with the stereotypical elite fears about the *sans culottes*, and with elite claims of *apres nous le deluge*. In Indonesia such fears are expressed with the words 'chaos' and 'radicalisation of the masses'. They have shaped the less than democratic conduct of elections under Suharto—not to empower, but to win consent from the masses. Despite a remarkably free election held on 7 June 1999, the same fears were soon pushing party elites to seek a 'consensus' government that essentially ignores the competitive nature of the election.

These reflections suggest that an elite seriously out of touch with the mass of the people has long led Indonesia. Yet nationalist support for them, at least in the heartlands, remains fairly broad-based. Almost the greater tragedy is that foreign commentators have often taken up their view that the centralist, non-democratic state is therefore justified by the chaos that would result from any alternative.

There is life in the regions

If Durkheim and his followers describe collective violence in the pathological language of 'breakdown', there is another view in the sociological literature that it might instead represent 'politics by other means'. Charles Tilly argues that violence can be a result of 'resource mobilisation' by those wanting change (Tilly 1978). Thus one person's breakdown is another's fresh start. Secessionist movements are peculiarly liable to be presented in either Durkheimian terms (by the central elite) or Tillian terms (by the secessionists and their sympathisers).

Contrary to the view long promoted by Jakarta that, left to themselves, the East Timorese are hopelessly fractious, we have many reasons to think of the victory of the local in East Timor as a victory not for chaos but for a new order. Especially in view of the intimidation practised against them by anti-independence forces, the 78.5% of East Timorese who voted for independence showed an extraordinary unanimity about their desired future. Through 24 years of resistance, the guerrilla army Falintil too has shown discipline and has rarely descended to violence against civilians. These are good omens for a peaceful future.

The East Timorese resistance has consciously steered away from adopting ethnic or religious themes to mobilise support. The Catholic hierarchy has mostly kept itself out of the political movement, allowing the latter to develop along secular, pragmatic lines. Whilst there are valid anxieties about how the resistance movement is to transform itself into a credible government, state officials especially in the West are showing every indication that they think they can work with these people.

Casting our eyes around the archipelago we soon discover more instances of conflicts that are described by the Jakarta elite in terms of breakdown, but are seen locally as hopeful and credible struggles for a better future. It is still difficult for us to understand these local movements well since, even today, the discourse they engage in is kept largely hidden by mainstream media that do not want to be seen promoting disintegrasi. Only some are secessionist in nature, but all are assertive against the centralised, non-democratic state. They want to reclaim local government, long hijacked by the interests of big capital and a brutal military, for the local community.

Everywhere local communities are forcing fresh negotiations with large mining companies or paper pulp mills that had raped the local environment with impunity throughout the Suharto years. The protests that stopped the giant pulp mill Indorayon in North Sumatra, and the quieter renegotiation for compensation being conducted with Rio Tinto (gold, East Kalimantan) and Inco (nickel, Sulawesi) are just three examples of an entirely responsible local assertiveness. Similarly, the 'anti-corruption' protests that forced hundreds of local government officers throughout the country to resign in 1998 show us, not the forces of anarchy and breakdown, but local communities who seek to protect legitimate interests.

If they are permitted to develop, these local forces can restore order at a level of the state that has been dysfunctional for a long time. If they are repressed, they may explode and end in a worse fate for Indonesia.

I have portrayed the alternatives to unitary centralism as potentially viable because much of the evidence suggests it is, and because the orthodox view has too arbitrarily and for too long ruled them out of order. However, I am keenly aware of counter-examples in which national elite views of the inescapably chaotic state of society in the regions seem all too realistic.

Local movements around the archipelago often have a xenophobic aspect, directed at 'foreigners' who may have lived in the area for generations and who are just as poor as the 'core' group. Ethnic and religious intolerance is an important mark of the intense Acehnese, Dayak (West Kalimantan) or West Papuan feeling that has exploded over the last year or two. Mind you, the locals think they are purifying and strengthening the community—the exact opposite of social breakdown. Achmad Kandang, an armed guerrilla leader, for example, is a hero in Aceh because young people are turning away from gambling and going back to prayer, as his father proudly told one interviewer.

We do not need to romanticise these local movements. The Free Aceh Movement GAM portrays its struggle in frankly racist (anti-Javanese) and religio-authoritarian terms (Johnson 1999). It drove a 100,000 Acehnese civilians from their homes for political purposes in the months around the June 1999 national election. Many hundreds have died in neighbour-kill-neighbour ethnic conflicts in West Kalimantan in 1997 and Ambon in 1999. The Free Papua Movement has repeatedly taken Javanese transmigrants or civil servants hostage, sometimes with fatal results, simply because they are non-Papuan. Several influential West Papuan figures (for example the late Thomas Wainggai) have adopted a millenialist Christian ideology that does not augur well for practical politics. Unlike the East Timorese and the Acehnese, the West Papuan movement has only an embryonic party structure and relies to a great extent on clerical leadership.

Then there is the possibility that, even if Indonesia does not break up into independent smaller units, the vertical dispersion of the state's powers will produce a local 'bossism' similar to that described for the Philippines by John Sidel (1997).

However, media commentary too often fails to recognise that local xenophobia is never the only factor at work. Over against it we usually find an admirable pragmatism practised by many local political players. Aceh, for example, has lately forced itself onto the attention of Jakarta less by any action of the xenophobic and uncompromising GAM, but by a variety of urban coalitions that are often quite critical of GAM. They are promoting an East Timor-style referendum, something that GAM views as unnecessary. Their efforts resulted in apparent approval of the idea from the leaders of four major national political parties on 15 September 1999.[5] Aceh's governor, by contrast with Jakarta, which refuses even to acknowledge them, sent emissaries to Bangkok and then to Sweden to hold discussions with GAM leader-in-exile Hasan di Tiro last July and August. Similarly responsible activism is seen in West Papua, where the coalition Foreri has sponsored

---

[5] Leaders of PKB, PAN, Partai Keadilan, and PPP, among them Abdurrahman Wahid and Amien Rais, together with Aceh governor Syamsuddin Mahmud, unveiled a billboard demanding a referendum at a mosque in Aceh (Serambi, 16 September 1999).

round-table discussions about alternatives. President Habibie met 100 Papuan delegates on 26 February 1999, though without immediate result.

The evident failure of the centralist, non-democratic state in Indonesia is spurring action not only along the democratising axis but also along the decentralising one. This second dimension of reform needs as much sympathetic attention from the international community as the first one. The reconstruction of local political life in Indonesia will be a huge task. Although there is a danger such sympathy will be viewed by national elites as sponsoring the breakup of Indonesia, its aim should be to transform the centralist, post-colonial Indonesian state and make it functional rather than to destroy it.

Prospects

At the end of the 19th century, the Netherlands Indies grew into a large colonial state because the Western powers conspired to carve up much of the world between them. The thousands of lives lost to establish it, particularly in Aceh, made no dent on that great power agreement. Similarly, during the long Cold War, particularly after 1965, Indonesia was an important Western ally, and the atrocities the state committed to maintain itself drew little international action. But the Cold War ended in 1991. While the US is not at all interested in promoting the breakup of Indonesia, its activism on East Timor culminating in 1999 marks a huge reduction in its tolerance of brutality by client states in remote places, no matter that this is the world's fourth largest nation.

US President Bill Clinton declared after the war in Kosovo, 'Whether you live in Africa, in Central Europe or anywhere else, if someone intends to commit massive crimes against innocent civilians, he should know that, to the limit of our capacities, we will prevent it.' Clinton may have been rhetorical, cynical or genuine, but his statement will not be reassuring to leaders of states inhabiting the dangerous corner of Rummel's field of modern states.

East Timor notwithstanding, the rise of the local does not have to portend the breakup of Indonesia. More likely, in the short term at least, is that it will signify a vertical dispersal of power as community movements adopt state-forming strategies. Even if Aceh does eventually split off, the same need for local empowerment will still have to be dealt with in other places.

Two arenas where Indonesian central state actors appear ready to make substantial concessions to local demands for more control are (ironically) the last Suharto-era parliament, as well as some of the parties competing in the 7 June election. The parliament elected in May 1997 continued to produce legislation for 16 months after Suharto resigned. Among the results was a law giving provinces greater authority to choose their own governor (law no.

22/1999), one returning a large percentage of locally raised primary resources revenues to the provinces (law no. 25/1999), and one that affirms Islamic syariah law in the 'special' province of Aceh. These laws still await implementing regulations.

During the last election campaign, the new party PAN openly stated it was willing to consider a federal model for the country. The Suharto-era party PPP won a majority in Aceh because it promised to lobby for Acehnese autonomy in the halls of power in Jakarta.

However, the counter-indications are also strong. Most of them are connected with the military. The army leadership has repeatedly rejected discussion of federalism as dangerous to the unitary state. It is establishing new garrison commands in 'difficult' areas around the country. Its abominable behaviour in East Timor after the ballot was widely interpreted as a warning of what systematic terror the state might unleash on any other peoples contemplating secession.

The Home Affairs Minister swore in three new governors on 12 October 1999, for two new provinces created in West Papua and one new province in Maluku, both areas of ongoing conflict. However, the appointments completely bypassed normal consultative mechanisms and seemed designed to strengthen central government control rather than empower restive areas (thus resembling the Dutch colonial 'federal' reforms).

The new Consultative Assembly (MPR) is at the time of writing considering a law designed to 'make it impossible' for any other province to follow the East Timor route. Meanwhile, an unelected military that has changed its thinking on the unitary state little if at all, is being courted by all factions within the MPR.

These contradictory movements at various levels of Indonesia's state and society probably mean nothing will be resolved quickly or cleanly. But the extreme violence that the centralist, non-democratic state has shown once more it is prepared to commit against entire local populations must make us agree to support those trying to re-conceive it for more human ends. Or else we may condemn Indonesia to a fate beyond anyone's control.

East Timor, Australia and Indonesia

Scott Burchill

When an extraordinary 98.6% of eligible East Timorese voted on 30 August 1999 to decide whether their political futures lay as members of an autonomous province of the Republic of Indonesia or as citizens of an independent state, the early signs were ominous for Jakarta and the pro-integrationists. It wasn't just the sight of people who had never decided their own political destiny queuing before dawn outside 800 United Nations polling stations scattered around the territory; it was the realisation that months of intimidation and terror by Indonesian-directed militias had failed to deter the East Timorese from determining their future political arrangements.

The result of the ballot was never in serious doubt. A decisive 78.5% of the population had spurned Jakarta's offer of special autonomy within the Republic of Indonesia, electing instead for independence. The commitment to self-determination by individual East Timorese is even more remarkable in light of their betrayal by so many over the last 25 years. After more than three centuries of colonial neglect, the Portuguese abruptly left in 1975 without preparing the territory for independence. Exploiting both the opportunity that followed Portugal's departure and the anti-communist sympathies of neighbouring states, Indonesia illegally invaded the territory in December 1975, falsely claiming to have been invited in by popular consent. It's subsequent brutal 24 year occupation, which cost the lives of more than 200,000 East Timorese or one third of the population constituted, in Noam Chomsky's assessment, the worst slaughter relative to a population since the holocaust (Chomsky 1999:42).

The invasion of East Timor and subsequent repression of its population would not have been possible without Western complicity. The United States and the United Kingdom gleefully sold Jakarta the weapons it needed to kill the civilian population and hunt down the military resistance, which had fled to the mountains. Australia's role was even more shameful.[1] The Whitlam Government made it clear to President Suharto in 1974 that it would prefer East Timor to be integrated with Indonesia, and would not insist on an act of self-determination. Jakarta's mistake, according to former foreign minister Gareth Evans, was that its 'military moved with less than decent haste to take

---

1 There are many excellent accounts of Australia's role, including: Dunn 1996; Chomsky 1996; Pilger 1994; 1998; Aubrey 1998; Jardine 1995; Macmillan 1992; Taylor 1991; Horta 1987; Jollife 1978; Cotton 1999.

the place of the hastily departed Portuguese colonists' (Evans and Grant 1995:200). The problem apparently was the speed of their arrival, which was embarrassing, rather than their crime of aggression or subsequent crimes against humanity.

In 1985 Indonesia's most important neighbour, Australia, gave explicit *de jure* recognition to Jakarta's illegal annexation of the territory so that four years later it could sign a treaty (1989 Timor Gap Treaty) with the occupying power to jointly exploit the oil and gas reserves of the Timor Sea—essentially an agreement to share stolen property. These actions placed Australia at odds with the United Nations and much of the international community. However, since Indonesia's invasion, Australian governments have routinely put commercial and defence ties before a concern for human rights, forging closer economic relations with the Suharto regime and training Indonesian military officers who had appalling human rights records in the treatment of their own people.

Setting the agenda: The Jakarta lobby

Amongst Canberra's policy elite, supporting Indonesia's existing territorial integrity has been widely seen as the best way of maintaining geo-political 'stability' in Australia's corner of Southeast Asia. And in such a diverse and disparate nation, Jakarta's firm control of the archipelago was accepted as the key to Australia's own territorial security. Suharto's iron grip, especially his intolerance of separatism and his pathological anti-communism, was therefore much appreciated by Australian governments throughout his presidency.

Canberra's consistent support for the Suharto regime can be largely credited to the Jakarta lobby, an informal group of bureaucrats, academics and journalists who tightly controlled Australian foreign policy towards Indonesia and East Timor. The Jakarta lobby has long regarded Australia's relationship with Indonesia as an exceptional case requiring careful management by 'experts' with a proper sympathy for and understanding of Jakarta's difficulties. As former Foreign Affairs head Richard Woolcott said in 1995, 'we cannot allow foreign policy [in this area] to be made in the streets, by the media or by the unions' (Woolcott 1995), or, in the case of the secretly negotiated 1995 Australia–Indonesia Security Agreement, by the Federal Parliament.

Until the atrocities in East Timor, the Jakarta lobby had been remarkably influential. Consider, for example, its success in presenting the Suharto regime in a favourable light to Australia's political leaders. A CIA report on the purges organised by the Indonesian military against the Indonesian Communist Party (PKI) shortly after Suharto came to power in 1966 claimed that 'in terms of the numbers killed the anti-PKI massacres in Indonesia rank as one of the worst mass murders of the 20th century, along with the Soviet purges of the 1930s, the Nazi mass murders during the Second World War and the Maoist bloodbaths of the 1930s' (CIA 1968:71). Historian Gabriel Kolko concurs, suggesting that 'the "final solution" to the Communist problem in Indonesia was certainly one of the most barbaric acts of inhumanity in a century that has seen a great deal of it; it surely ranks as a war crime of the same type as those the Nazis perpetrated' (Kolko 1988:181).

No-one seriously contests Suharto's responsibility for the bloodbath. He is as clearly culpable for it as Pol Pot was for Year Zero in Cambodia, though no Australian politician has suggested that he be charged with crimes against humanity. On the contrary, Suharto has been lauded by former Prime Minister Keating for producing a 'tolerant society' and bringing 'stability' to the region (*AFR* 1994),[2] praise that has been echoed by Opposition leader Kim Beazley, who in 1989 claimed that 'Australians pay far too little attention to the value to us of the stability' the Suharto dictatorship 'brought to the Indonesian archipelago'. If the PKI 'had been victorious in the mid 1960s,' says Beazley, 'our security prospects over the last two decades would have been very different from the favourable circumstances we enjoy today' (Henderson 1993). Half a million deaths clearly had not weighed too heavily on the conscience of the leadership of the Labor Party.

Nor did they on the Australian government of the day. In July 1966 Prime Minister Harold Holt told the River Club of New York City that 'with 500,000 to 1,000,000 Communist sympathisers knocked off, I think it is safe to assume a reorientation has taken place' (*New York Times* 1966).

In Australian government circles, praise for Suharto and his achievements regularly sidestepped the issue of human rights and his invasion of East Timor. In 1998 the then Deputy Prime Minister, Tim Fischer, recommended that 'when magazines look for the man of the world of the second half of this century, they perhaps should not look much further than Jakarta'. While Suharto's victims looked elsewhere, the Jakarta lobby insisted that his human rights 'failures' should be balanced against his 'economic achievements'—now only a fading memory, and which were in truth rather modest by regional standards.

Suharto's regime was characterised as 'moderate' by Professor Jaimie Mackie, an Indonesian specialist at the ANU (Mackie 1974), and in a eulogy

---

2 Keating's remarks prompted the following response from Indonesian human rights lawyer Buyung Nasution: 'If you were in our position, people who were oppressed, harassed, some of us were arrested unlawfully, even tortured...of course we could not expect too much—that foreign countries will jump in and help us or get us relief but that at least we would expect that foreign governments would not praise oppressive measures' (*Australian* 1994).

that would have made him blush, journalist Greg Sheridan has argued that 'even in human rights there is a case for Suharto' (Sheridan 1998a). It shouldn't therefore come as a surprise that in three biographical reviews written in May 1998 by Mackie, Sheridan and his colleague Paul Kelly in the *Australian*, Suharto's role in one of the century's worst bloodbaths was passed over in silence (*Australian* 1998). Can anyone imagine an obituary for Pol Pot that failed to mention the killing fields?

The 'friends of Indonesia' never spoke out on behalf of Indonesia's political prisoners (tapols) as they did so consistently for 'refuseniks' in Easter Europe, but they regularly demonised Jakarta's critics. Ordinary people concerned about human rights under Suharto and those who campaigned for East Timor's independence were regularly defamed by Sheridan and Woolcott as 'anti-Indonesian' and 'racist' (Woolcott 1992:81; Sheridan 1998b). The implication was always clear: Indonesia comprised Suharto and the military elite that ran the state. No-one else mattered. Criticism of them was a slander on the entire Indonesian nation.

Apologising for Suharto led his Australian supporters into a state of denial. Shortly before Suharto's downfall in May 1998, Richard Woolcott was arguing that in Indonesia 'there will be no people power movement, comparable to that in the Philippines in 1986' (Woolcott 1998a), a view endorsed by Paul Kelly in the *Australian*: 'Indonesia in the 1990s is not a re-run of The Philippines of the 80s…There is no political reform movement' (Kelly 1998).

The exculpation of Jakarta for each outrage committed by ABRI (the Indonesian military, now TNI) in East Timor became almost reflexive behaviour for policy elites in Canberra and in sections of the Murdoch press. It was a behavioural trait that continued, even as the TNI and its militia proxies attacked those East Timorese civilians who voted overwhelmingly for independence on 30 August 1999. Their strategy, as articulated by Woolcott just prior to Indonesia's invasion of East Timor in 1975, has been to 'act in a way which would be designed to minimise the public impact in Australia and show private understanding to Indonesia of their problems' (Toohey and Wilkinson 1987:179–80).

Predictably, the two separate massacres in Dili in November 1991 sprang the Jakarta lobby into damage control mode. Concerted efforts to offset community outrage, deflect moral judgement and mute public criticism were made. The number of victims was minimised and evidence of a second massacre dismissed entirely. Sheridan and Woolcott seemed to blame Portugal for the killings, while former ANU Economics Professor Heinz Arndt called the massacre a tragedy, not because of the loss of life but because it inflamed anti-Indonesian hate campaigns in Australia (*Australian* 1991).

Australians were urged to show understanding to the perpetrators of the crimes, rather than the victims. Such was the success of the disinformation campaign in exculpating Jakarta for the Santa Cruz killings, Foreign Minister Evans found himself describing the latest in a long list of atrocities as 'aberrant local behaviour' by Indonesia's armed forces (*Herald-Sun* 1995), and even flew to the US to berate the editorial board of the *New York Times* for its unhealthy preoccupation with Suharto's human rights record (Toohey 1994).

In the light of the post-ballot slaughter, the Jakarta lobby was again seeking to shift responsibility for TNI atrocities away from Jakarta by blaming the Australlian Prime Minister, John Howard. Howard's letter to President Habibie in late December 1998, which encouraged the Indonesian president to resolve the East Timor issue, was portrayed as a naïve investment in a lame-duck leader who didn't have the support of the Indonesian military. According to the Jakarta lobby, Howard's enthusiastic support for the UN-supervised referendum was ill-timed: it should have waited until a legitimate government had convened in Jakarta in November. Howard was therefore not only responsible for the killings and the forcible displacement of the majority of the population of East Timor, he was also guilty of a much greater sin in the eyes of the lobby—abandoning 'good relations' with Jakarta (Woolcott 1999; Dalrymple 1999; Sheridan 1999).

The strategy of blaming the Howard Government for the killings in East Timor was difficult to reconcile with history. Australia was not a party to the flawed tripartite agreement signed in New York on 5 May 1999, and had little if any influence over its content. Howard's Christmas letter recommended an extensive period of autonomy—up to ten years—before the holding of a referendum, and his Government's own preference was for autonomy within Indonesia rather than independence. Habibie rejected this recommendation, opting instead for an immediate ballot, with tragic consequences. Blaming the Howard Government for the atrocities committed in the lead-up to and after the 30 August ballot was little more than another attempt to exculpate the perpetrators of those crimes.

Even as the full extent of the post-ballot slaughter in East Timor was revealed, ANU Indonesianist Harold Crouch was warning the Howard Government not to increase the size of the Australian Army because it might be misinterpreted in Jakarta. At the same time his former colleague, Jamie Mackie, was also concerned that if a war crimes tribunal investigating the killings in East Timor were held in Australia it could lead to a dangerous deterioration in Australia–Indonesia relations (Barker 1999a; Colebatch 1999). Old habits, it seems, are hard to shake.[3]

However, it's not just the Jakarta lobby's moral credentials that are under question. As recent events have shown, their political assessments have been as deeply flawed—a case study of professional negligence and malpractice.

Mistaken assumptions

Jakarta's closest supporters in Australia believed the issue of East Timor was the only significant irritant in the bilateral relationship, and should therefore have been removed from both domestic and international concern. In 1982 former Prime Minister Gough Whitlam appeared at the UN General Assembly Fourth (Decolonisation) Committee arguing the case for withdrawing the issue of East Timor from the business of the United Nations. Whitlam had long been an enthusiast for integration and a vocal opponent of independence. The magnitude of his failure can only be truly measured against the success of the United Nations in staging an independence ballot on 30 August, and the Security Council's subsequent authorisation of a multi-national peace enforcement mission led by soldiers of the Australian Defence Forces to support the result of the ballot.

Only four earlier, Australia's most prominent pro-integrationist, Richard Woolcott, claimed that 'the East Timor lobby should accept that the time for an act of self-determination after 20 years has passed and that demanding independence is a lost cause which raises false hopes, prolongs conflict and costs lives' (Woolcott 1995). Similarly, former Foreign Minister Evans repeatedly argued that Indonesia's takeover of East Timor was 'irreversible' and that 'it's quite quixotic to think otherwise' (*Age* 1994).

The poverty of this analysis is now obvious to all. However, the political changes that have recently begun in Indonesia are already proving to be a concern for those who mistakenly equate 'stability' in the region with supporting the status quo. This error is at the heart of Australia's regional foreign policy failure.

In the wake of Suharto's departure in May 1998, defence analyst Paul Dibb claimed that 'a unified Indonesia is vital to Australia's national interest' and that its possible Balkanisation is 'something we must make absolutely sure doesn't happen' (Dibb 1998). Richard Woolcott agreed, arguing that 'it is

---

3 Richard Woolcott still refuses to call the Suharto regime a 'dictatorship', preferring the more considerate description 'authoritarian' (*PM* 1999). Similarly, it wasn't until the Indonesian election on 7 June 1999 that an Australian Government official (Foreign Minister Alexander Downer) described the Suharto regime as a 'dictatorship'.

foolish to suggest the fragmentation of Indonesia into a number of independent states need not concern Australia' (Woolcott 1998b).

Putting to one side the question of Australia's right or capacity to prevent such a development, one lesson of the post-Cold War period seems to have been lost on 'experts' such as Dibb and Woolcott: political and territorial boundaries are clearly not immutable. It is quite normal for nation-states to come into and go out of existence, as it is for boundaries to shift. The incorporation of the Baltic states into the Soviet Union was once said to be irreversible. Czechoslovakia was a single state before it peacefully bifurcated. East and West Germany, like North and South Yemen, were separately recognised before their sudden unification. Few predicted the disintegration of Yugoslavia or the collapse of the Soviet Union. The lesson to be gained from these examples is clear: political communities are fluid and transient. Sometimes, when groups reconsider their political arrangements, violent struggles ensue: but often they don't. Woolcott's claim that 'historically, no state has willingly accepted dismemberment' (Woolcott 1995) is demonstrably untrue.

Far from being a threat to Australia's national security, the partial fragmentation of Indonesia could defuse ethnic, regional and religious tensions that have been simmering throughout the archipelago for many years. Centrifugal forces there are a reaction to the assumption that the unity and territorial integrity of the Indonesian state based on the boundaries of the Dutch East Indies and ruled from Java was beyond question. In fact, the artificial and contrived nature of Indonesian nationalism, the absence of common national values, and anti-Javanese resentment in the outer provinces produced a post-colonial structure that was much more fragile than its champions in Australia were prepared to admit. The revolt against Jakarta in Aceh, West Papua, Kalimantan, East Timor and elsewhere, has intensified in recent years. Consistent Australian government support for Suharto's authoritarian control over 13,000 islands and 300 ethnic groups was noticed and resented.

Secret diplomacy

Indonesia's unilateral withdrawal from the Australia–Indonesia agreement on security in September 1999 brings to an end a period in bilateral relations when military ties reached their closest point. It was an era characterised by a wide disparity between popular and elite opinion in Australia towards Indonesia, when the negotiation of foreign policy in Australia was effectively driven underground.

'Secret diplomacy' was the expression coined by late-19th-century liberals to describe the way unrepresentative elites practised international relations in the pre-democratic era. Liberal-democrats disputed the view that foreign policy was a specialised art best made by professional diplomats behind closed doors and away from the influences of national politics. Too many conflicts had been caused by a 'warrior class' bent on extending their power and wealth at the expense of the masses who bore the burdens of war.

It was felt that the spread of democratic processes and institutions would break the power of the ruling elites and curb their propensity for violence. Wars would become less likely, if not impossible, because democratic rulers would have to respond to public opinion.

Despite their misplaced faith in the pacific tendencies of democratic states, liberals have left at least one important mark on modern political thinking. Since the end of the the First World War, it has been assumed that in democracies the affairs of state should be open to the scrutiny of the people and their representatives. After all, it is the idea of popular consent in the form of majority rule and public participation in decision making that confers legitimacy on government behaviour. The ultimate consent for diplomacy in general, and war-making specifically, now rests with the citizens of the state.

How then should we have viewed the decision of the Australian Government in December 1995 to sign a security agreement with the Indonesian Government? Not only did the Keating Government give no indication to the public or the Parliament that such a foreign policy initiative was even being considered, let alone negotiated, it also withheld details of the agreement from the Australian people until after it had been signed by the foreign ministers of both countries.

At the time the Government's justification for the secrecy was remarkably honest. Foreign Minister Evans said it was 'difficult to do things in a fishbowl' (*Australian* 1995) and went on to claim that the treaty 'was discussed in private, as these things often need to be if you are to have a sensible process of negotiation and if it's not to be thrown off the rails by people getting very excited about things before it's appropriate' (*Age* 1995a). Prime Minister Keating was even more frank: 'if there had been a more public process, there probably wouldn't have been a treaty' (*AFR* 1995). What both men conceded is that if the public had participated in the decision-making process it would not have supported the agreement. In other words, the democratic process had to be suspended because the Government believed that public opinion was opposed to its policy. This was a remarkable admission for democratically elected officials to make.

If we accept the principle that it is popular consent that confers legitimacy on public policy, the agreement, though not illegal, was always illegitimate. As the editor of the *Age* pointed out, 'secrecy is almost always inimical to public acceptance of government actions' (*Age* 1995b). It is not the right of democratically elected governments to negotiate treaties on the public's behalf that is being questioned, but the value and status of agreements that the public has been prevented from considering. This is the risk governments take when they abandon due process. Does the electorate feel bound to honour the commitments made on its behalf in such an arrangement?

The manner in which the Australia-Indonesia security agreement was negotiated raised a broader question: What role does the foreign policy establishment in Australia see for the public in foreign policy making? Are we returning to the era of 'secret diplomacy, when the public were spectators rather than participants in decision-making?

The secret agreement reached between Canberra and Jakarta lacked substantive content. Promises to consult regularly on common regional security issues and consider actions in response to 'adverse challenges' to common security interests were about as meaningless as diplomatic phraseology can make them.

Its conclusion, however, delighted the Jakarta lobby. The foreign editor of the *Australian* described the agreement as 'a fantastic slap in the face for the anti-Indonesian protest groups...it declares definitively that the protest groups cannot set the agenda in the Australia–Indonesia relationship' (Sheridan 1995a). Although the Australian Government 'will be pilloried by the anti-Indonesian lobby...and its treaty will be denounced up hill and down dale by East Timorese groups, some church groups, many aid groups, human rights organisations and the Left inside and outside the Labor Party...Keating has made it clear that while he is prime minister these myriad groups will not drive Australian foreign policy, certainly not towards Indonesia. This of itself is of first order importance' (Sheridan 1995b). Michelle Grattan in the *Age* similarly argued that as a result of bipartisan support for the treaty, 'the anti-Indonesian lobby will have nowhere to go' (Grattan 1995).

Three points can be made about this curious episode in Australia's diplomatic history:

First, security alliances between a liberal-democracy and a dictatorship are often problematic. They only temporarily disguise deep cultural and political divisions between the parties. And frequently they are morally suspect.

Second, in a democracy the public will not and should not feel under any obligation to support international agreements that are secretly negotiated on their behalf. Popular scrutiny and consultation are critical to the legitimacy of public policy (this could be said to also apply to Whitlam's unilateral support for Indonesia's incorporation of East Timor).

Third, secret diplomacy only widens the gap between popular and elite opinion on foreign policy issues. A new relationship with Indonesia can only be started and sustained if this gulf is immediately narrowed by Australia's political leaders. The era of the 'Indonesian foreign policy specialist' and 'special relationships' is over.

From joy to tragedy

Despite the best efforts of Canberra, London and Washington to remove East Timor from the international diplomatic agenda, the extraordinary courage and resistance of the East Timorese was finally acknowledged in 1996 with the awarding of the Nobel Peace prize to East Timorese Catholic Bishop Carlos Belo and resistance leader Jose Ramos Horta. Predictably, the awarding of the prize to Horta in particular was attacked in the Murdoch press in Australia and by the Jakarta lobby generally. Suharto apologist Heinz Arndt went as far as to suggest that Indonesian Foreign Minister, Ali Alatas, was a more deserving recipient, though the Keating Government had already bestowed an Order of Australia on Jakarta's international spokesman (Arndt 1999).

Two years later, in May 1998, Suharto's fall from power in Jakarta provided a new window of opportunity for the resolution of the East Timor conflict. Portugal and Indonesia, under President Habibie, recommended negotiations at the United Nations that eventually resulted in an agreement, signed on 5 May 1999, to give the people of East Timor the choice of independence or integration with Indonesia in a 'popular consultation'. The result of that ballot, announced by UN Secretary-General Kofi Annan on 4 September, recorded a decisive 78.5% in favour of independence. But the announcement of the ballot result also triggered an all out attack on the civilian population by those who had been firmly rejected: the TNI and their militia proxies.

Despite the skill of UNAMET—the United Nations Assistance Mission in East Timor—and the overwhelming preference of the East Timorese for independence, the Popular Consultation was not held in either a peaceful or a free and fair environment. East Timor's resistance leader Xanana Gusmao was unable to campaign during the popular consultation, remaining under house arrest in Jakarta. His international spokesman Jose Ramos Horta was barred from entering his homeland by the Habibie Government.

The orchestrated reign of terror in the territory exposed a major flaw in the tripartite agreement. Article 3 of the agreement states that 'the Government of Indonesia will be responsible for maintaining peace and security in East

Timor in order to ensure that the popular consultation is carried out in a fair and peaceful way in an atmosphere free of intimidation, violence or interference from any side'. It was a responsibility Jakarta insisted on taking. To say that the Government of Indonesia did not fulfil its obligations under the agreement is to fail to convey the barbaric behaviour of Indonesia's security forces in East Timor.

Before the referendum, Colonel Tono Suratman, the TNI commander in Dili, warned of what was coming: '...if the pro-independents do win...all will be destroyed...It will be worse than 23 years ago' (Toohey 1999a). He was good as his word. In the days following the ballot, pro-Jakarta militias freely roamed East Timor killing suspected independence supporters and locally-engaged UN staff, harassing and attacking journalists and evacuating provincial towns. Hundreds of thousands of East Timorese were forcibly driven into West Timor, where many were attacked by militias, and others deported to outlying provinces within Indonesia.

Death squads, which were given a licence to exact revenge against anyone associated with the ballot, were clearly the creation of Indonesia's security forces, directed by Indonesian intelligence operatives and, courtesy of the local Indonesian police, immune from prosecution and agreements demanding their disarmament. Prior to the arrival of multinational InterFET forces on 20 September, East Timor rapidly descended into state-organised anarchy as Indonesia's security forces openly colluded with the militias in the slaughter of the population throughout the territory. The foreign media and the United Nations were driven out of the territory. More than half the population were estimated to have been internally displaced, triggering an enormous humanitarian crisis. Meanwhile at the United Nations, Indonesian Foreign Minister Ali Alatas told the General Assembly that although Jakarta had made some mistakes it would leave East Timor 'honourably, peacefully and amicably' (ABC 1999).

The responsibility of the international community

Indonesia's security forces were free to terrorise the population because, under the 5 May tripartite agreement, Portugal and the UN granted Indonesia its demand to be solely responsible for maintaining law and order up until the conclusion of the ballot. UN Security Council resolution 1246 (1999) confirmed that it was 'the responsibility of the Government of Indonesia to maintain peace and security in East Timor...in order to ensure that the consultation is carried out in a fair and peaceful way and in an atmosphere free of intimidation, violence or interference from any side and to ensure the safety and security of United Nations and other international staff and observers in East Timor'. In the behaviour of its security forces in East Timor, Indonesia clearly and brazenly breached international law.

The moral responsibility for the atrocities committed in East Timor after the ballot, however, must be shared by those states that waited for Jakarta's permission before sending in an armed peacekeeping force on 20 September. In contrast to the case of Kosovo where national sovereignty was unsuccessfully invoked to deter outside intervention, there is no legal basis for Indonesia's sovereign claim on East Timor. East Timor was legally a non-self-governing territory of the United Nations General Assembly (UN Charter, Chapter XI) and Portugal was the administering authority. Only Australia explicitly recognised Jakarta's annexation of the territory; the United Nations did not. From the perspective of the international community, the need for permission before the deployment of troops therefore should not have arisen.

Intelligence briefings leaked in Australia suggested that the Australian government was fully aware that the militias were directed by senior TNI officers and that an attack on the civilian population after the ballot was highly likely. There is also evidence that earlier in the year the Australian government discouraged the United States from co-planning for a peacekeeping force that could have been quickly deployed either before or immediately after the referendum. Again it seems clear that many East Timorese lives have been shattered by the reluctance of Western states to upset the ruling elite in Jakarta (Toohey 1999b; Toohey 1999c; Toohey 1999d; Barker 1999a).

According to Article 6 of the tripartite agreement, following the vote for independence, 'the Government of Indonesia shall take the constitutional steps necessary to terminate its links with East Timor thus restoring under Indonesian law the status East Timor held prior to 17 July 1976, and the Governments of Indonesia and Portugal and the Secretary-General shall agree on arrangements for a peaceful and orderly transfer of authority in East Timor to the United Nations. The Secretary-General shall, subject to the appropriate legislative mandate, initiate the procedure enabling East Timor to begin a process of transition towards independence'. Indonesia does not have the discretion to reject the outcome of the referendum. Given the clear result of the ballot and the fact that its implementation is not contingent on Indonesia's domestic constitutional and legal processes, East Timor's independence is now a formality.

On 15 September the UN Security Council unanimously adopted resolution 1264 (1999). Acting under Chapter VII of the Charter of the United Nations, the Security Council authorised the establishment of a multinational force 'to restore peace and security in East Timor, to protect and support UNAMET in carrying out its tasks and...to facilitate humanitarian assistance operations'. The multinational force was empowered by the UN to 'take all necessary measures' to fulfil its mandate. The resolution also stressed that it was 'the responsibility of the Indonesian authorities to take immediate and effective measures to ensure the safe return of refugees to East Timor'.

This force, called InterFET, was largely put together by the Australian Government at the APEC heads of government summit in Auckland, with support from New Zealand, the United States, the United Kingdom and a number of ASEAN countries including the Philippines and Thailand. InterFET was not a UN peacekeeping mission even though it was authorised by the UN Security Council. Rather, it was a 'coalition of willing states'—20 in all—that was hastily mobilised and deployed in anticipation of a handover to a formally constituted 'blue helmets' mission. UNTAET—United Nations Transitional Authority in East Timor—was established by a unanimous vote of the UN Security Council on 25 October (resolution 1272 (1999)), and will take over in February 2000.

Given almost a quarter of a century of bipartisan appeasement of Indonesia, how can Australia's leading role in establishing InterFET be explained? There are three broad reasons. First, public opinion in Australia was horrified by the television images broadcast from East Timor after the announcement of the ballot result. The Howard Government, which has been reluctant to stray far from public sentiment on any issue since it was elected in 1996, was overwhelmed with demands for a military response to the slaughter.

Secondly, in foreign policy the Howard Government has been seeking 'product differentiation' from its predecessor which was closely identified with Asian engagement. Breaking with diplomatic orthodoxy towards Indonesia and the opportunity for a conservative government to 'deliver' an independent East Timor after years of Labor Party failure, proved irresistible.

And thirdly, confronting Indonesia by leading an interventionary force in East Timor was consistent with the Howard Government's distaste for the rules of engagement with Asia advocated by the Hawke and Keating Governments. If the price of acceptance in the region is cultural deference and a diminished commitment to universal values such as human rights, it is a cost John Howard seems unwilling to bear.

Future relations

The slaughter in East Timor represented an enormous moral and strategic failure for Australia. Three decades of obsequious fawning towards and appeasement of Jakarta resulted in the collapse of Canberra's foreign and defence policy. Closer military ties between Australia's armed forces and TNI, symbolised by joint training exercises and the secretly negotiated 1995

Australia–Indonesia Security Agreement, clearly gave Australia no influence whatsoever—professionalising, civilising or strategic—over Indonesian security forces. Indonesia's generals became unacceptable partners in any security alliance, a situation unlikely to change until TNI ends its dual function and is firmly placed under civilian control.

The undue influence of the Jakarta lobby within the Foreign Affairs bureaucracy also needed to end. By placing a premium on 'stability' within the Indonesian archipelago and deeper economic relations with Jakarta, Canberra ignored the ethical implications of close ties with a repressive dictatorship. The lobby's 'big picture' meant ignoring Jakarta's human rights abuses, distorting the history of Suharto's rise to power, and subjugating the legal rights of the East Timorese. A normal bilateral relationship with Indonesia depended on an honest review of this unfortunate history and the realisation that political and territorial boundaries, even in this part of the world, are rarely immutable.

Australia's regional relations will have to factor in dealing with an independent East Timor. Canberra will sometimes need to tread carefully in this new relationship for fear of confronting Indonesia, yet provide as much friendship and financial assistance as possible. Canberra will have an important role to play in brokering relations between a battered East Timor and its giant neighbour. Blood cannot be measured in dollars or goodwill, but the responsibility born of complicity in East Timor's tragedy is substantial.

The Jakarta lobby glossed over the important issues of human rights and democracy, frequently invoking 'Asian values' on behalf of Indonesia's rulers as an excuse for political repression. The lobby was even opposed to raising democratic goals as an instrument of diplomacy if the unity and stability of Indonesia was questioned, or if economic growth was seen to be under any kind of threat. At times it was clear that Australia's foreign policy elite had a greater affection for the unitary Indonesian state and its dictatorial rulers than it did for the citizens of that country.

Rebuilding the diplomatic relationship with Jakarta was suspended until the new government was convened in November 1999, just as restoring 'good relations' with Malaysia has to wait until Mahathir's departure from office. The Jakarta lobby's obsessive emphasis on order as a necessary pre-requisite to economic growth enabled it to ignore issues of human rights and the need to develop accountable democratic institutions throughout the Indonesian archipelago. Like those who peddle 'Asian values', the Jakarta lobby believed that Indonesians faced a choice between economic or political development: for reasons never explained, they couldn't have both.

The exclusion of alternative interpretations of post-1965 Indonesia from policy debates in Australia has left a foreign and defence policy void. Instead of wishful thinking, Canberra needs to develop cogent policy responses to scenarios based on the potential break-up of the Indonesian state as it is currently constituted. How will Australia respond if West Papua slips out of Jakarta's grip? This is now a possibility. The revenue that Jakarta bleeds out of the province far exceeds what it puts back. West Papua was, after all, as fraudulently acquired as East Timor was. Few believe that if given a free choice, the indigenous people there would opt for continuing integration with Indonesia.

In Aceh the levels of anti-military hostility are high. Would a seriously weakened and impoverished Jakarta have the stomach, much less the capability, for an attenuated ethnic conflict there? And what if Ambon erupted into a full-blown religious war? It may be that the fracturing of Indonesia would make the disintegration of the old Yugoslavia look mild in comparison. These centrifugal forces have gathered strength because of resentment generated by years of Javanese repression and the frustrations people feel at being denied their just political freedoms. The federalisation of Indonesia and the prospect of a confederation of states around the Indonesian archipelago may have to be seriously explored.

The so-called 'Howard doctrine' puts forward the idea that Australia could play the role of regional 'deputy' to the United States in future peacekeeping operations (Brenchley 1999). This was a silly and possibly offensive posture for a middle power in East Asia to take, and was wisely retracted shortly after its annunciation. Other aspects of the doctrine, however, had some merits. That Canberra was no longer prepared to maintain 'good relations' with Indonesia 'at all costs' signalled a positive break with a now discredited diplomatic orthodoxy. Prime Minister Howard's reversal of what he described as 25 years of 'over-accommodation of Indonesia' long overdue (Barker 1999b). If the killing of priests, the rape of nuns and the forced displacement of the population of East Timor by Indonesian security forces did not justify a cooling of relations with Jakarta, it is difficult to imagine circumstances that would.

Exploding the myth of 'special relationships in Asia' and a growing unwillingness to conform with regional cultural expectations also demonstrated a higher level of political maturity and sophistication. A more consistent and open projection of liberal democratic values was likely to reduce perceptions of ambiguity and opportunism amongst Australia's northern neighbours. Contriving an artificial sense of belonging to the region did not prove to be very convincing to a sceptical domestic audience. At the very least, the inspiring example of the East Timorese in pursuing their political rights against enormous odds and sustained resistance forced Australia to review its diplomatic history in a more honest light, and recast its regional foreign policy outlook.

Conclusion

Damien Kingsbury

From the perspective of those who had face to face contact with the militias during the period surrounding the 30 August 1999 ballot in East Timor, it was apparent that they were a gutless gang of thugs who rarely had any idea of what it was they were actually doing. However, what they did, they did with particular arrogance and brutality. In one on one confrontations, they would often become afraid, their sense of bravado only coming from numbers. From this experience it became clear that, should a proper, disciplined and genuinely neutral police or military force enter the territory, the violence would disappear almost immediately.

Although many claim, with some justification, that the international response was too late, when it did come in late September 1999, it had the almost immediate effect of dispersing the militias to the Indonesian side of the land border. As expected, despite their frequent bragging that they would shed the blood of international soldiers, virtually none wanted to stay and fight when the international force, InterFET, arrived. The two clashes between the forces resulted in small losses to the militia and the Indonesian police. The TNI, so long a law unto itself in East Timor, was increasingly relegated to the position of impotent and unwanted thugs whose time had passed. On 29 October 1999, the withdrawal of Indonesian soldiers that had been taking place since late September was concluded, and the Indonesian flag in East Timor was hauled down. The TNI shuffled back across the border to West Timor, to return to the rest of the archipelago. They were a humiliated force, defeated by the will of a people, embarrassed in the eyes of their fellow countrymen for both their defeat and the shameful way in which they had acted. In the eyes of the international community, the TNI had become a pariah force that had brought opprobrium upon the state they had vowed to serve and protect.

East Timorese who had fled to the mountains or across the border began to trickle back into their villages and towns, in most cases to find them destroyed. Destruction, undertaken by the retreating TNI as a part of a scorched earth policy was estimated at around 70% of all buildings. Infrastructure such as electricity, water supply and telecommunications was also destroyed. If shelter was scarce, food was even more so, and a major international relief operation began to address the immediate needs of the people of East Timor, as well as try to start planning for the future.

The leadership of the CNRT returned to East Timor to begin the process of rebuilding. It was not without difficulties, however, with tensions between the CNRT and aid agencies and even between the CNRT and UNTAET surfacing. It was a difficult time, in which the immediacy of so many pressing issues tested even the closest and best meaning of relationships. But the reconstruction had begun and, as Xanana and Belo noted at the beginning of this volume, there were moves towards reconciliation with some militia members.

At the time of writing, no-one really knows how many people were killed in the pre and post-ballot period. Bodies, often in mass graves, were still being discovered, many more were believed to have been dumped in the shark-infested ocean and a disturbingly high number of people, as many as 80,000, had still not been accounted for. Many were scattered, certainly, but their shadow left a chilling sensation in anyone who stopped for a moment to consider the implications of such unaccountability.

The broad response in Indonesia to this crisis was one of belligerent nationalism, of offence at having their state 'insulted', of accusations of interference in domestic affairs and of ignoring the pride of the Indonesian people and not adequately appreciating their own long suffering, including throwing off the shackles of colonialism in 1945–49 and dealing with dangerous communist and separatist movements. But for many outsiders, and even many Indonesians, it was difficult to feel sympathy for these protestations. Certainly the TNI and its policies in East Timor did not represent the Indonesian people, or even the government, but they did operate under the red and white flag. When this flag was burned, especially in Australia, many Indonesians were deeply upset. Perhaps they should have been as upset, or more so, by the activities conducted under it.

It would be easy here to talk also of the atrocities committed by the TNI in West Papua and in Aceh, in Ambon, East and West Kalimantan and in other parts of the archipelago, including Jakarta. There is no doubt that Indonesia faces an extraordinarily difficult time at the beginning of the 21st century, and there is some doubt as to whether the state will last intact, or whether it will accept a modification of itself, perhaps as a federation, to retain some unity. But all of this has become largely redundant to the people of East Timor. They, or their leaders, will have to continue to be very concerned by affairs in Indonesia, given its proximity to the tiny new state and the potential for its problems to spill across a sometimes poorly defined and historically less respected border. But, they say, Indonesia must look after itself, as East Timor—Timor Loro S'ai—will also have to assume responsibility for itself. The international community will care for it, but not forever.

If the brutality surrounding East Timor's ballot for self determination could be said to stand as a signature for the closure of the 20th century, perhaps the formal creation of the new state can stand as something more hopeful for the 21st century. It is perhaps naïve to believe that human beings will fundamentally alter the violent responses they have exhibited since time immemorial, but it is not naïve to believe that civil behaviour could become the preferred and accepted option for the resolution of interstate (and intrastate) problems. East Timor's experience stands in many respects for all that has been wrong, indeed evil, about the 20th century. But to talk to East Timorese people about the future, to see their open smiles, to listen to their enthusiasm, is to believe that there are grounds for hope.

About the authors

Peter Bartu has worked with the United Nations in Cambodia (1991–1993, 1998), the Democratic Republic of the Congo (1998) and East Timor (1999).

Carlos Belo is the Catholic Archbishop of East Timor and is joint holder of the Nobel Prize for Peace 1997.

Scott Burchill is a lecturer in International Relations at Deakin University and longstanding critic of Australia's policy on East Timor.

Annemarie Devereux teaches and undertakes research at the Faculty of Law, Australian National University. She continues to practise law, specialising in international law.

Hidayat Djajamihardja is an Indonesian citizen and longtime journalist for Radio Australia.

Former Asia correspondent **Sue Downie** is completing *Inside Peace-keeping: the UN in Cambodia* and is the author of *Down Highway One: Journeys Through Vietnam and Cambodia*. She is undertaking a PhD on peace-keeping and development and was a UN-accredited observer for the East Timor referendum.

Xanana Gusmao is President of CNRT and Supreme Commander of Falintil, the armed wing of the independence movement. He was a political prisoner in Jakarta from 1992 until 1999.

Damien Kingsbury is Executive Officer of the Monash Asia Institute and author or editor of five previous books on aspects of Southeast Asian politics.

Anthony Smith is a lecturer in International Relations, with a focus on Southeast Asian politics, at the International Pacific College, Palmerston North, New Zealand.

Gerry van Klinken teaches Asian Studies at Griffith University. He edits the quarterly *Inside Indonesia*.

Helene van Klinken is an Indonesian language teacher, and has worked as an International Mission Consultant for the Uniting Church in Australia.

Bibliography

ABC (Australian Broadcasting Corporation) 1999, Online news, 24 September.

ACFOA (Australian Council for Overseas Aid) 1991, *East Timor: keeping the flame of freedom alive*, Development Dossier No 29.

ADF (Australian Defence Department) 1999, representatives at a peace-keeping policy workshop, Canberra, 8–9 July.

AETA (Australia East Timor Association) 1983, *East Timor: Betrayed but not beaten*, Melbourne.

AFR (Australian Financial Review) 1994, 17 March.

Age 1994, 27 June.

—— 1995a, 18 December.

—— 1995b, editorial 19 December.

Agreement between the Republic of Indonesia and the Kingdom of the Netherlands Concerning West New Guinea (West Irian), New York, 15 August 1962, reprinted in Siekmann, Robert C R 1989, *Basic documents on United Nations and related peace-keeping forces* (Second Enlarged Edition), Martinus Nijhoff Publishers, Dordrecht, Boston, London.

Alvarez, J E 1999, 'Crimes of states/crimes of hate: Lessons from Rwanda', *Yale Journal of International Law* 24.

Arndt, Heinz 1999, *Australian Financial Review*, 23 April.

Aubrey, Jim (ed) 1998, *Free East Timor*, Vintage, Milson's Point.

Australian 1991, 6 December.

—— 1994, 13 September.

—— 1995, 21 December.

—— 1998, 20 May.

—— 1995, 19 December.

Barker, G 1999a, *Australian Financial Review*, 21 September.

—— 1999b, *Australian Financial Review*, 28 September.

Bassiouni, M C 1996, 'Accountability for international crime and serious violations of fundamental human rights: Searching for peace and achieving justice: The need for accountability', *Law and Contemporary Problems* 59.

Berry, Ken 1997, *Cambodia—From red to blue: Australia's initiative for peace*, Allen & Unwin, St Leonards.

Bourne, Don 1993, adjunct to Canadian contingent, author interview, Phnom Penh, 18 August.

Bradley, C, A, and Goldsmith, J L 1999, 'Pinochet and international human rights litigation', *Michigan Law Review* 97.

Brenchley, F 1999, *Bulletin*, 28 September.

Brownlie, I 1991, *International law and the use of force by states*, Clarendon Press, Oxford.

Budiardjo, C and Leong, L 1984, *The war against East Timor*, Zed Books, London.

Budiman, Arief 1999, talk at seminar 'Restoring peace and building a state: prospects for East Timor', Melbourne Town Hall, 21 September.

Carney, Timothy and Tan Lian Choo 1993, *Wither Cambodia? Beyond the election*, Institute of Southeast Asian Studies, Singapore.

Cassese, A 1995, *Self-determination of peoples: A legal re-appraisal*, Cambridge University Press, Cambridge.

Chen, Lung-Chu 1976, 'Self-determination as a human right' in Reisman, W M and Weston, B H (eds), *Toward world order and human dignity*, Free Press, New York.

Chinkin, C 1992, 'The merits of Portugal's claim against Australia', *University of NSW Law Journal* 15.

Chomsky, Noam 1996, *Power and prospects*, Allen & Unwin, St Leonards.

—— 1999, *The new military humanism: Lessons from Kosovo*, Common Courage, Monroe.

CIA (Central Intelligence Agency) 1968, *Intelligence report: Indonesia—1965, The coup that backfired*, Directorate of intelligence.

Clark, R S 1980, 'The decolonisation of East Timor and the United Nations norms on self-determination and aggression', *Yale Journal of World Public Order* 7.

Colebatch, T 1999, *Age*, 25 September.

Colombijn, Freek 1999, 'A peaceful road to freedom', *Inside Indonesia* no 60, October–December.

Cotton, James (ed) 1999, *East Timor and Australia*, Australian Defence Studies Centre, Canberra.

Cribb, Robert and Brown, Colin 1995, *Modern Indonesia: A history since 1945*, Longman, London and New York.

Dalrymple, R 1999, in *Australian Financial Review*, 21 September.

Delaney, J and Langford, M 1996, 'Nonsense upon stilts? East Timor and the International Court of Justice', *Australian Journal of Human Rights*, 3(1).

De Matos, A 1974, *Timor Portugues 1515–1769*, Universidade de Lisboa, Lisbon.

Dibb, Paul 1998, *Australian Financial Review*, 23 May.

Doyle, Michael W 1995, *UN peacekeeping in Cambodia: UNTAC's Civil Mandate*, International Peace Academy, Lynne Rienner, London.

Doyle, Michael W and Ayaka Suzuki 1995, 'Transitional authority in Cambodia' in Weiss, Thomas G (ed), *The United Nations and civil wars*, Lynne Rienner, Boulder, Colorado.

Dunn, James 1996, *Timor: A people betrayed*, ABC, Sydney.

Elliot, P D 1978, 'The East Timor dispute', *International and Comparative Law Quarterly* 27.

Evans, Gareth and Grant, Bruce 1995, *Australia's foreign relations*, Melbourne University Press.

Feith, Herbert 1962, *The decline of constitutional democracy in Indonesia*, Cornell University Press, Ithaca.

Franck, T M and Hoffman, P 1975–6, 'The right of self-determination in very small places', *New York University Journal of International Law and Politics* 8.

Garnadi, H 1999, Memo M53/TM p4-OKTT/7/99 (General Assessment if Option 1 fails), Office of the Minister of State for Co-ordinating Politics and Security, Republic of Indonesia, Dili Command Post, 3 July.

Grant, Bruce 1996, *Indonesia*, (3rd ed) Melbourne University Press, Melbourne.

Grattan, Michelle 1995, *Age*, 15 December.

Gusmao, J 1999a, 'We will forget the past', *Asiaweek*, 3 September.

—— 1999b, at press conference, UN Headquarters, New York, 28 September.

Harbottle, Michael 1971, *The blue berets*, Leo Cooper, London.

Herald-Sun 1995, 12 March.

Hastings, P 1999, 'Timor—some Australian attitudes, 1941–1950' in Cotton, James (ed) *East Timor and Australia*, Australian Defence Studies Centre, Canberra.

Heder, Steve and Ledgerwood, Judy (eds) 1996, *Propaganda, politics, and violence in Cambodia: Democratic transition under United Nations peacekeeping*, M E Sharpe, Armonk and London.

Heininger, Janet C 1994, *Peacekeeping in transition: The United Nations in Cambodia*, Twentieth Century Fund Press, New York.

Henderson, Gerard 1993, *Courier Mail*, Brisbane, 29 January.

Hiorth, F 1985, *Timor: Past and present*, South-East Asian Monograph No 17, James Cook University, Townsville.

Horta, Jose Ramos 1987, *Funu: The unfinished saga of East Timor*, Red Sea, Lisbon.

HRWA (Human Rights Watch Asia) 1997, *Communal violence in West Kalimantan*, December.

—— 1999, 'The violence in Ambon', www.hrw.org/hrw/reports/1999/ambon/, March.

Hughes, Caroline 1996, *UNTAC in Cambodia: The impact on human rights*, Institute of Southeast Asian Studies, Singapore.

ICJ (International Court of Justice) 1971, 'Advisory opinion on Namibia', in *Advisory opinion on Western Sahara* [1975].

—— 1975, *Advisory opinion on Western Sahara*.

Jardine, Matthew 1995, *East Timor: Genocide in Paradise*, Odonian, Tucson.

—— 1999, *East Timor: Genocide in Paradise*, Odonian/Common Courage Press, Monroe, Maine.

Johanson, Vanessa 1999, 'The Sultan will be Dr Hasan Tiro', *Inside Indonesia* no 60, October–December.

Jollife, Jill 1978, *East Timor: Nationalism and colonialism*, University of Queensland Press, St Lucia.

Joyner, C C 1998, 'Redressing impunity for human rights violations: The Universal Declaration and the search for accountability', *Denver Journal of International Law and Policy* 26.

Kell, Tim 1995, *The roots of Acehnese rebellion 1989–1992*, Cornell Modern Indonesia Project, Ithaca.

Kelly, Paul 1998, *The Australian*, 25 February.

Kingsbury, Damien 1998a, 'Watch these five!' *Inside Indonesia* No 53 January–March.

—— 1998b, *The politics of Indonesia*, Oxford University Press, Melbourne.

Kolko, G 1988, *Confronting the Third World* , New York.

Kompas 1999, 1 May.

Legge, J D 1961, *Central authority and regional autonomy in Indonesia*, Cornell University Press, Ithaca.

Leitao, H 1956, *Vinte e oito anos de historia de Timor*, Agencia Geral do Ultramar, Lisbon.

Lillich, R B 1995–6, 'The growing importance of customary international human rights law', *Georgia Journal of International and Comparative Law* 25.

Lutz, E L 1989, 'After the elections: Compensating victims of human rights abuses' in Lutz, E, Hannum, H and Burke, K J (eds), *New directions in human rights*, University of Pennsylvania Press, Philadelphia.

Mackie, Jamie 1974, *Australian Outlook*, no 28.

MacLeod, Andrew 1999, seminar at Northcote Town Hall, Melbourne, 29 September.

Macmillan, Andrew 1992, *Death in Dili*, Hodder, Rydalmere.

McBeth, J 1999a, 'Cameo Role', *Far Eastern Economic Review*, 18 March.

—— 1999b. 'Military challenge', *Far Eastern Economic Review*, 2 September.

—— 1999c, 'Bitter Memories', *Far Eastern Economic Review*, 16 September.

Meron, T 1983, 'Note and comment: On the inadequate reach of humanitarian and human rights law and the need for a new instrument', *American Journal of International Law* 77.

—— 1989, 'Human rights and humanitarian norms as customary law', Symposium on customary international human rights law, (1995–6) *Georgia Journal of International and Comparative Law*.

Morris, M H 1996, 'Accountability for international crime and serious violations of Fundamental Human Rights: International Guidelines Against Impunity: Facilitating Accountability', *Law and Contemporary Problems* 59.

Murphy, D and McBeth, J 1999, 'Scorched Earth', *Far Eastern Economic Review*, 16 September.

New York Times 1966, 6 July.

Nicol, B 1978, *Timor: The stillborn nation*, Widescope International Publishers, Melbourne.

Osborne, Robin 1985, *Indonesia's secret war—the guerilla struggle in Irian Jaya*, Allen & Unwin, St Leonards.

Petrasek, D 1998, 'Current development: Moving forward on the development of minimum humanitarian standards', *American Journal of International Law* 92.

Pilger, John 1994, *Distant voices*, Vintage, London.

—— 1998, *Hidden agendas*, Vintage, London.

Pomerance, M 1982, *Self-determination in law and practice*, M Nijhoff, The Hague.

PM 1999, ABC Radio, 27 September.

Ratner, S R 1998, 'The schizophrenias of international criminal law', *Texas International Law Journal* 33.

—— 1999, 'New democracies, old atrocities: An inquiry in international law', *Georgetown Law Journal* 87.

Resink, G J 1968, *Indonesia's history between the myths: Essays in legal history and historical theory*, Van Hoeve, The Hague.

Rikhye, Indar Jit 1984, *The theory and practice of peacekeeping*, C Hurst & Company, London.

Robinson, Mary 1999, UN High Commissioner for Human Rights, Press Release 14 September.

Rummel, Rudolph J 1997, *Power kills: Democracy as a method of non-violence*, Transaction, New Brunswick.

Schiller, A 1955, *The formation of federal Indonesia, 1945–1949*, Van Hoeve, The Hague/Bandung.

Senate Debates 1994, Response of Senator Evans, 10 November.

Serambi 1999, 16 September.

Sheridan, Greg 1995a, *Australian*, 15 December.

—— 1995b, *Weekend Australian*, 16 December.

—— 1998a, *Australian*, 20 May.

—— 1998b, *Australian*, 30 October.

—— 1999, *Australian*, 22 September.

Sidel, John T 1997, 'Philippine politics in town, district, and province: Bossism in Cavite and Cebu', *Journal of Asian Studies*, Vol 56 no 4.

Simma, B and Alston, P 1992, 'The sources of human rights law: Custom, jus cogens and general principles', *Australian Yearbook of International Law* 12.

Simpson, Gerry 1997, 'Conceptualising violence: Present and future developments in international law…Didactic and dissident histories in war crimes trials', *Albany Law Review* 60.

Singh, B 1995, *East Timor, Indonesia and the world: Myths and realities*, Singapore Institute for International Affairs, Singapore.

Spencer, G 1999, 'Indonesia's leader's deal on East Timor rejected', *Seattle Times*, 21 June.

Sunga, L S 1992, *Individual responsibility in international law for serious human rights violations*, M Nijhoff, Dordrecht.

Suter, K 1982, *East Timor and West Irian*, London Minority Rights Group Report No 42.

Sydney Morning Herald 1999, 24 May.

Tapol 1999a, *The TNI's 'dirty war' in East Timor*, Tapol, London.

Tapol 1999b, *The dismissal and indictment of TNI officers for human rights violations in East Timor*, Tapol, London.

Tavares, J 1999, *Kesiapan dan kesiagan pasukan pejuang integrasi (milisi) dalam menyikapi perkembangan situasi dan konisi di Timor-Timur*, PPI, Balibo, 17 July.

Taylor, John G 1991, *Indonesia's forgotten war*, Zed, London.

Tesoro, J 1999, 'Voting for the future', *Asiaweek*, 10 Setpember.

Tilly, Charles 1978, *From mobilization to revolution*, Addison-Wesley.

Tomuschat, C 1993, *Modern law of self-determination*, M Nijhoff, Dordrecht.

Toohey, Brian 1994, *Australian Financial Review*, 24 November.

—— 1999a, *Australian Financial Review*, 14 August.

—— 1999b, *Sun-Herald*, 29 August.

—— 1999c, *Sun-Herald*, 5 September.

—— 1999d, *Australian Financial Review*, 28 September.

Toohey, Brian and Wilkinson, Marion 1987, *The Book of Leaks*, Sydney.

Ummat 1999, 'Berliku talak tiga Timor Leste', 15 February.

UN (United Nations) 1960, Declaration on the Granting of Independence to Colonial Countries and Peoples, 14 December, Resolution 1514 (XV);

—— 1970, Declaration of Principles of International Law Concerning Friendly Relations Among states in Accordance with the Charter of the United Nations, 24 October.

—— 1976a, Documents A/AC.109/526, 28 May.

—— 1976b, Documents A/AC.109/527, 15 June 1976.

—— 1976c, SCOR, 31st year, Supplement for April, May and June, Doc S/12104, 21 June.

—— 1976d, *Report of the Secretary-General Pursuant to Security Council Resolution 389* (1976), UN Doc S/121066, 22 June.

—— 1991a, S/23097, 'Report of the Secretary-General on proposals for a United Nations Advance Mission in Cambodia (UNAMIC)', 30 September, reprinted as Document 17 in United Nations 1995, *The United Nations and Cambodia* 1991–1995, UN Department of Public Information, New York.

—— 1991b, S/RES/717, 'Security Council Resolution on UNAMIC and political settlement of the Cambodia situation', 16 October, reprinted as Document 18 in United Nations 1995, *The United Nations and Cambodia* 1991–1995, UN Department of Public Information, New York.

—— 1991c, S/23218, 'Report of the Secretary-General on UNAMIC', 14 November, reprinted as Document 22 in United Nations 1995, *The United Nations and Cambodia* 1991–1995, UN Department of Public Information, New York.

—— 1992a, *Agreements on a comprehensive political settlement of the Cambodia conflict: Paris, 23 October 1991*, UN Department of Public Information, New York.

—— 1992b A/47/277-S/24111, *An agenda for peace*, June.

—— 1994, A/48/935, *Agenda for development*, May.

—— 1995, *The United Nations and Cambodia* 1991–1995, UN Department of Public Information, New York.

—— 1996, A/51/761, Agenda for Democratization, General Assembly, Fifty-first session, Agenda item 41, 20 December, letter from the Secretary-General to the President of the General Assembly.

—— 1999a, *Agreement between Indonesia, Portugal and the Secretary General of the United Nations*, 5 May.

—— 1999b, 'Code of conduct for participants: East Timor Popular Consultation' UNAMET Electoral Unit, (signed) 9 August, Dili.

—— 1999c, Security Council Resolution S/RES/1264, 15 September.

—— 1999d, *Questions and answers: The United Nations and East Timor*, 1 October, at www.un.org/peace/etimor/Qna_frame.

—— 1999e, News Service, 5 October, at www.un.org/news/dh/latest/page2.

—— 1999f, Spokesman at noon briefing, UN Headquarters, New York, 5 October.

UNGA (United Nations General Assembly) 1975, Resolution 3485 (XXX), 12 December.

UNHCR (United Nations High Commissioner for Refugees) 1999, *Report of the High Commissioner for Human Rights on the human rights situation in East Timor*.

UNSC (United Nations Security Council) 1975, Resolution 384, 22 December.

—— 1976 Resolution 389, 22 April.

United Nations websites:
  UNCI (Commission of Inquiry)
  www.un.org/News/ossg/etimor_report.htm
  DPO (Department of Peacekeeping Operations)
  www.un.org/Depts/dpko/field/pkeep.
  DPAa (Department of Political Affairs),
  www.un.org/Depts/dpa/docs/website8.
  DPAb (Department of Political Affairs),
  www.un.org/Depts/dpa/docs/website3.
  DPA (Department of Political Affairs)
  www.un.org/Depts/dpa/docs/website10,11,12,13.
  DPIa (Department of Public Information), www.un.org/depts/dpko/pk_50.
  DPIb (Department of Public Information), www.un.org/depts/dpko.

Van Boven, Theo 1993, 'Study concerning the right to restitution, compensation and rehabilitation for victims of gross violations of human rights and fundamental freedoms: Final report', Special Rapporteur, Commission on Human Rights, Sub-Commission on Prevention of Discrimination and Protection of Minorities, 45th Sess, Item 4, UN Doc E/CN.4/SUB.2/1993/8.

Van Klinken, Gerry 1995, 'The contemporary roots of East Timorese resistance, and prospects for peace', *Antara Kita* (bulletin of the US-based Indonesian Studies Committee) no 43, October.

—— 1999a, 'Democracy, the regions and Indonesia's future' in Blackburn, Susan (ed), *Pemilu: the 1999 Indonesian election*, Monash Asia Institute, Clayton.

—— 1999b, 'What caused the Ambon violence?', Inside Indonesia no 60, October–December.

Weekend Australian, 1995, 2 September.

Whittaker, David J 1995, *United Nations in action*, UCL Press, London.

Woolcott, Richard 1992, 'Myths and realities in our approach to Indonesia', *Sydney Papers*, Winter.

—— 1995, *Weekend Australian*, 22–23 April.

—— 1998a, *Age*, 16 January.

—— 1998b, *Australian Financial Review*, 3 June.

—— 1999, *Australian*, 17 September.

Glossary

ABRI	Angkatan Bersenjata Republic Indonesia, Armed Forces of the Republic of Indonesia
ADF	Australian Defence Department
Aditla	Associacao Democratica Intergracao Timor-Leste Australia, Democratic Association for the Integration of East Timor into Australia
AETIVP	Australia–East Timor International Volunteers Project
AHI	militia group, meaning unknown
ANFREL	Asian Nations for Free Elections
APEC	Asia-Pacific Economic Co-operation
APMT	Associacao Popular Monarquia de Timor, Popular Association of Timorese Monarchists
Apodeti	Associacao Popular Democratica de Timor, Timorese Popular Democratic Association
ASDT	Timorese Social Democrats, an early name for Fretilin
ASEAN	Association of South East Asian Nations
BAIS	Badan Inteligen Strategi, Intelligence and Strategy
BIA	Badan Inteligen ABRI, Indonesian Military Intelligence
Brimob	Mobile Brigade (Indonesian paramilitary police)
BRTT	Barisan Rakyat Timor Timur, Peoples Front for East Timor
CAT	Convention Against Torture
CEDAW	Convention on the Elimination of All Forms of Discrimination Against Women
CERD	Convention on the Elimination of All Forms of Racial Discrimination
CivPol	Civilian Police
CNRM	National Council of Maubere Resistance

CNRT	Conselho Nacional de Resistencia Tomorense , National Council for Timorese Resistance
CPLP	Community of Lusophone Countries
CPP	Cambodian People's Party
CROC	Convention on the Rights of the Child
CSIS	Centre for Strategic and International Studies
Dandim	Komandan Distrik Militer, District Military Commander
Danrem	Komandan Resort Militer, Provincial Military Commander
DEO	District Electoral Office (of UNAMET)
DEPLU	Departemen Luar Negeri, (Indonesian) Department of Foreign Affairs
DKPO	United Nations Department of Peace-Keeping Operations
DPP-IMPPETU	pro-independence group
DPRD II	Dewan Perwakilan rakyat daerah, District Representative Council
DSMTT	Dewan Solidaritas Mahasiswa Timur Timor, East Timorese Students' Solidarity Council (pro-independence student group)
Falintil	Forcas Armada de Liberacao Nacional de Timor L'Este, Armed Forces for the National Liberation of East Timor, was the armed wing of Fretilin and later of the Council of National Timorese Resistance
Familia	pro-independence group
Fitun	pro-independence group
FPDK	Front for Peace, Democracy and Justice
Fretilin	Frente Revolucionaria de Timor L'Este Independente, Revolutionary Front for an Independent East Timor
GAM	Free Aceh Movement
Gardapaksi	Youth Guard for Upholding Integration
ICCPR	International Convention on Economic, Social and Cultural Rights
ICJ	International Court of Justice

ICTR	International Criminal Tribunal for Rwanda
ICTY	International Criminal Tribunal for the former Yugoslavia
IDP	International Displaced Person
IFET	International Federation for East Timor
InterFET	International Forces to East Timor
Kodim	Komando Distrik Militer, District Military Command
Kopassus	Special Forces
Koramil	Komando Rayon Militer, Sub-District Military Command
Korem	Komando Resort Militer, Provincial Military Command
KOTA	Klibur Oan Timur Aswain, Sons of the Mountain Warriors
KPP-HAM	Indonesia's Commission of Inquiry into Human Rights Violations in East Timor
KSAD	Kepala Staf Angkatan Darat, (Indonesian) Army Chief of Staff
Markus Besar	Main Headquarters (UNAMET)
MPR	People's Consultative Assembly
NATO	North Atlantic Treaty Organisation
NCO	Non-commissioned officer
NGO	Non-government organisation
NTT	Nusa Tenggara Timur, the eastern islands of south-eastern Indonesia
Ojetil	pro-independence group
Opjlatil	pro-independence group
Opsus	Special Operations
Pangab	Panglima Angkatan Bersenjata, Armed Forces Commander
Pangdam	Panglima Daerah Militer, Provincial Military Commander
Polri	Republic of Indonesia Police
PPI	Pasukan Pejuang Integrasi, Integration Struggle Troops (militia)

Renetil	Restencia National dos Estudantes de Timor L'Este
Sagrada	pro-independence group
SGI	Satuan Tugas Inteligen, Intelligence Duty Unit
SNC	Supreme National Council, Cambodia
SOC	State of Cambodia
TNI	Tentara Nasional Indonesia, Indonesian National Armed Forces
UDT	Uniao Democratica de Timor, Timorese Democratic Union
UNAMET	United Nations Assistance Mission to East Timor
UNAMIC	United Nations Advance Mission in Cambodia
UNDP	United Nations Development Program
UNSF	United Nations Security Force
UNTAC	United Nations Transitional Authority in Cambodia
UNTAET	United Nations Transitional Administration in East Timor
UNTEA	United Nations Temporary Executive Authority (in West Papua)
UNTIM	University of East Timor
UNV	United Nations Volunteer

Also published by Monash Asia Institute

To Be Free: Stories from Asia's struggle against oppression

Chee Soon Juan, 1998, $24.95. ISBN 0 7326 1173 3.

This popular and controversial book tells the personal and political stories of people who have been persecuted because they stood up for freedom and democracy in Asia: Chia Thye Poh in Singapore, Aung San Suu Khi in Burma, Pramoedya Ananta Toer in Indonesia, Benigno Aquino in the Philippines, Kim Dae Jung in South Korea and Shih Ming-teh in Taiwan. Chee Soon Juan challenges the myth that 'Asian values' should deny human rights and democracy in Asia and prevent the international community from being concerned about these issues.

Reformasi: Crisis and change in Indonesia

edited by Arief Budiman, Barbara Hatley and Damien Kingsbury, 1999, $24.95. ISBN 0 7326 1179 2

This extensive book brings together academic and grassroots commentators from Indonesia and Australia to explain why Indonesia is currently in political, social and financial turmoil, and examines the likely outcomes. It looks at the economy, political parties, military, violence, rapes, riots, ethnic, religious and gender divisions, and the reformasi total movement that calls for democratisation.

Women creating Indonesia: The first fifty years

edited by Jean Gelman Taylor, 1997, $24.95. ISBN 0 7326 1156 3.

The first half of the twentieth century was a period of intellectual ferment in the new colonial state when thinkers, writers, politicians and workers of all religious and ethnic groups were debating and organising to generate a new society. This book brings together papers first presented at the Asian Studies Association of Australia's fourth Women in Asia conference, which was held in Melbourne in October 1993.